PRAISE FOR *THE MOTHERHOOD MYTH*

"This book is nothing short of a revelation—raw, timely, and deeply needed. In a world where women, especially mothers, are drowning under impossible expectations, Vanessa Bennett doesn't just name the problem—she offers a way through. With profound psychological insight and deep soul wisdom, she gently unravels how we got here and powerfully guides us back to ourselves. This book speaks to the woman who has always felt the tug between who she was told to be and who she truly is. It's a lifeline for any mother ready to stop repeating patterns and start reclaiming her power."

Shefali Tsabary, PhD
New York Times bestselling author of *The Parenting Map*

"*The Motherhood Myth* is the book every woman needs on her nightstand. Vanessa Bennett gives women the permission, the tools, and the wisdom to reclaim their sense of Self—without guilt. This book is a game changer."

Melissa Wood-Tepperberg
founder of Melissa Wood Health

"Vanessa Bennett has written the book that so many of us have been yearning for—one that doesn't just challenge the myths of motherhood but gives us the language and tools to transform them. *The Motherhood Myth* is a rare blend of intellect and soul, making depth psychology and Jungian thought accessible while guiding us toward a radical reconnection with ourselves. It is both a critique of the systems that shape us and a deeply personal invitation to step into a new way of being. This book is a must-read for any woman ready to reclaim her wholeness."

Terri Cole, MSW, LCSW
psychotherapist and author of *Boundary Boss* and *Too Much*

the motherhood myth

ALSO BY VANESSA BENNETT, LMFT

It's Not Me, It's You: Break the Blame Cycle.
Relationship Better., with John Kim

the motherhood myth

A Depth Therapist's
Guide to Redefine Parenting,
Reimagine Intimacy,
and Reclaim the Self

vanessa bennett, LMFT

BOULDER, COLORADO

Sounds True
Boulder, CO

© 2025 Vanessa Bennett

Sounds True is a trademark of Sounds True Inc.
All rights reserved. No part of this book may be used or reproduced in any manner without written permission from the author(s) and publisher.

No AI Training: Without in any way limiting the author's and publisher's exclusive rights under copyright, any use of this publication to "train" generative artificial intelligence (AI) technologies to generate text is expressly prohibited. The author reserves all rights to license uses of this work for generative AI training and development of machine learning language models.

This book is not intended as a substitute for the medical recommendations of physicians, mental health professionals, or other health-care providers. Rather, it is intended to offer information to help the reader cooperate with physicians, mental health professionals, and health-care providers in a mutual quest for optimal well-being. We advise readers to carefully review and understand the ideas presented and to seek the advice of a qualified professional before attempting to use them.

Published 2025

Cover design by Jess Morphew

Jacket and book design by Charli Barnes

Printed in the United States of America

BK07102

Library of Congress Cataloging-in-Publication Data

Names: Bennett, Vanessa, author.
Title: The motherhood myth : a depth therapist's guide to redefine parenthood, reimagine intimacy, and reclaim the self / Vanessa Bennett.
Description: Boulder, CO : Sounds True, 2025. | Includes bibliographical references.
Identifiers: LCCN 2024058734 (print) | LCCN 2024058735 (ebook) | ISBN 9781649633415 (trade paperback) | ISBN 9781649633422 (ebook)
Subjects: LCSH: Motherhood. | Parenthood.
Classification: LCC HQ759 .B457 2025 (print) | LCC HQ759 (ebook) | DDC 306.874--dc23/eng/20250212
LC record available at https://lccn.loc.gov/2024058734
LC ebook record available at https://lccn.loc.gov/2024058735

"There is no good answer to how to be a woman;
the art may instead lie in how we refuse the question."

—Rebecca Solnit, *The Mother of All Questions*[1]

contents

INTRODUCTION — 1

PART 1: THE MYTHS OF MOTHERHOOD — 27

CHAPTER 1: From Maiden to Mother — 29

CHAPTER 2: The Loss of the Village . . . and Ourselves — 51

CHAPTER 3: The Cult of Busy — 75

CHAPTER 4: Martyrdom Is Not Mothering — 99

PART 2: THE MYTHS OF SEX — 117

CHAPTER 5: The Mother Wound — 119

CHAPTER 6: The Father Wound — 145

CHAPTER 7: Sex Was Never about Me — 165

CHAPTER 8: The Wild Woman's Role in Our Evolving Feminism — 187

PART 3: THE MYTHS OF RELATIONSHIPS — 205

CHAPTER 9: Liberation through Responsibility — 207

CHAPTER 10: Belonging to Ourselves — 227

CHAPTER 11: Is It Love or Fear? — 239

CHAPTER 12: The Trouble with Couples Therapy — 257

CONCLUSION: THE JOURNEY CONTINUES — 271

ACKNOWLEDGMENTS — 273

NOTES — 275

ABOUT THE AUTHOR — 287

introduction

The Motherhood Myth was born out of countless hours sitting with female clients and couples, and reflecting on my own journey through the many stages, twists, and turns of motherhood. It emerged from a pattern of the same aching questions: "What's wrong with me?" "Why isn't this easier?" "Why am I not happier?" Witnessing so much struggle, tears, anger, and confusion, I couldn't help but begin a journey to seek answers. Have mothers always been this overwhelmed and disillusioned with parenting? Were couples always so dissatisfied with each other once they became parents? Was there always this much emotional and psychic turmoil? Why did some women and couples seem to experience more ease and happiness? What was the cause? The root? What was the collective psyche trying to reveal to us?

Every mother I've met has experienced a profound identity shift upon becoming a parent, yet many lack the language or support to process and integrate this change. This gap leaves them wondering how they can evolve while also relying on the wisdom of deeply intuitive ancestral knowledge. Many of the mothers I work with come to me seeking to make sense of their journey, to turn it over in their hands and inspect it from every angle.

The Motherhood Myth challenges the overarching myth—the deeply ingrained cultural belief—that motherhood, partnership, and relationships should be inherently easy and fulfilling. It explores the dissonance between societal expectations and lived reality and examines how these myths leave us feeling like we're failing. This book delves into the challenges I observed in both my clients and myself during our transitions from Maiden to Mother, from couple to family, and from an uninitiated, uncertain Self to one that questions why, listens to its own voice, and champions its wisdom—even if it ruffles feathers and disrupts the status quo. Throughout the book, I will provide context, solidarity, and strategies to help you navigate not just the initial shift into parenthood but also the continual evolution with more ease, authenticity, and self-compassion.

While I advocate for building a strong sense of Self, this does not mean disconnecting from others or abandoning community. Healthy community is only possible when we relate to others from a place of self-awareness and internal strength. Many people mistakenly equate personal accountability and self-trust with isolation or selfishness, but the reality is quite the opposite: by cultivating a grounded, sovereign sense of Self, we can participate in deeper, more authentic connections.

A codependent society, which I believe is what we have existed in for generations, where relationships are built on external validation, fosters shallow connections driven by fear, control, and the need to prove our worth and lovability. These dynamics fuel the epidemic of loneliness and disconnection we see today. Codependency is a relational pattern rooted in fear and externalized power, where self-worth hinges on others' approval. As feminist scholar and activist Silvia Federici noted, pre-capitalist societies relied more heavily on collective support, a stark contrast to the isolating individualism encouraged by capitalist structures. Similarly, bell hooks has written extensively on how true love and community thrive on mutual respect and self-determination rather than dependency or control.

In contrast, interdependence arises from an internalized sense of worth, where individuals engage in relationships from a place of security and autonomy. Interdependence allows for personal sovereignty while creating deep, meaningful connections built on true reciprocity, trust, and esteem. By clarifying this distinction early, we can dispel the myth that prioritizing a strong sense of Self means isolating from others. Instead, it means engaging in relationships that honor both individuality and connection, free from fear-driven behaviors.

As Harriet Lerner writes in *The Dance of Anger*, "The goal is not to end relationships but to end the dynamic of dependency and rescuing, so that true intimacy can grow."[1] When we step out of codependent patterns, we open the door to relationships built on mutual care, not obligation—connections where love and respect are given freely, not earned through sacrifice. In these interdependent relationships, intimacy thrives and, with it, the healing of the widespread disconnection and loneliness that pervade our culture.

My hope is that this book speaks not only to mothers experiencing the shifts deep in their bones, but also to those hoping to better understand the women in their lives. This is not an exhaustive account of every issue that arises in motherhood; each chapter could have been its own book. Motherhood is a vast, evolving journey that varies across cultures and experiences, and no single work can capture it all. If you're feeling overwhelmed by all of the change, please know you are not alone.

While my perspective as a white, cisgender, heterosexual woman shapes this narrative, I've included diverse viewpoints drawn from my work with clients from varied backgrounds and integrated varied research from multiple disciplines. This book cannot encompass every experience, but it aims to offer inclusive and insightful reflections for all. My hope is that each reader finds something within these pages that resonates, regardless of their unique background or journey.

THE LIE WE WERE SOLD

I want to shout from the rooftops that life is not meant to be simply "gotten through" or endured. Generations have passed down beliefs rooted in collective traumas: you work, you have kids, and you die. Most of my clients over the years have struggled to unpack the beliefs that have been passed down in the phrases they heard growing up:

- Suck it up.

- Life is pain.

- Pull yourself up by your bootstraps.

- I'll give you something to cry about.

- Boys don't cry.

- Stop being so dramatic.

- Children should be seen and not heard.

- If I wanted your opinion, I would have asked for it.

- Because I said so.

- You have no idea how easy/good you have it.

- After all I've done for you . . .

Many of us were taught we could "have it all" and "be anything," but at the same time, we were raised to follow authority blindly and put our heads down and grind, and were then told that wavering from that path meant we were ungrateful. For women, "having it all" meant having a successful career, being a wife and a mother in a heterosexual marriage, and, although statistically working the same hours outside of the home as her partner, doing the majority of the domestic labor and child rearing inside the home. Meanwhile, men were taught "having it all" meant being a stoic and successful financial provider (also heterosexual) without the emotional or relational skills necessary for deeper connection. These expectations have left many of us feeling disconnected, unfulfilled, and unsure of our roles.

This book challenges the myths and norms that have dictated motherhood, bringing light to the unconscious beliefs that drive us and offering tools for reclaiming our voices and values. It is an invitation to question, disrupt, and find a new way forward for mothers and their families. To see and use the tumult of the transitions themselves as a springboard for radical self-development, evolution, and acceptance. The journey of motherhood is not just about caring for our children; it's about rediscovering and redefining ourselves and the future for all.

This narrative isn't exclusive to one gender, cultural, or economic group. I've worked with many clients from diverse backgrounds, including those from the LGBTQIA+ community and immigrant families, who also feel the weight of these expectations. While the specifics might differ, the underlying messages remain strikingly similar: conform, don't question, and above all, perform your roles as defined by society.

Through exploring both personal and client stories, as well as historical and cultural contexts, I aim to provide a guide for understanding how we got here—and how we might begin to chart a new path. I have found time and again that pretending I am not a human with similar struggles to my clients does nothing more than make them feel more alone. So throughout this book, I will share personal anecdotes as well as stories from my clients (with permission and anonymity maintained) to illustrate the common struggles and triumphs that define the motherhood journey. It is through this shared vulnerability and honesty that we find connection and healing.

The human psyche requires an understanding of its place in the collective, to know that we are not alone in our struggles, to have a deep sense of context, and to feel that there is a larger purpose to it all. We are, by nature, meaning-making creatures, and it is by reconnecting with collective wisdom and stories that we can change our relationship to our suffering. We heal in community through seeing ourselves in others and in witnessing the trials, tribulations, and learnings others who have come before us have experienced. Motherhood is not a burden to be endured, but a transformative journey—a narrative we have the power to reshape.

WE DON'T KNOW WHO WE ARE

Many in modern Western cultures have lost touch with the stories and ancestral knowledge that once guided us through major identity shifts and ego explosions like motherhood. As a depth-oriented psychotherapist, I often use myth, metaphor, dream, and story in my work and personal journey. Mythic and archetypal forms and stories remind us of our place in the collective, and I found myself connecting to many on my journey into and through early motherhood. In this book, through sections I have called "Myths as Maps," I will acquaint—or reacquaint—you with Baba Yaga, Circe, Cinderella, Kali, Lilith, Eros, Psyche, and many others. Their traits and stories empower and teach us to understand and reclaim aspects of ourselves that have been lost, suppressed, or left dormant. These myths also reveal how society devalues the feminine—not only in people of all gender identities, but in the Earth herself.

This book also explores techniques to help you identify which beliefs and values are truly yours and which have been handed down to you. From this strengthened inner discernment, you can work toward crafting a life that feels aligned with your truth. I combine depth psychological approaches, feminist perspectives on outdated cultural structures, and embodied practices to provide strategies for navigating the very real conflict, vulnerability, and discomfort that show up on this journey of rediscovering the Self (capital *S*) and in our attempts to strengthen and deepen connection with others.

Finding and acting on inner discernment isn't easy. It requires a commitment to leaning into discomfort and sometimes facing intense inner challenges. It takes a commitment to leaning into what feels uncomfortable *at best* and what feels acutely painful and like you might actually die *at worst*. I felt, and still feel, immensely challenged to listen to that inner voice.

SEXPECTATIONS: THE STRUGGLE TO CONNECT TO MY DISCERNMENT

I was so lost in my head, trying to rationalize my choice, that I barely noticed he finished.

I was staring down at myself from the ceiling, my body going through the motions but my heart shaking its proverbial head at me, disappointed that I had once again said yes when I wanted to say no. And my mind? It was screaming obscenities at me. It was the ultimate mind/body/soul disconnection.

I hadn't seen him in a week, since he was on a business trip. We were at a hotel after a romantic dinner. "I should *want* to have sex with my partner," my mind kept telling me all throughout dinner. But I didn't.

I showed up to the evening anxious, knowing there was an expectation that sex would happen at the end of it. That because we hadn't seen each other in a week and he had planned a nice night, I would fuck him . . . not just fuck him, but do so with enthusiasm.

Truthfully? I was annoyed that he had planned the night at all. I wished he had come home from the trip after I was sleeping and just slipped into bed without any expectation of fanfare. I had enjoyed the week without the pressure, without the constant lingering feeling that I was letting him down, hurting his feelings, not meeting his needs, being a disappointment of a partner. The week had been so smooth. My daughter and I had gotten along better, I was less stressed, I had yelled less and laughed more. I had been able to read half a book in four days because I had three to four hours of glorious alone time each evening after she had gone to bed.

My mind was reeling as my body went through the motions. I couldn't believe he didn't even notice or care that I didn't seem to want to do this. Maybe I didn't want to be in this relationship. Maybe he wasn't my person. Maybe I was meant to parent alone. Maybe, maybe, maybe . . .

When all was said and done, I was angry. At him but mostly at myself. Over ten years of working on my codependent bullshit and the ways I self-abandon, and there I was. Again.

SHAME IS ALWAYS THE THROUGH LINE

If I had a dollar for every story a female client shared that felt similar to mine, I'd be rich. I share this one with you to remind you, as I will over and over, that you are not alone in your experiences and feelings. While the details might differ between the stories I've heard from women, the emotional through line is always the same: *shame*.

Shame around feeling:

- that they don't want their partner to touch them
- like they don't want their children to touch them
- like it might be easier to do if they were alone
- that their partner is just another child to take care of
- like they don't recognize themselves anymore
- short-tempered and burnt out
- like they are letting everyone down
- like they made a mistake in having children
- that they made a mistake in their choice of partner
- on the verge of tears or yelling
- like they sometimes want to rip their skin off
- a strong urge to pack a bag and disappear in the night

Here's the thing about shame. Most of us can agree that it is a horrible feeling, and yet it serves a psychological purpose. Shame encourages us to adhere to social norms and values and maintain social cohesion. It can motivate us toward more ethical and prosocial behavior, including triggering us to learn from our mistakes and change our behavior toward others. Shame encourages apologies and making amends. Plus, it prods us to look inward at areas we need to focus on for inner growth. From an evolutionary perspective, shame's purpose is to ensure we are not ostracized from the group or community, since, as social creatures, ostracization essentially meant death for our ancestors.

One of the biggest problems with shame, however, is that while we feel shame when we violate the social norms we *believe* in or *want* to adhere to, we also feel shame for violating the social norms we have been *conditioned* to believe in or adhere to. Because of this, shame is used as a weapon to control and manipulate people into compliance. It's wielded against us to ensure we don't rock the boat, question social norms we disagree with or find troublesome, stray too far from the group through exploration, gain new knowledge and inner growth, or challenge the pecking order in a society. Shame is used against us to make us feel that something is wrong with us. Because if we feel we are flawed, we will work extra hard to hide that part of ourselves, to prove we are "good." We will start the habit of hiding our true selves, our needs, and our desires, performing for our belonging and love. And once this codependent way of relating to others is formed, it's really hard to change.

Most of us are raised to believe in a very shame-based and conditional way of loving others and ourselves. This shame-based, codependent approach pervades all our relationships, not just romantic ones. This way of relating says, "I need to look and act a certain way to be loved, and so do you." We learn early to believe that our safety, value, and lovability depend on conforming to expectations—both ours and others'. This mindset drives us to preserve connections at any cost, even if they are unhealthy or unfulfilling, leading to manipulation, control, and self-contortion in pursuit of approval and a sense of safety. Part 3 of this book delves deeply into understanding and unpacking these dynamics of codependency.

Mothers, in particular, are told from all sides what good mothering and good mothers should look and act like—from family, friends, places of worship, social media, advertising, and experts. Almost none of it is realistic. And almost all of it is by design. Being *in* our shame maintains the status quo of patriarchal, economic, racial, gendered, cultural, political, educational, and healthcare systems that have been designed to benefit only a select few. When women are consumed with shame, they are too busy performing for their belonging to ask questions about why things are the way they are or challenge what doesn't feel right. They are too busy performing for their belonging to explore and follow what gives them a feeling of aliveness. They are too consumed with everything they "should" be doing to find time to nurture their Soul and question their larger purpose. Their energy is too overwhelmed by the feelings of not being enough to be channeled into changing what feels off-balance in their relationships or the broader systems that impact them.

I am going to make a bold statement here: Keeping women overwhelmed and feeling as though they are failing is how the current paradigm sustains itself. If a group as large in numbers as mothers collectively woke up and began questioning the patriarchal ideals of motherhood, challenged the social structures that keep them exhausted and feeling like they're drowning, and prioritized their own alignment and fulfillment, the entire structure of society would begin to shift.

The good news is it's already shifting. We are in an unbelievable moment in history right now. Never before in the upward of seven thousand years of living in a patriarchal society have there been so many people, not just women, questioning and challenging it all. We see this in the growing focus on mental health, community, and environmental care. It's reflected in the global women's marches of 2017; the rise of young people, women, BIPOC, and LGBTQIA+ individuals taking political office; the "escape the corset" and 4B movements in South Korea; and the 2022 "Woman, Life, Freedom" uprising in Iran. Yet this shift also faces fierce resistance from those threatened by change, evident in actions like the overturning of *Roe v. Wade* in the

US, the surge of restrictive legislation, and continued conflicts and wars rooted in dominance, hierarchy, and fear.

As Jungian-oriented psychotherapist Maureen Murdock aptly states, "Hate arises as women's power emerges."[2] This resistance is a sign that change is underway and that the structures designed to keep us small are beginning to fracture under the weight of collective awakening.

THE SWING OF THE PENDULUM

Many women, including myself and those in my practice, are struggling with fear and anxiety around what is happening socially, politically, economically, and to the Earth. We know that much of how we live is unsustainable—whether it's how we produce food, the isolated way we live, the relentless pace of life, the pedestalized culture of war, or the exploitative approach to healthcare and wages. In order to not be paralyzed by the fear, I actively work to reframe this tense time in history as a natural response to an unnatural environment. The pendulum is swinging, which is a pattern we have seen throughout human history.

The Pendulum Theory, or Hegelian Dialectic, proposed by eighteenth-century German philosopher Georg Wilhelm Friedrich Hegel, offers a lens through which to understand this pattern. The theory describes a constant push toward a more harmonious world through a cyclical process of challenge and integration. While rooted in a Western worldview, it can be a helpful tool for mitigating the anxiety many feel about the state of the world.

This complex process can be simplified into three stages, mirrored by the motion of a pendulum:

> Stage 1: A state of "knowing," where something is believed as an absolute truth. Here, the pendulum rests off-center, leaning toward one extreme. This certainty creates tension, sparking a natural curiosity or desire to explore the opposite perspective, leading to . . .

Stage 2: The push against the knowing or a challenge to the initial truth. The pendulum swings to the opposite side, representing a period of questioning, dismantling, and reevaluating established beliefs. This phase is characterized by opposition and disruption as old ideas are deconstructed.

Stage 3: The pendulum begins to swing back toward the center. However, rather than coming to rest, it lands just off-center on the original side, reflecting a new synthesis of ideas. This is a state of elevated awareness where opposing truths are reconciled, integrating past knowledge with new insights. Importantly, the pendulum never rests perfectly in the middle; instead, it tilts slightly, marking the beginning of another cycle as this new "truth" becomes the starting point for future questioning.

The key takeaway is that each swing of the pendulum propels us forward. We don't regress but instead build upon the learnings from past struggles. Our starting point for the next swing is where we left off from the last swing. We don't go backward, so to speak. Our journey is one of continuous growth, moving "up" in consciousness with each cycle.

Currently, we are in the midst of stage two, the pushback on what we once accepted as absolute truth. We are challenging long-held beliefs about gender, power, relationships, and the world itself. It's a time of dismantling outdated norms and reimagining a more inclusive and balanced future. While unsettling, this period of questioning is a crucial step toward the next stage of collective awareness and growth.

WHY WRITE THIS BOOK NOW?

Women have been feeling angry and burnt out for a long time, but given where we are on the axis of the pendulum, there's something different about this moment. Many factors have converged, making now a pivotal time for change.

1: Women now have more power to speak up honestly about their experiences.

Social media platforms have facilitated a shared language around experiences previously considered private, such as challenges related to the mental load, perceived weaponized incompetence, and movements like #MeToo.

A shared sense of urgency and a subtle (or not so subtle) feeling of panic that climate change and global unrest brings seems to be fueling the honesty of the shares in my therapy sessions and groups. I remember being deep in meditation prior to getting pregnant with my daughter, and the biggest inner conflict I had about bringing a child into this world was the state of the world itself. According to a 2021 Pew Research Poll, 9 percent of non-parents ages 18–49 cited "the state of the world" as the reason for them not wanting children, 5 percent cited "climate change/the environment," and 17 percent cited "financial reasons."[3] If we add all of those people together who are choosing to stay childless because of fear and struggle, we're at 31 percent.

Not only are we openly discussing and actively dismantling unhealthy relational, societal, and parenting structures, we are also feeling the pressure to live our lives more authentically, to reconsider what we've been taught in the face of many concurrent climate, financial, and humanitarian crises.

2: Social media has connected women worldwide, fostering a global support network.

I have a love-hate relationship with social media. It truly can bring out the worst in human beings, but it is also a powerful tool for connection and solidarity. At this moment in history, people are simultaneously feeling more depressed and isolated and yet are more accessible than ever before. I have come to understand that it's not the platform itself that causes disconnection but how it's used. When harnessed for genuine interaction, community building, and social change, it can be transformative. I have first-hand experience in creating and running online therapeutic groups and communities that have had huge positive impacts on people's mental, emotional, and even social lives, including bringing relationships they made online out into the real world.

Women are using these spaces to share their dissatisfaction with their partnerships and the cultural and social structures of motherhood, their struggles to regain some semblance of autonomy and selfhood after becoming parents, and their desires to redefine what it means to be a mother. Hashtags like #touchedout, #momrage, and #honestmotherhood have upward of five million related pieces of content and reflect a growing movement of women publicly challenging cultural expectations.

3: Society is evolving its expectations of men.
In just a couple of short generations, men face new pressures to be emotionally available partners and fathers. While this evolution is necessary, it's also met with resistance and fear, and many men are grappling with the balance between traditional roles and these emerging expectations.

While the fathers of today (Gen X and Millennials) are more present and emotionally attuned than even just one generation prior, I think it's fair to say that all of us are feeling the struggle of that stage two pendulum swing. Many of the straight women, with varying economic, religious, and ethnic backgrounds, in my therapy practice talk about not only wanting a male partner who is emotionally available and attuned to the needs of her and the family, but also someone who is a complete equal around the home, truly sees and respects her for the individual she is, has high emotional intelligence (EQ) and self-awareness, has communication and conflict resolution skills, and is actively working on improving themselves.

The men who are "doing the work," however, find themselves many times in a catch-22. As much as women express wanting these more emotionally mature men who are in touch with their feelings, they then struggle with what to do when the feelings presented are negative or painful.

In her groundbreaking book *The Will to Change*, American author, theorist, educator, and social critic bell hooks talks about this paradox through her personal experience with her partner and then through her research of other couples.

> When I was in my twenties, I would go to couples therapy, and my partner of more than ten years would explain how I asked him to talk about his feelings and when he did, I would freak out. He was right. It was hard for me to face that I did not want to hear about his feelings when they were painful or negative, that I did not want my image of the strong man truly challenged by learning of his weaknesses and vulnerabilities. Here I was, an enlightened feminist woman who did not want to hear my man speak his pain because it revealed his emotional vulnerability.
>
> I did not want to hear the pain of my male partner because hearing it required that I surrender my investment in the patriarchal ideal of the male as protector of the wounded. If he was wounded, then how could he protect me?[4]

4: The vice of societal control is tightening.

In recent years, we've witnessed a surge in restrictive legislation and social backlash aimed at maintaining traditional power structures. In the West, over the past decade, we have seen a massive uptick in the systemic stripping away of vulnerable people's rights. Anti-choice laws, attacks on LGBTQIA+ rights, and other regressive measures are symptoms of an old guard fighting to preserve its hold. However, these actions also signal the fear of those in power as they witness an unstoppable wave of change led by marginalized voices.

In my view, what we are witnessing globally is an extinction burst—a psychological concept that describes a dramatic spike in an unwanted behavior when attempts are made to stop or change it by removing reinforcement. This surge occurs as the behavior fights for survival but eventually diminishes if not reinforced. Simply put, things often get worse before they get better.

We experience smaller versions of extinction bursts in the work of self-development. When we try to change a maladaptive behavior in ourselves, we might realize a huge uptick in anxiety, anger, or resistance as our old patterns fight to stay. This also happens in relationships. Have you ever noticed that as you begin to work on, say, setting boundaries where there weren't any boundaries before, you might get passive-aggressive or guilting responses to your attempts? People resist change because it forces them to confront their own behaviors and beliefs, often without their consent or readiness.

In the face of an extinction burst, it's easy to panic, retreat, or revert to old ways. But we have a choice: to stay the course, deepen our education and awareness, cultivate empathy, and support both our growth and the growth of others. By doing so, we expand our consciousness and contribute to broader, more meaningful change.

I'm going to rattle off some very interesting stats here. Although it's important to note that these studies are often concentrated in the US and Europe and may not fully capture the experiences of all classes, religions, and ethnicities, they offer a glimpse into broader trends occurring at this moment in history:

- Since the COVID-19 pandemic, there has been a notable increase in divorces and separations, with 76 percent of new divorce cases initiated by women, up from 60 percent pre-pandemic. Researchers and therapists attribute it to increased time spent together revealing unresolved issues and the expectation that working from home would balance household responsibilities, which often did not materialize. Studies indicate that working women still spend an average of fifteen hours more per week on unpaid domestic labor compared to their male partners.[5]

- Nearly half of women in opposite-sex marriages now earn as much as or more than their husbands, a share that has tripled since the 1970s,[6] with nearly one-third of American women in opposite-sex relationships now earning more money than their spouse or partner.

- According to a Pew Research Study, dads now represent 18 percent of stay-at-home parents, up from 11 percent in 1989, highlighting a shift in traditional caregiving roles.[7]

- US birth rates have declined by 20 percent since 2007 (as have many other countries' birth rates). Reasons cited include cultural and climate uncertainty, financial concerns, and shifting social norms, such as waiting longer to marry and have children or choosing to remain child-free in favor of pursuing education and careers.[8]

While these statistics paint a picture of evolving norms, the emotional reality of these shifts is also palpable. In my private practice, group therapy, and retreats, I've observed a swell of unrest in my clients. Many are questioning why more than ever before, challenging what they have been taught they should or shouldn't do, expecting more of themselves emotionally but also more from their partners in every way, regardless of gender. This moment represents a collective reevaluation of home, community, and partnership. As society evolves, we face a choice: dig in our heels and resist, or buckle up and embrace opportunities to create more balanced and authentic ways of living.

ANGER AS A MOTIVATOR

While there has been a noticeable increase in books about parenting, mothering, relational struggles, and critiques of the patriarchy, I have yet to find the book I'm craving—a depth psychological exploration that weaves together the language of the Soul, the collective unconscious, and the cultural, social, and psychological forces that have shaped our experience of motherhood and relationships today.

In comparing many of these books, I've noticed two prevailing themes. On one side, there are instructional, affirming guides full of tips and practical advice on setting boundaries, asking for help, giving ourselves more grace, and gaining some insight into how we're feeling. These resources are valuable and have helped many. In my opinion, however, there tends to be a safe and almost distant feeling to many of them. They often place the responsibility of relational struggles solely on the mother without fully acknowledging the broader social systems and programming that impact her.

On the other side are the books fueled by women's (very justifiable) anger and rage. These are the books that pour gasoline on the smoldering coals of our injustices. They illuminate the deep-rooted issues of patriarchy, misogyny, and classism, igniting a fierce response in readers. These books got and get me going. Make my blood boil. Make me want to get up and scream. They also sometimes make me feel like my options for action are limited to FUCK ALL MEN. I'M GETTING DIVORCED, TAKING MY KID, AND GOING TO LIVE IN A COMMUNE OF ALL WOMEN *or* stay in the reality that is my reality, holding this hot coal in my hands without having tangible steps to move from rage to meaningful action.

Psychologically, anger is often viewed as a secondary emotion—what lies beneath it is often hurt, rejection, sadness, frustration, powerlessness, or fear. Many of us experience anger as a protective layer because it feels less vulnerable than confronting deeper emotions. We feel anger first but also have a tendency to cling to it. In many cultures, anger is more socially acceptable, particularly for men, while emotions like sadness and fear are often judged and suppressed.

As a therapist, I encourage my clients to explore what lies beneath their anger without bypassing it too quickly. In 2018, I wrote an article called "The Danger of False Positivity and Spiritual Bypassing." It spread faster than I expected and was referenced in numerous online publications. I wrote the article in response to what I felt and still feel is a fakeness in pop psychology and mainstream spirituality. Pushing for "positive vibes only," ending relationships with people who "bring you down" or don't have a "growth mindset," or labeling those who we don't agree with as "toxic" without deeper introspection is, in my professional opinion, a dangerous space to occupy. This mindset, while appealing, can bypass the crucial emotional work that anger signals—a need to address crossed boundaries or unhealed wounds. Like it or not, the ugly and uncomfortable parts of our humanity are where the most growth can occur.

Anger, when processed healthily, can be a powerful motivator for change, prompting us to set boundaries, speak up, or take action. However, our society often teaches men and women to respond differently to anger. Men are generally conditioned to express anger and repress emotions deemed feminine and weak, such as sadness or fear. Many are taught young that there are really only two feelings that are socially acceptable: lust and anger. Women, conversely, are taught that anger is unbecoming, leading to repression that can manifest as depression or anxiety.

In *Women Who Run with the Wolves*, Jungian psychoanalyst Dr. Clarissa Pinkola Estés notes that "it is a mistake for others to think that just because a woman is silent, it always means she approves of life as is."[9] She reminds us that while releasing anger is necessary at times, unchecked rage can corrode hope and fuel deeper pain. Understanding and integrating our anger is key to using it constructively.

As a depth psychotherapist, my work dives into the depths of the darker, shameful, and unbecoming parts of ourselves so that we can be curious and use them as catalysts for transformation. This book aims to balance the paradox of embracing our anger while not becoming consumed by it. By understanding the forces that shape our emotions and having the tools to express and process them, we can create meaningful change in our lives and relationships.

We need to be educated on the history, the truth, about how we got here. The truth about why so many women are talking about things like Mom Rage. To understand that patriarchy promises women they get to hold onto their righteous anger in exchange for being submissive and grateful for the breadcrumbs we get in our romantic relationships. We also need to have tangible tools to help us express ourselves, set boundaries, and self-soothe in the face of the inevitable emotional activation our partners and children will bring up in us. The big *but* here, the missing link between the two sides of this scale, is, in my opinion, the paradox. It is paramount that we hold both sides of the scale *at the same time*. That we don't stay too long in either the state of righteous anger or the sometimes endless loop of self-betterment. Staying in anger too long without metabolizing it and putting it into action can lead to bitterness, resentment, and a sense of victimhood. Conversely, staying in the emotionally disconnected place of focusing solely on self-improvement without acknowledging the underlying anger of why *we* have to be the ones to constantly strategize, learn more, do more, and be more to keep the family unit intact and functioning can have the *exact* same results.

If societal expectations of motherhood and womanhood remain unchallenged, the divide between genders will only grow. As a depth-oriented psychotherapist who studies the macro, the *collective* psyche, as much as the micro, the *individual* psyche, I see this leading to deeper societal rifts. My hope is that this book will guide you in holding space for both the anger that drives change and the self-compassion that sustains it, helping to bridge the gap between where we are and where we need to be.

DEPTH PSYCHOLOGY 101

Depth psychology, encompassing analytical, Jungian, and archetypal psychology, is rooted in the work of Carl Jung and is often referred to as the psychology of the Soul. Another hope I have in writing this book is to make Jung's work and depth psychology more accessible. These concepts can often feel dense and out of reach, and only a small percentage of modern therapists are even familiar with them.

Throughout the book, I will break down key depth psychological terms to demystify them and make them more approachable.

As a depth psychotherapist, I focus on what lies beneath the surface of consciousness, exploring the spiritual and transcendent aspects of the human experience. Modern psychology often views spirituality as merely a tool for community or comfort and, at times, as something unscientific. However, neuroscience now shows that our brains are wired for spirituality, suggesting that recognizing our interconnectedness is crucial for a meaningful life,[10] something Jung nodded to in what he called the "Religious Function" of the psyche.

Depth psychology integrates personal spirituality—not in a dogmatic sense, but in the understanding that healing involves more than just the intellect. A large part of healing comes from a deep sense of unity with the cosmos. The essence of depth psychology is moving beyond the concrete intellect to the symbolism and metaphor of the unconscious, so I use dreams, myths, stories, and archetypes to help clients tap into deeper understanding and reconnect with ancient guides for navigating life's challenges.

Depth psychology is non-pathologizing and strength-affirming, going beyond the logical and biological to engage with aspects of ourselves that we cannot fully grasp on those levels. My work as a depth psychotherapist focuses on both my client's personal journey of individuation and the undeniable interconnectedness of all beings, offering another way to make meaning and feel connected to something greater than ourselves.

DEPTH 101

Psyche: Latin for "Soul."

Numinous: That sometimes overwhelming feeling or sense of spiritual or religious quality. Mysterious, awe-inspiring, often inexplicable and non-rational, indicating or suggesting the presence of divinity.

Individuation: A lifelong journey toward wholeness and self-realization, achieved by exploring life's meaning and purpose within the larger community and involving integration of the shadow Self and making the unconscious conscious through self-awareness, ego breakdowns, and initiations.

Shadow: Repressed parts of ourselves (good or bad) deemed unacceptable by society or upbringing. These traits, buried in the unconscious, must be discovered and integrated to avoid being unconsciously driven by them.

Collective Unconscious: The deepest layer of the psyche, separate from both the conscious and unconscious mind and shared by all humanity. This collective layer originates in the inherited structure of the brain and is the source of instincts, myths, legends, and archetypes.

Archetype: A primal or universal symbol or pattern within the collective unconscious that connects humanity and helps give the logical mind a framework through which we can interpret numinous experiences. Most archetypes have both golden qualities—those that are easily recognized for their positive impact—and shadow qualities, which may be more challenging but ultimately offer powerful lessons for personal growth.

Language and storytelling are unique human skills that have always been used to pass down experiences and wisdom through generations. Myths, fairy tales, and folklore provide narratives for how our lives might unfold—a relatable path, character, or archetypal image that shows us that we are not alone and what life's initiatory experiences might look like, sometimes warning us of life's lessons to prepare us and temper the fear of something otherwise unexpected.

Humans, especially in modern Western societies, have made great efforts to remove the sacred from their daily lives, placing increasing reliance on science and logic. While we often believe that this reliance will provide a greater sense of security, it has instead left many of our psyches starved for the connection that our souls once had to the ineffable—those things that can't be captured by words or reason but must be felt and experienced. Joseph Campbell, who extensively studied the role of myth and initiation in human psychology, noted, "This is our problem as modern, 'enlightened' individuals, for whom all gods and devils have been rationalized out of existence."[11] Instead of feeling safer, we often feel more disconnected and out of control.

For some, there may be a familiarity with stories from the Bible, Greek mythology, or the fairy tales popularized by the Brothers Grimm, while others might be more connected to the themes in texts like the Bhagavad Gita, the Vedas, or the Quran. These examples represent just a few of the many mythic and archetypal narratives that have shaped human understanding. In contemporary times, stories are often conveyed through movies and TV shows rather than oral or written traditions. Due to our disconnection from the numinous—the spiritual aspect of life—we often view these stories merely as entertainment, filtering them through a purely cognitive lens. However, the psyche absorbs these images and stories, using them as lessons and life maps, whether we are aware of them consciously or not.

The danger lies in our lack of awareness of this process. Without proper understanding of the metaphorical and archetypal meanings, modern interpretations can unintentionally reinforce harmful stereotypes by inadvertently conditioning our girls into "princesses" and grooming our boys to conform to the patriarchal system, perpetuating the unbalanced order of things.

THE PATH FORWARD

Throughout this book, I'll guide you through some myths that shape our experiences as women and parents. In part 1, we'll dismantle The Myths of Motherhood—the beliefs that we should instinctively know how to parent and that the way we mother today is the way it's always been done. We'll explore how modern society isolates mothers by stripping away communal support, glorifies busyness and productivity at the expense of well-being, and upholds the harmful narrative that martyrdom is an essential part of mothering.

In part 2, we'll unpack The Myths of Sex—the cultural narratives that shape our understanding of gender, power, and our sense of Self. These myths impact not only our public lives, but also our relationship with sex—our desire, pleasure, and agency. By naming and dismantling these myths, we can reclaim our authentic sexual selves and move toward a more liberated, embodied existence.

In part 3, we'll examine The Myths of Relationships, where we explore how becoming a mother transforms our relationship not only with ourselves, but also with our partners, children, friends, families, and communities. We'll dive deep into the ways a codependent society uses fear to keep women from knowing themselves, maintaining power structures that prevent authentic connection.

Throughout each chapter, you'll be invited to explore some of my most personal stories, gain insights from my work with clients, and reflect on how we arrived at this pivotal moment in history. Some of these stories might be challenging to hear. They are raw, real, and unpolished, exploring hard topics like birth trauma and sexual coercion. I'll also present myths and thought-provoking questions to help you engage more deeply with the material, offering opportunities to apply these reflections to your life and personal growth.

I hope that the insights, stories, and therapeutic techniques I provide in this book can serve as a flashlight on a path that can sometimes feel quite dark and lonely. This book is an invitation to explore the unknown territories of your inner world, to challenge the myths that have shaped your experiences, and to reclaim your voice, your body, and your truth. Together, we will navigate this journey of self-discovery and healing and, in doing so, pave the way for more fulfilling and balanced relationships with others and with ourselves.

Part 1

the myths of motherhood

> "We need women who are so strong they can be gentle, so educated they can be humble, so fierce they can be compassionate, so passionate they can be rational, and so disciplined they can be free."
>
> —Kavita Ramdas[1]

Part 1 sets the stage for our collective awakening to the forces that have shaped and, in many ways, suppressed our most natural ways of being. The weight of dominator social structures, the crushing expectations of motherhood, and the pervasive narratives that tell us to shrink ourselves—these are not just stories we inherit; they are lived realities that have seeped into every corner of our lives. But now, we are beginning to remember. Remember the wisdom that existed before these narratives, and remember that reclaiming our stories is an act of courage, a quiet revolution of the Soul.

1

from maiden to mother

"Birth is the death of the life we have known; death is the birth of the life we have yet to live."

—Marion Woodman, *The Pregnant Virgin*[1]

I felt like a starfish, arms spread across a T-shaped metal table, a curtain from my chest down blocking my vision. I was numb, unable to see more than the anesthesiologist on my right and my partner on my left. There were people all around my body, touching and moving and poking it, talking about me, some I couldn't see and many never actually acknowledging me.

Time had become strange and distorted the past five days in the hospital leading up to this point. Lack of sleep, a constant painful barrage of interventions and medications, being confined to one room—mostly in an uncomfortable bed—and a small hallway had blurred the lines between reality and a nightmare. And now, I was splayed out on a cold table where more than half the people in the room acted as if my body and I were separate entities.

I suddenly felt my body being pulled upward. I felt pressure and then release as they pulled my daughter's six-pound-twelve-ounce body from mine. There was no sound other than beeping and murmured medical speak as the nurses rushed the baby to a table just outside my vision. They were all talking at once, making it impossible to make out what was being said. Then, I heard my daughter scream . . . and scream. No one came to tell me what was happening. I frantically yelled at my partner to go to her. To find out what was going on. More crying and screaming. And still no one told me anything.

I finally yelled, "What is happening?! Someone tell me what the fuck is going on!" with every ounce of strength I could muster.

A nurse, annoyed and hurried, rushed over and hissed, "The baby has meconium in her lungs; we're suctioning her." Then she was gone. I lay there quietly, alone, warm tears streaming down my face. No one noticed.

This was not how it was supposed to happen. I was supposed to labor comfortably at home for as long as possible, then make my way to the hospital calmly, where my doula would meet us, string up twinkly lights, and put on some good music and a lavender essential oil diffuser. I was supposed to get in a tub. Be unmedicated and untethered to monitors and screens. Feel my transition from early to active labor. Get lost in the primal dance of birth. Be supported by my partner and mother. Feel an ancestral connectedness to the millions of women who had crossed this threshold before me as I naturally pushed my daughter into the world.

I had read Ina May, taken birth preparedness classes, and created a birth preferences list—none of this was on it. Instead, my daughter was cut from my body in a rushed decision made out of panic and exhaustion. A room full of nurses and interns crowded around my bed, strapping oxygen to my face, injecting me with terbutaline, and tossing my body around to find the heartbeat they had lost moments earlier as I sat on the toilet.

It took me nearly a year to be able to recount my birth experience without tears. Even still, emotion comes suddenly when certain memories creep their way into my consciousness. There were many more horrible things that happened in the five days leading up to my emergency C-section, but the point of this book is not to belabor (pun intended) every detail of my birth trauma. It is, instead, an abbreviated version of my story, given as an offering at the altar of an overlooked, undervalued, rushed through, and downright disrespected sacred initiatory experience. An altar that more of us stand at together, in solidarity, than I ever realized.

FROM PREGNANT PRINCESS TO POSTPARTUM PAUPER

In the United States, around 82 percent of women claim to desire a natural birth or one with an epidural and vaginal delivery. Yet 32.3 percent of those labors end in C-sections. Similar rates are seen across Europe (except for a few outliers), slightly higher in Australia, and somewhat lower in Canada. In other parts of the world, those rates vary significantly based on factors like access to hospitals, maternal and paternal education, wealth, and cultural and religious views on childbirth. The World Health Organization (WHO) recommends a cesarean rate of around 15 percent and only when medically justified. Yet, in places like South America and the Caribbean, C-sections account for 43 percent of all births. According to WHO, the cesarean rate in Africa is as low as 11.9 percent in Uganda and as high as 75 percent in private sector hospitals in South Africa.[2]

Studies conducted in Japan, Turkey, and the United States show that around 45 percent of new mothers report a traumatic birth.[3] In Sweden, a correlation was found between a woman's perception of her birth experience and her mental health up to seven years later, with negative experiences often resulting in long-lasting emotional struggles affecting relationships with partners and even their children.[4] I have often wondered, how much of this trauma can be explained by the over-medicalization of the birthing process in Western cultures? From our disconnection with a more grounded, natural, physical, and psychological approach to pregnancy, birth, and early motherhood?

The average pregnant woman in the United States sees her doctor ten to fifteen times over about seven to eight months. We're poked and prodded, and the baby is measured in every possible way. Outside of the countries that seem to be the gold standard in many of their approaches to medical care, such as Denmark or Sweden, rarely does modern Western medicine give us access to birthing, breastfeeding, newborn care, maternal mental health, or relationship classes. Those we must seek out and, most often, pay for ourselves. Alternatively, how many times does the average postpartum woman see her doctor in the United States? *Once.* Six weeks after birth, with no comprehensive physical exam.

In some cultures, pregnancy is idealized to the point of fetishization. It is not uncommon for people to hold open doors for you or for strangers to smile at you on the street or touch your stomach without asking. Comments about "glowing" appearances or guesses about the baby's gender based on the shape or height of the belly are frequent. Elaborate gender reveal parties—complete with fireworks, balloon releases, or smoke bombs—are often staged for social media, with friends and family capturing these moments for viral TikTok videos. This idealization can even extend into societal norms, laws, and policies.

The moment you have the baby, the doctor appointments stop and people's curiosity feels as though it evolves into judgment. Smiles turn into exasperated sighs when the baby cries in public, and unsolicited advice replaces compliments. This cultural transition—what we call in depth psychology "Pregnant Princess to Postpartum Pauper"—is stark and isolating.

THE CULTURAL DISCONNECT

In many societies, the early transition to motherhood is recognized as a profound shift in identity, not merely a temporary phase. These cultures often emphasize a significant postpartum rest period, lasting between twenty to forty days, to support a mother's physical, emotional, and spiritual healing. For instance, Mexico's *la cuarentena* and China's *zuo yue zi* provide thirty to forty days of complete support, where the community ensures the mother focuses solely on recovery and bonding with her newborn. Similar practices exist in Korea, Japan, and across Islamic, Vedic, and Indigenous traditions, reflecting a universal understanding of the need for extended postpartum care.

These practices also reflect a broader global perspective in which the birth of a child is considered the birth of a new woman and, by extension, a new family. This perspective contrasts sharply with norms in the US and many other Western cultures, where new mothers are often expected to "bounce back" to their pre-pregnancy routines, bodies, and lives as quickly as possible. The idea that birth fundamentally changes a woman—chemically, hormonally, and in terms of identity—is deeply embedded in many non-Western traditions. Meanwhile, the trajectory of much of modern Western culture, influenced by factors such as patriarchal capitalism, liberalism, and individualism, often overlooks this significant transformation, emphasizing instead a quick return to the "normal" of life before childbirth.

Two days after my own C-section, I was sent home alone with my partner, mother, and newborn. Five days later, my mother had to leave to return back to New York. One week after giving birth, it was just the three of us—two adults attempting to care for a baby who needed attention around the clock while also trying to feed and care for ourselves somewhere in between. It was a lonely time centered on survival and little else.

THE MYTH OF INNATE MOTHERHOOD

There is a pervasive and damaging myth that women will just "know" what to do when it comes to birth and motherhood. That the transition from childfree to mother will be beautiful, even easy. That we will instinctively know how to breastfeed, change diapers, and manage our emotional responses to a brand-new, tiny person who we have never met and who needs us—our bodies, minds, emotions, energy—around the clock. But often, it doesn't happen like that. Many of our births were not magical or intimate. We did not experience gushing happy tears and didn't have immediate bonds with our babies.

Early motherhood is not the serene image often portrayed in the media. We are not draped in white gowns, floating around the home with a glow as we lovingly stare down at our babies (in full hair and makeup, of course). Instead, we are raw and primal, coping with swelling, blood, adult diapers, greasy hair, milk and spit-up stains, and dark circles under sleepless eyes.

The immediate shift in how society views new mothers, paired with the lack of support, contrasts sharply with the myth that this will be one of the happiest periods of our lives. This dissonance leads many women to feel duped, overlooked, isolated, abandoned, and, in many cases, angry. Few have people to talk to about these very real and very normal experiences, as it feels like most of our loved ones just want to hear how grateful for and in love with our new baby we are. They stop by to hold the baby for an hour, they might bring food, and then they rush back to their equally busy lives and jobs. Or, in my case, because I had my daughter two weeks before COVID sent Los Angeles into full lockdown, no one was even allowed to come see us or the baby until she was almost six months old.

Rarely do people ask about the pain, struggle, fear, and even rage that being a new mother elicits. Mothers-to-be in Western (and often white) cultures are celebrated and carried on the shoulders of society up to the threshold of birth, only to be dropped there without the proper support or initiation into who and what we now embody. It's no wonder so many new mothers feel lost, confused, and overwhelmed.

A CULTURE OF UNINITIATED CHILD-MOTHERS

Dr. Clarissa Pinkola Estés calls the uninitiated mother the "child-mother"—a woman who is old enough to have babies but lacks the mothering she herself needs to feel supported, grounded, and secure in her new role.[5] Many of our mothers and grandmothers were also child-mothers, entering motherhood without the guidance of wise elders and disconnected from the ancestral wisdom that had once provided crucial support. Their initiatory process of matrescence, a term introduced by Dana Raphael to describe the psychological and physical transition from maiden to mother, was thwarted. Instead of moving through the natural evolution from child-mother to queen mother, their transition was disrupted by societal forces that replaced internal knowing with external expectations. Instead of being guided by generational wisdom, they experienced childbirth and child-rearing in a fragmented, medicalized system that prioritized institutional authority over intuition.

This mothering, guidance, and support by wise elders was once essential not only for developing our own intuition, but also for providing the emotional and spiritual support that is so necessary for this profound transformation. Without experienced and initiated women to mentor them, new mothers remain psychologically uninitiated, struggling to integrate their experiences and access their deeper knowing. If we did not encounter major thresholds or transitional experiences throughout our lives, such as childbirth, we would forever experience the world through the eyes of our child selves with no integration of experience or realized potential. The wise elders of our past ensured that this transition into motherhood was not just physical, but also psychological and spiritual, helping women move from uncertainty to embodied knowing and allowing them to make sense of the often traumatic initiatory experience of birth.

Much of this connection to Self has been disrupted by a society that values external authority and materialism over internal wisdom. We live in a world that worships the mind, intellect, and reason, encouraging dichotomous thinking and a lost connection to the nuanced wisdom of the human experience, the spiritual realm, the innate cycles of the body, and the intuition. At some point, our mothers' mothers stopped listening to their ancestors and their own internal knowing, and the tree of wisdom was chopped down. This rupture in the lineage of maternal wisdom left future generations to navigate motherhood without the guidance and grounding that had once been essential.

Marion Woodman, a pioneer in depth psychology, wrote in *The Pregnant Virgin*, "One of the central and most potentially destructive issues women face is that of beginning various psychological initiation processes with initiators who have not completed the process themselves."[6] With no models for secure and integrated motherhood, many women were left grasping for guidance in a culture that offered little beyond rigid expectations and judgment. Nowhere is this severance more evident than in the way childbirth itself became a medical event, stripped of its intuitive and communal nature.

For example, practices like twilight births were common in the West until the early 1970s. Women would wake up with a child in their arms, having no recollection of the traumatic birthing experience they had just endured. Nurses recounted stories of the horrific self-harm and psychotic behaviors in mothers and spoke of infants who reacted horribly to the cocktail of heavy drugs given to the birthing mother. The iconic image of the doctor holding the newly born infant upside down and smacking their bottom? This practice originates from this era, when almost catatonically drugged babies were sometimes unable to breathe on their own. These traumatic birthing practices, driven by a medicalized and detached approach, highlight how deeply women relied on external authority figures over their own bodies and instincts. In many cases, women were not only physically severed from their own birthing experiences, but psychologically disconnected from their power as creators of life.

Today, we still see echoes of this disconnection. Many of us seek out the emotional support and encouragement that were once provided by a small and close-knit community of family, friends, and wise elders, but we now find it from outside sources, including strangers or on social media. While social media can be a valuable tool for information, it can also be a mine field of "mom shaming" and advice from well-meaning but unqualified influencers. We are confused, lost, and tired, hoping someone will give us the right answer on how to get our baby to sleep longer, how to breastfeed painlessly, how to find time to take a shower and clean ourselves up so we might still look attractive to our partners, how to find the mental time and capacity to call our friends, and how to feel like some semblance of ourselves . . . whoever that even is anymore. It's unsurprising we continue to be a culture of child-mothers seeking validation from outside of ourselves, much like our mothers and grandmothers before us, who also lacked access to generational wisdom.

This trend is exacerbated by the generational shift away from communal living. Older Gen Z, Zillennials, Millennials, and some younger Gen Xers often lack a supportive group of elders, not just in child-rearing, but for life in general. A 2019 Pew Research Center study found that Millennials are much less likely than previous generations to live with a family of their own—whether that includes a spouse, children, or both. Only 55 percent of Millennials live in such family structures, compared to 69 percent of Boomers and 85 percent of the Silent Generation.[7] Millennials are also more likely than other groups to live with a child and no spouse, and many are waiting longer to marry and have children due to factors like labor and housing shortages and economic instability.

Even when Millennials do have children, they are often parenting in isolation, within nuclear families where one or two adults do all of the work of raising children while working full-time jobs. Many families lack the resources to hire outside help, such as nannies, night nurses, or even day care. While some may have grandparents or aunties and uncles living close by, the lineage of passed-down wisdom remains sparse. This lack of intergenerational support and wisdom has left many of us feeling like child-mothers, disconnected from the community, support, and guidance that were once foundational to the maternal experience.

THE TRANSFORMATIVE POWER OF RITUAL

Rituals connect us to the community, the divine, the numinous. They give our Soul, our psyche, a deep understanding of the cycles of and our place in the universe, of the importance of change. They test who we are, allowing us to reflect on and integrate all we have learned up to that point on our path of individuation, and then move into our next phase of life prepared for the discomfort of the psychic death that happens as our identity changes. This is particularly important during major life transitions, such as becoming a mother, where there is a profound need for containment and support.

Not only do humans crave ritual or initiation to help move them forward on their path, but these are imperative to our flourishing as we mature. After a particularly chaotic few years in my early thirties, I wrote my psychology grad school thesis titled "The Archetype of Initiation: A Physical Manifestation through Psychically Co-created Trauma." Through this work, I explored the importance of initiation for the psyche and the phenomena of how far our psyche is willing to go to experience it.

What I found was that when we do not honor our innate need for initiation, our psyche unconsciously seeks it out. In the absence of formal and sanctioned initiations in modern culture, our psyche often co-creates or gravitates toward chaotic or traumatic experiences to fulfill this need. Meaning, a deep, instinctual part of us, the part connected to our inner wisdom and something greater, may seek out or even stir up a significant event as a catalyst, forcing us into the transformation it knows we require. If you find your eyes widening in response to this seemingly wild claim, just know, mine did as well.

DEPTH 101

Initiation/Ritual/Rite of Passage: Essentially interchangeable terms. A process in which the ego is broken down, self-reflection and self-exploration become paramount, and a new way of understanding the Self is achieved. This leads to a more integrated and often transformed version of us in the world, having been rebuilt with the new understandings that came from and through this process.

Formal, Sanctioned, or Cultural Initiations: Rituals still respected by our society and considered part of our modern culture. Some of these include weddings, bar/bat mitzvahs, Aqiqah, Ritusuddhi, Holy Communion, Dastar Bandhi, Seijin-no-Hi, Ji/Guan Li, quinceañeras, Apache Na'ii'ees, graduations, and funerals.

Psychically Co-created Trauma/Chaos: The trauma or chaos that our psyche seeks out or creates to provide the initiatory experience it knows it needs to evolve, but that our ego isn't willing or able to acknowledge the need for yet. It's the proverbial push off the ledge we aren't willing to jump from because we don't trust ourselves or the process of growth.

This need for ritual and initiation is particularly relevant for new mothers, who are often left without a sense of ritualized support or acknowledgment of their transformation. Instead of being supported through this initiatory process, they can feel unanchored and adrift, struggling to find meaning and identity in the chaos of early motherhood. The sheer act of birth, or really any way in which you become a mother—surrogacy, adoption, fostering—is, in and of itself, an almost immediate explosion of the ego, of who you thought you were, regardless of the books you've read or classes you may have taken.

Like any other major transition, the shift from the state of child-mother to mother, or from what we might call in depth psychology the embodiment of the Maiden archetype to the Mother archetype, requires a supportive and stabilizing container or platform on which to take place. Nurturing matrilineal lines, myth, fairy tales, and even therapy can provide this containment.

DEPTH 101

Maiden Archetype (or Child-Mother Archetype if a mother): The archetype of the uninitiated girl or woman. The golden qualities of the Maiden embody youth, innocence, vitality, independence, and curiosity. She is full of potential and represents new beginnings. However, her shadow side reflects naivety, powerlessness, and a sense of victimhood, often portrayed as the "damsel in distress." In myths and fairy tales, the Maiden is frequently depicted as being asleep, imprisoned, or captured—symbolically or literally—waiting to be rescued, typically by a male figure, and often wronged by an external villain.

Mother Archetype: An initiated feminine archetype. The golden qualities of the Mother embody nurturing, generosity, attentiveness, service, care, power, and wisdom. She is a source of life and unconditional support. However, the shadow side of the Mother can manifest as over-giving, neglecting herself, and falling into patterns of codependency or martyrdom. She may struggle with her sense of identity, be preoccupied with fears of abandonment, and develop an overbearing need to be needed.

The concept of matrescence encompasses more depth than simply the psychological and physical transition into motherhood. According to psychologist Dana Raphael, matrescence marks a profound reorganization of a woman's identity.[8] As women move through this process, they must navigate new responsibilities, social expectations, and evolving relationships with the world around them. Psychologist Daniel Stern further elaborates on this transition with his theory of the "motherhood constellation," which explains how becoming a mother activates new mental frameworks focused on the survival and well-being of the infant, often at the expense of the mother's own needs and desires. This internal conflict—where mothers feel pulled between their own identity and societal ideals of self-sacrifice—can lead to feelings of isolation and identity loss, particularly in societies that idealize motherhood as martyrdom.[9]

We certainly don't need ritual or community support to *physically* transition from Maiden to Mother. Just like we don't need it to go from childhood to adolescence to adulthood, or from middle age to old age. These physiological transitions happen whether we like them or not. But as a therapist, more often than not, the clients I see in my practice who come to me in a state of crisis, complaining of stuckness, anxiety, confusion, or even a general sense of relational or life dissatisfaction and disconnection, are almost always in the midst of a life transition in which they feel very alone. Alternatively, they are on the other side of a transition without a clear sense of Self, finding themselves now defined by the chaos or trauma that triggered the transition, but not having made meaning of it, and with no understanding of their new life's purpose or identity. They cling to old emotional and psychological tools from previous life phases, baffled that nothing works as they try to white-knuckle the change.

This is what we call the phase of transition or the liminal space—when you are between the old and new sense of Self. Liminality is a time of darkness. The tunnel. The forest. It is in this space where a deeper sense of knowing yourself emerges. Where the process of alchemy breaks us down and a truer, more integrated version of ourselves can emerge . . . but not without struggle.

> ## DEPTH 101
>
> *Liminal Space/Liminality*: A sociology term derived from the Latin word *limen*, which means "threshold" or "in between." The phase between the old and new sense of Self, or between pre-ritual and post-ritual status, where there is struggle, disorientation, and learning.
>
> *Alchemy*: Originally the precursor to chemistry, alchemy involved breaking down and understanding matter. However, many practitioners brought their mystical knowledge and practices with them, so in depth psychology, we understand the process as a way to break down, study, rebuild, and integrate the psychic components of our life journey (i.e., the process of individuation).

Liminality often compels individuals to confront and acknowledge the state of struggle they are in. During these times, clients, especially mothers, frequently report an experience of deep disconnection and ruptures with partners, friends, and loved ones. They may feel lost in their own identity and report overwhelming levels of postpartum anxiety.

I want to emphasize that it is *not coincidence* that so many new mothers come to therapy all discussing similar struggles in a society that does nothing to support or usher us into this new identity. Many of us act out in self-sabotaging ways, such as neglecting our self-care and health (including emotional and mental). Self-sabotage can look like holding perfectionistic and unrealistic expectations of ourselves and our partners, overextending ourselves and failing to uphold boundaries, and neglecting personal interests and relationships. Additionally, we put faith in relationships we intuitively know are emotionally unsafe only to have the inevitable betrayal deepen our sense of isolation and mistrust in others and ourselves. These are all chaotic ways that our psyche begs us to:

- Wake up.

- Go inward and pay attention.

- Create and lean into support systems and social networks.

- Learn, dig, go deeper into knowledge we have been cut off from.

- Become our own fierce self-advocate in a society that does not advocate for us.

- Practice, learn, and integrate more emotionally mature ways of showing up for ourselves and our relationships.

- Build a deeper sense of meaning and connection to something greater than ourselves.

- Emerge an embodied and self-assured Self that's prepared for the next phase of life we have transitioned into.

THERAPY AS AN INITIATORY CONTAINER

When we first started working together, Sam had a two-year-old. Her intake form read like a mom influencer's Instagram infographic of common mother struggles: low-level depression, anxiety, insomnia, brain fog, fatigue, irritability, loneliness, not feeling like herself, and feeling disconnected from her husband and her daughter.

During our first session, she cried for twenty of the fifty minutes. She complained of being "so tired" and continually apologized for crying. She talked about not being the mother she wanted to be, how it was so much different than she had anticipated. She told me she had always been so career-driven and had decided on a whim to get pregnant because she was in her thirties, was sick of the fast-paced city life, and thought it was time she get serious and settle down. Now, two years after moving states and to the suburbs, becoming a mother, and transitioning from a full-time career to freelance and part-time work, she was grappling with regret, and then guilt for feeling regret.

She didn't know who she was anymore outside of wife and mother. She didn't have anyone to talk to because all her friends in her new town only seemed to want to talk about their kids, and it made her "want to scream." All she wanted to do was *not* talk about her kid. She longed for deep conversations about the meaning of life, amazing books she had read, politics, self-development—anything beyond the endless chattering about kids that dominated her new social circles. She felt alone and often like she was "climbing the walls" of her own life.

Over the course of our two years working together, we explored passion, career, community, and codependency recovery. We delved into initiation, ritual, liminality, and individuation. Sam made strides in speaking up about her needs with her husband, setting boundaries with her parents, taking time for herself, and making space for her creativity. She practiced playing and resting, allowing her husband the space to parent without her standing over his shoulder, and reconnecting with the sexual side of herself that she felt she had lost in her transition to motherhood.

I witnessed Sam grieve the death of her inner Maiden, wrestle with her new identity as a Mother, and ultimately embrace the Queen archetype—a woman confident, self-assured, and integrated in her evolving roles.

> **DEPTH 101**
>
> *Queen Archetype*: Another initiated feminine archetype, represented by the golden qualities of confidence, leadership, strength of heart, grace, dignity, sovereignty, and empowerment. She rules with wisdom and a sense of purpose. However, the shadow side of the Queen can emerge as arrogance, a hunger for power, control, and vindictiveness. In this shadow form, she may misuse her authority, becoming more concerned with dominance than leadership.

I fell deeply in love with her as a person. If we had lived in the same city (and I wasn't her therapist, of course), I could have seen us being friends. We wrapped up our work together in the beginning of 2020, right as I was about to have my first baby. We both cried, and she imparted some of her maternal wisdom to me, having made it through the newborn, infant, and toddler stage ahead of me.

Two years after that last session, we connected over Zoom. I opened by apologizing, feeling I could have been a better therapist for her. After becoming a mother myself, I gained an even deeper appreciation for Sam's experience. We spoke about the hard and often lonely realities of early motherhood and how it involves a profound dissolution of the Self. We also discussed how therapy had provided a safe container for her initiation, allowing her to fully grieve, sit in the liminality, and ultimately emerge feeling grounded and confident in her new identity.

Every initiation follows a similar archetypal story: the catalytic event that separates us from who we were (death), the passage through darkness (liminality), and ultimately, rebirth. In the darkness, we confront deep discomfort, face inner challenges, and encounter the "dragons" that need to be slain. This phase demands exploration, respect, and true acceptance, along with an active surrender to the unknown, allowing us to integrate the lessons learned during the "death" or separation phase.

Through the process of writing my thesis all those years ago, I came to understand how therapy itself can serve as an initiatory stage or a container where a new version of the Self can be discovered and integrated. But it was my work with Sam that truly brought this deep understanding to life, showing how therapy can guide someone through these stages toward rebirth.

In *Transpersonal Psychotherapy: Theory and Practice*, Valerie Coumont Graubart identifies three key elements that help a person navigate major transitions: inner security, a loving and supportive network, and a storyline that ultimately gives meaning.[10] For most of us, these must be consciously cultivated, as modern Western society rarely provides them.

Prioritizing the creation of inner security, fostering a loving and supportive network, and finding meaning isn't selfish; it's imperative. Healthy, well-adjusted parents are crucial for raising healthy, well-attached children. Inner security allows us to trust the ego-dissolving process of transformation, a loving and supportive network (which can include your therapist) helps us navigate the darkness, and finding meaning in suffering helps us integrate and move through that suffering toward rebirth.

Without honoring the full process of initiation, integration is lost and we are left in the darkness, stuck in the phase of transition—no longer who we were, yet unclear about who we are becoming: the child-mother. As Graubart aptly states, "What makes change so difficult for us is that in order for the new to come, the old must decay, crumble, or die, sometimes with violent suddenness. Change, even in its benign manifestations, always carries a component of loss, even when it is change for the better."[11] Our rebirth lies on the other side of this loss.

MYTHS AS MAPS
Sarah's Journey from Maiden to Queen Through the Labyrinth

A modern myth that illustrates the transition from Maiden to Queen is the 1986 fantasy film *Labyrinth*, directed by Jim Henson. This film offers a powerful depiction of how one can move from the shadow aspects of the Maiden archetype to embody the empowered Queen archetype through self-discovery and integration. Sarah, played by Jennifer Connelly, is a teenage girl who embarks on a quest to rescue her baby brother Toby from the Goblin King, played by David Bowie.

At the start, Sarah is portrayed as childlike, despite being sixteen. She plays dress-up with her dog; argues with her stepmother and father; sits in her room surrounded by dolls, stuffed animals, and other toys; and wishes someone would save her from her life. She feels victimized by her parents' expectations of her to help with her baby brother and their disapproval of her desire to hold onto her childlike ways.

Her character reflects both the golden and shadow sides of the Maiden archetype. While the Maiden embodies qualities such as creativity, playfulness, and innocence, its shadow side manifests as naivety, victimhood, and powerlessness. Sarah embodies this shadow when she feels wronged by her parents' expectations and resists the responsibilities of growing up.

In a moment of frustration, Sarah wishes that someone would take her brother away. "I wish the goblins would come and take you away . . . right now." In a flash of thunder and white drapes, feathers, and the most glorious '80s mullet you have ever seen, Jareth, the Goblin King, is there to fulfill her wish, taking her brother to his castle and giving Sarah thirteen hours to solve the labyrinth before he turns her brother into a goblin forever.

This event catalyzes Sarah's Heroine's Journey, a feminine expression of the Hero's Journey—a process of initiation and transformation that follows a metaphorical path of death, darkness, and rebirth. The labyrinth, a maze-like puzzle, symbolizes the internal journey of self-discovery and is the backdrop for the film. We see Sarah's character transform from a naive and stubborn young girl who's most repeated line is "It's not fair!" into a self-possessed young woman who learns to listen to her intuition, forge deep friendships, and problem-solve in mature ways.

In the final confrontation with Jareth, Sarah's external battles culminate in an internal reckoning. He pleads with her to stay with him and let him rule her as his Queen, but Sarah is confident, self-possessed, and clear. Having integrated the lessons she's learned, along with both the golden and shadow aspects of the Maiden archetype, she no longer views herself as a victim. Instead, she is now ready to reclaim her agency and step into her power. She rescues her brother and returns home, where we see her putting away her dolls and toys—symbolic of her readiness to step into the next phase of her life.

SEEING OURSELVES IN THE MYTH

Reflecting on Sarah's journey in *Labyrinth* provides a powerful lens through which we can examine our own paths. Where in your life do you see yourself embodying the qualities of the Maiden? Consider both the positive (creativity, playfulness, innocence) and shadow aspects (naivety, victimhood, passivity). Recognizing these shadow qualities, noticing at what moments in our life they overtake us, and then beginning to understand where they come from allow us to consciously choose another way forward.

Similarly, reflect on the qualities of the Mother (often nurturing and generous) and Queen (embodying confidence, leadership, and grace) archetypes and how they manifest in your life.

Think about your current initiation journey—your Heroine's Journey. Are you in a period of struggle, transition, or liminal space that brought you to this book? While you may have experienced other initiations in your life (and will likely face more), reflect on the one unfolding now. Understanding where you are on your path can help you navigate the challenges ahead and move toward embodying your inner Queen.

GOING DEEPER

Expand

Deeply consider the postpartum practices of your own and other cultures. While we can't singlehandedly change our hyper-individualistic society, we can start by educating ourselves about what exists—or once existed—in our own and other cultures. Read stories about how women around the world are supported during the postpartum period. Ask your parent friends or older family members about experiences they had that felt nourishing and supportive during that time in their lives. Be a bit of a researcher here. Think about what kind of support would feel grounding for you in such a transition. If you are already a parent, reflect on what would have felt supportive and allow yourself to acknowledge and feel the grief or even anger around what may have been lacking.

You might not be able to create your ideal scenario (or maybe you can, and that's amazing!), but it may give you some clues to smaller changes and support systems you can put in place for yourself, regardless of where you are in your motherhood journey. Remember, we have more power to shape our circumstances than we think we do. The hardest part sometimes is asking for help or going against what society tells us we "should" want or be able to handle.

Many of us do not live in a society that is conducive to multiple generations of families supporting us in close proximity for a myriad of reasons. But I hope you have created a network of *chosen* family to pull from, and if you haven't, pregnancy and early parenthood is a great time to befriend those also going through it. Trust me, I know you're tired. I know you may be working full-time; you may even have other children at home to tend to, but we need to begin with prioritizing ourselves. Join your local chapter of La Leche League, search for online communities through Facebook or mom influencers, or if you can afford it, try a paid community builder such as Peanut. I'm not here to stand on a soap box of privilege. I do not have insight into the realities of your world, your finances, or your capability to create support structures. However, as a therapist, I do have insight into what will ultimately affect your long-term postpartum mental health in a positive way, and a support system made up of more than one other person is a huge part of it.

Honor

A therapist of mine once gave me homework around honoring my C-section scar. It felt weird at first, but she pushed me to take it seriously. Once I did, I had a few unexpected emotional releases, as I found myself feeling gratitude instead of anger for the first time around aspects of my birth story. Regardless of how your child came into this world, honor their portal. Sit for a few moments each morning or evening and bring your focus to the area of your body or to the person who carried and birthed your child. Thank it or them for the work done in supporting the growth of this life. If it was through your body, place your hands directly on your belly, scar, or pubic area. Focus love and warmth, reverence and gratitude toward the area. My advice, if you can, is to sit for as long as it takes to feel the actual emotions of love and gratitude in your body, not just to simply think the thoughts. Gratitude, as a practice, is a feeling-based experience, not a logical one.

Explore

Reflect on who you were before becoming a parent, or who you are now if you are considering becoming one. What were your passions? What filled you up? What was important to you? How did you show the people in your life love? How did you show yourself love? How did you like to receive love? How do these aspects of yourself manifest now, in your identity as a parent or soon-to-be parent? Are there areas that feel charged or unresolved? Write down any thoughts or emotions that arise, and allow yourself to sit with them. This process of exploration can help you reconnect with parts of yourself that may feel lost or distant.

2

the loss of the village ... and ourselves

> "Why were we taught to be afraid of the witches
> and not the people who burned them alive?"
>
> —Unattributed

I watched Tanner over Zoom as she wept silently into her hands. We had been meeting weekly for about five months. She sought me out after hearing an episode of my podcast where I lamented and raged about how we are not meant to mother alone. I had recorded it just three months into my motherhood journey, during the early pandemic lockdown, isolated with just my partner and our newborn daughter, feeling trapped and climbing the walls. I remember the feeling vividly, even all these years later. Tanner's message to me echoed the same feelings of sadness, frustration, loneliness, and anger.

She was angry—angry at her wife's job for not giving her any paid leave, at her wife for how profoundly her own life had changed while her wife's seemed largely unaffected, at her mother for not living closer, at her mostly childless friends for getting uncomfortable when she complained and cried when they visited, and at all the pregnancy advice she'd received that didn't tell her what to *really* expect when the baby came. Most of all, she was angry with herself for not being able to "handle it."

In the first few months after her son was born, she cried every day. She felt confused at how often she was crying because, up until then, she "wasn't a crier." She felt profoundly lonely, despite her son being basically attached to her body, whether through feeding, baby wearing, or napping. She had a wife who wanted to help with the baby. She was as supportive of Tanner as she could be when she was home, but she wasn't home most of the day. Tanner's wife didn't qualify for either maternity *or* paternity leave under her company policy, so she was back at work one week after their son was born. She tried to help when she was home, offering to do night feedings or take their son out so Tanner could rest or call friends. But Tanner often declined, feeling she had to do it all herself because "no one understood her son like she did." She frequently snapped at her wife for not knowing his needs or schedule as intimately as she did.

One late night, she found herself irrationally angry when their son had a horrible cold. He was having a hard time breathing through his nose, which was impacting his ability to feed and sleep and, in turn, causing him to be cranky, overtired, and inconsolable. She had been up for hours, trying to soothe him through rocking, bouncing, walking, and shushing, but nothing worked. Meanwhile, her wife slept soundly in the other room, seemingly undisturbed. Tanner found herself imagining dropping him out of the window of their three-story home and then smothering her wife with a pillow. The fantasy felt disturbingly soothing to her, and she was so engrossed in it that she didn't notice her son's spit-up dripping down her arm. She recounted to me, through tears, that she had calmly cleaned herself and her son, changed his clothes, reswaddled him, and put him in his crib. Without a word to her wife, she put in earplugs, crawled into bed, and fell asleep—even as she could hear him screaming down the hall.

The next morning, her wife, who had been awakened by the cries and had gone to soothe their son, nervously confronted her. "I think you should talk to someone," she suggested after Tanner took the baby from her without a word. As Tanner sat on the couch with her son in the morning light, the details of the night returned to her: the violent visions, the eerie calm she felt, and how easily she had slept through his cries. She didn't cry as she recalled these moments; instead, she felt fear. She didn't recognize herself and wondered what else she might be capable of.

That same morning, she allowed her wife to call a friend of a friend who was a psychiatrist and make an appointment for her. She was fortunate to get an appointment quickly through a personal connection, as the typical waitlist was four to six months. They met the following week over Zoom, the office still not seeing people in person because of the pandemic. The psychiatrist asked her about ten questions, the session, in total, was about thirty minutes, and it cost her $350 out of pocket. At the end, she had a prescription for an anti-depressant and a recommendation to find a therapist.

So there we were, deep in our therapeutic work together. Me explaining how common intrusive thoughts were and are, especially when under extreme stress and sleep deprivation, while working to help her gain compassion for herself. Plus working to unpack how she had reached that breaking point, how to safeguard herself from spiraling deeper into a depression, and how to learn and practice tangible tools to keep herself on the slow climb out of the emotional hole she found herself in.

Much of my work with Tanner, and with many mothers who come to me for therapy, follows a similar structure:

1. Normalizing the anger, depression, loneliness, and feelings of failure and being let down when the reality of motherhood doesn't match the myths we are fed (much of what we talked about in chapter 1).

2. Processing birth trauma, which often creates a feeling of a complete loss of control and disconnection with the body.

3. Educating them on how our species was *actually* designed to parent: in community. In some current hunter-gatherer

cultures, biological mothers only do about 30 percent of the child-rearing, showing that the idea of mothers doing it all alone in nuclear families is far from our natural wiring. Communal caregiving, or alloparenting, aligns with how we've evolved to raise children and benefits everyone's well-being. Research also shows that when mothers lack this kind of support, they're more likely to struggle with postpartum depression and anxiety.[1]

4. Helping them regain a sense of connection to Self (or sometimes building a sense of Self for the first time) and reclaim some autonomy through codependency recovery. Codependent tendencies show up in *all* of our relationships but seem especially poignant in early motherhood.

5. Encouraging them to create support systems, ask for help (sometimes for the first time in their lives), and redefine what type of woman—and mother—they want to be, but also who they want their children to watch them become and embody.

MOVING WOMEN INSIDE

The challenges of parenting without community could fill volumes, but it is crucial to address this issue to understand why so many of us feel disillusioned with our roles as parents and women today. Much of this discontentment stems from the fact that we are parenting within structures that our species was never meant to parent in, yet we believe these structures are "normal." We believe what we see and what we have seen for the past few generations is normal, so *we* must be abnormal for struggling. This is simply untrue.

The entanglement of capitalism and patriarchy has significantly shaped the creation of the nuclear family and the isolation that comes with it. The research I reference largely focuses on Europe, the region that heavily influenced Western approaches to living and child-rearing. Through colonization, globalization, and the spread of capitalist systems, these approaches have permeated societies worldwide.

Approximately ten thousand years ago, human societies began transitioning from nomadic hunter-gatherer lifestyles to settled agricultural villages. This change from a more nomadic lifestyle to one focused on the domesticity of plants and animals created a period with a larger focus on stable community. Evidence from Old Europe shows that many of these agricultural societies were egalitarian and matrilineal, meaning descent was traced through the female lines, and many times the woman's family home was the home in which the next generations were born and raised. Men and women shared the responsibilities necessary to keep the community alive and thriving, from tending crops and animals to construction and other physical labor, while continuing to engage in communal childcare, eldercare, and caregiving for the sick.[2]

By the eighth century, feudalism was established in Europe. While our high school social studies class taught us that this era wasn't particularly joyful for the average person—plagues, famine, and war—some aspects of prior communal living persisted. Peasants lived on communal land provided by lords and shared spaces that were central to daily life, from washing and sewing to childcare and socializing.

However, by the twelfth century, with the establishment and strengthening of trade routes, the royalty and lords who controlled the land began seeing not only the potential profit of what could be created, harvested, and exported *from* the land, but also the profit in the land *itself*. This realization led to the "enclosure" movement in England, where communal lands were taken over by the elite for private agricultural profit. Through enclosure, villages and communal spaces were destroyed. Peasants had little to no land to live upon, and the system of needing to work for wages to survive, of making money off the sale of either time or product (i.e., capitalism), was born.[3]

More importantly, in this very simplified version of history I am providing, is the recognition of the shift in how we viewed nature, life, and each other. Through a capitalistic lens, nature and people become something to be dominated and profited off of. We begin working *for* someone else rather than for the survival of ourselves, our family, and our community. In order to justify the dominance, control, and exploitation that this way of living inherently creates, we have to disconnect and dehumanize. Whoever and whatever does not add to or bring in profit becomes less valued and less protected, mainly women and especially older women, based purely on perceived differences in physical strength.

This period marked the emergence of a patriarchal social system. As wage labor became the economic standard, opportunities for paid work were primarily reserved for men. Women were pushed to the margins of society, then eventually confined to the home. Although the work within the home remained vital for survival, it was not recognized as economically valuable. As a result, financial control and violence against women by men increased.

During this time, the institutionalization of prostitution and rape, as well as the criminalization of women as witches and heretics, began to emerge as tactics to further control women and solidify a hierarchy based on gender and wealth. The rise of capitalism and patriarchy set in motion the isolation of Western women, disconnecting them from their communities and creating a hierarchical system of supremacy and financial dependence.[4]

While ten thousand years might seem like a long time, it is but a blip in the timeline of human evolution. *Homo sapiens*, the first modern humans, evolved between two hundred thousand and three hundred thousand years ago, and many researchers argue that our social way of living, hunting, and caring for our young is the primary reason we have survived over other species like Neanderthals, *Homo erectus*, and *Homo floresiensis*.[5] For nearly 290,000 out of three hundred thousand years, our species thrived through a way of living that was systemically stripped away from us *only* ten thousand years ago. So the next time you beat yourself up for getting overwhelmed, feeling like you are losing your mind, or feeling like a failure of a mother because you can't "handle it all," please remember this expectation is historically and evolutionarily inaccurate.

IT'S IN OUR DNA: THE WITCH WOUND

As a therapist who works regularly with intergenerational trauma, I am a bit embarrassed to say I hadn't considered the biological impact of the witch trials that swept across Europe and North America—and the generational trauma of women since, whether they are of European descent or not. Research shows that trauma leaves a chemical mark on a person's genes, which can then be passed down to future generations. This epigenetic process of trauma transmission has been studied in Black Americans who are the descendants of enslaved people and in those whose family survived the Holocaust. It stands to reason then that descendants of women persecuted during the socially and religiously sanctioned witch hunts and murders—alongside those pitted against each other; those who lost mothers, sisters, and grandmothers; the African, Latin American, and Asian enslaved people; and the massacred Native population of North America—would also carry this trauma.

During the nearly three hundred years of witch hunts in Europe and North America (and continuing today in places like India, Nepal, and parts of Africa), women were targeted and preyed upon for providing support and protection to other women. Seen as a threat to the expansion and solidification of capitalism and patriarchy, women's connection to each other, to their ancestral knowledge, to the land, and to themselves was systematically vilified. Many accused women held herbal medicinal knowledge, led community rituals, were respected elders sought out for advice, served as midwives, and often publicly and vocally opposed enclosures and the shift toward cash crops. While the history is fuzzy due to poor record keeping, researchers have documented that many accused women were poor, some widows, and many did not have children to take care of them as they aged.[6]

The archetype of the Witch—popularized in Disney movies, *The Wizard of Oz*, and Halloween imagery—often depicts an old woman with gray hair, a hunched back, and a black cloak. This image may have resembled the older rural women in the sixteenth and seventeenth centuries who had become a thorn in the side of conformity and misogynistic, patriarchal practices. While prior to the development of capitalism, widows, elderly, and the poor were financially provided for as part of the then common social order, under this new system they became a drain—a nuisance that needed to be eliminated.

In her book *Caliban and the Witch*, scholar and feminist activist Silvia Federici examines this dynamic, explaining how the witch was often a woman whose behavior defied imposed norms of femininity. "At times she was a healer, and a practitioner of various forms of magic that made her popular in the community. But this increasingly signaled her as a danger to the local and national power structure in its warfare against every form of popular power."[7] In this new era, women who were self-assertive, independent, or outspoken were dangerous. Self-preservation often meant blending in and not standing out, as highlighted by Barbara Ehrenreich and Deirdre English in their book *Witches, Midwives, and Nurses*: "To be or behave otherwise was to open oneself to suspicion of witchcraft."[8]

The Witch Wound is not confined to the distant past. The control and punishment of women who stepped outside societal norms persisted well into the twentieth century. In the 1920s and 1930s, women labeled as "promiscuous" could be institutionalized or forcibly sterilized for their perceived "feeble-mindedness." This practice continued for women of color, poor women, and those seen as sexually deviant into the 1960s. Moreover, lobotomies were still being used as a "cure" for depression in women until that same decade.[9]

It's hardly surprising then that standing out, being unique, standing unabashedly in our power, embracing our sexuality, being outspoken, taking up too much space, or being seen as too smart feels risky or makes many of us uncomfortable to this day. After all, it's in our DNA.

I DON'T TRUST OTHER WOMEN: THE SISTER WOUND

My client Sherry, a white woman in her mid-sixties, illustrates how the suspicion among women, cultivated centuries ago, continues to isolate and divide us today. After a year of therapy focused on processing the grief of losing both her mother and her best friend, Sherry was ready to re-engage with the world.

I asked about her other female friends. What had they done over the past year to support her? Had she reached out to them? Could she now? Could she set up some dinners with them? Concerts? Hikes? Her response was immediate and firm.

"I HATE women," she said. I was a bit taken aback by the intensity of her statement. "Women backstab, they're catty, they always play the victim, they care more about themselves than anything. I don't trust them. I only trust men."

Unfortunately, Sherry's reaction isn't unique. Distrust among women has deep roots in historical manipulation—origins I believe can be traced back to the witch hunts that sowed seeds of internalized misogyny. Today, we see this in women who claim to be "guys' girls" because they "don't like other women," women who emotionally gang up on other women, fight other women over the possession of a man, and who are disconnected from community, their mothers, their mothers' mothers, and themselves.

DEPTH 101

The Witch Wound: The generational trauma that women carry due to the over three hundred years of persecution related to the witch trials, causing fear around being perceived as unconventional, independent, or outside societal norms.

The Sister Wound: Historical animosity among women, not necessarily biologically related, characterized by betrayal,

> jealousy, insecurity, gossip, and various other cruel interpersonal dynamics.
>
> *The Mother Wound:* Cultural and generational trauma carried and perpetuated by mothers, rooted in internalized patriarchy and misogyny, and designed to keep current structures unquestioned and functioning.

By creating an environment in which women couldn't trust one another, those in power could effectively isolate, silence, and bully half of the population into submission for political and financial gain. The witch hunts turned neighbors against neighbors, family members against family members, women against women. Ehrenreich and English tell us that "anyone failing to report a witch faced both excommunication and a long list of temporal punishments."[10] During this time period, we even saw a change in language as a way to further separate and malign the close relationships of women. The word "gossip," originally from the Old English "godsibb," meaning "close friends or godparents," began to shift in meaning around this time, becoming a term for idle talk, rumor-spreading, and immorality in women.

What could constitute being a "witch" in those days? Aside from gathering with other women in private or in public (gossiping), it could have been a myriad of things, including political subversion and open criticism, lewdness, blasphemy, being argumentative with your husband, having a visible birthmark, having sex out of wedlock, your neighbor's livestock or child becoming ill and dying, your neighbor's livestock or child becoming ill and recovering, or someone simply telling someone else that you were . . . a witch. A common misconception is that many of the women murdered as witches were still practicing paganism, when in fact, by the height of the witch hunts, the majority were Christian.

In addition to the Witch Wound, most women today have experienced the Sister Wound. When writing this chapter, I polled my social media community (which at the time of writing is just under 170,000 people—90 percent women, 10 percent men, primarily between the ages of twenty-five and forty-four, mostly based in the US with meaningful representation elsewhere throughout the English-speaking world) and found countless examples of how this wound manifests in everyday life:

- Mom shaming and guilt that comes directly from other mothers.

- Waking up at a sleepover when you were thirteen and overhearing your friends talking about you.

- Women tearing each other apart on social media.

- Older female relatives ganging up on each other or talking about each other behind their backs.

- Women at work using things you have told them in confidence to gain footing in their own career.

- A friend sleeping with your current or ex-partner.

- Assumptions and judgments from women who don't know you.

- Being slut shamed and/or being shamed for being a prude.

- Jealousy of another woman's success rather than support.

- Friends not being happy for you in your moments of joy.

- Choosing sides among female groups or family members.

The Sister Wound is also reinforced through popular culture and art:

- *Sex and the City*'s depiction of single women as social pariahs among their married friends.

- The movie *Black Swan*, where rivalry between two female dancers leads to psychological breakdown and death.

- *Sharp Objects*, both the Gillian Flynn novel and the subsequent TV series exploring deep-seated family issues and trauma among female relatives.

- The tendency of women, especially white women, to vote against their interests or vote vocal misogynists into various political offices.

- Not believing female victims or falling into the victim-blaming stance of "What did she do to bring it on herself?"

- *Mean Girls*, where cruelty and sabotage are used to navigate social hierarchies.

But mean girls aren't only in the movies. Sherry's harsh words about hating women, especially coming from a woman in her sixties, reminded me of how deeply ingrained this wound is. It's not just about how we've been affected by the Sister Wound, but also about recognizing how we have, knowingly or unknowingly, participated in perpetuating it. For centuries, we have been conditioned to believe it's us versus them, that either we betray the sister or we betray ourselves. Capitalism ingrains the idea that there's only so much to go around—a zero-sum game.

But this belief is entirely constructed and false. What is good for other women is good for us, and there is, in fact, plenty of pie to go around. We will get into tangible ways to excavate and begin to heal this wound in the Going Deeper section.

CLOSING OUT THE TRINITY: THE MOTHER WOUND

The most painful traumatic life moment for my client Sofia, a Latina woman in her early forties, rests almost entirely on the shoulders of the Mother Wound.

"The only clear memory I have from that night is sitting on the couch sobbing uncontrollably while no one comforted me. My mom, stepmom, and dad were all in the kitchen arguing about whose fault this was, and I just remember feeling so alone, ashamed, and scared."

I sat listening to Sofia recount the horrible night when she was raped by a twenty-nine-year-old man after sneaking out of her house at age fourteen. Her first sexual experience.

"I remember my dad yelling at me. I remember them taking me to the hospital and having to do a rape kit. As I lay there in the bed and they performed that embarrassing process, no one came near me. Not my mom, not my stepmom. They just stood in the doorway while I cried. I was so mortified. After we got home, no one talked to me about it. Then, suddenly, it was like everyone forgot about it and started acting as if it had never happened. So I never brought it up again." She looked down.

I could feel rage bubbling up inside of me. We had been unpacking why, as an adult, she struggled with intimate relationships with men. Why she had struggled with disordered eating her entire life. Why she hated her father so much. This was the first time we ever really spoke about her mother or stepmother outside of surface information gathering.

I couldn't contain myself any longer. I was visibly shaking.

"Sofia, I have to express something that is coming up for me in this moment. As a mother myself, I am ENRAGED. I feel so much protection for that little girl. I cannot, in my wildest imagination, picture a universe in which my young daughter was raped by a grown man and I didn't go looking for him with a shotgun. I am *so* angry at every single adult in your life, but especially your mother. I am so sorry."

I was sitting on my knees in the chair by this point. Sofia was quiet. She watched me with what looked to be a blank expression on her face. I worried that I had gone too far. My training as a therapist to stay calm and neutral, "a blank slate," contradicted my training as a depth psychotherapist to allow myself the space to work with whatever was alive in the room (within reason) and with my human horror at what I was being told.

"You know, I've actually told two other female therapists this story before meeting you, and they both sat and listened with no emotion and calmly asked me how it made me feel. I felt ashamed and embarrassed and told myself that the whole thing was obviously my fault and that I should stop talking and thinking about it. And then, after, we just sort of moved on and didn't ever really talk about it again. Thank you . . ."

Her voice trailed off as she looked down. "I found out years later that my stepmom had been raped by a family member when she was twelve." She looked up at me again. "I don't remember feeling empathy for her. I only remember feeling angry at her for not hugging me and telling me that night as I lay in the hospital bed. I feel horrible for feeling that way."

Sofia is not alone in feeling deeply betrayed by her mother and stepmother. Many of us, across genders, carry a heritage of matrilineal pain rooted in internalized patriarchy and misogyny. While this pain manifests differently for men and women, its origins are the same.

Internalized patriarchy leads our mothers to blame us for our sexual abuse, avoid holding men accountable, and become jealous of us as we grow into our beauty and radiance, diverting the male gaze from them to us. It teaches them to shame us for our bigness and applaud us for being nice and compliant, to expect more from us than our brothers, and to see us as an extension of themselves. Internalized patriarchy causes our mothers to give us the cold shoulder or shut us down when we express big emotions or assert our independence, to treat us like a friend she confides in with an expectation that our childlike selves can hold these adult truths without issue, and to smother us with love only when we perform or achieve.

This isn't to blame mothers for all of our issues; mothers already unfairly shoulder most of the responsibility and the weight of dysfunction in families. But I hope that by examining the Mother Wound, we can understand the fear driving these behaviors and work to break the cycle, preventing trauma from being passed down any further.

If patriarchy teaches us that women are subservient to men, emotions are weak and dangerous, men's sexual urges are impossible to control, men are inherently violent and volatile, and women are the weaker and dumber sex, it follows that in order to protect themselves and their children, mothers project their generational fears onto their daughters and sons. That they mold them into what feels safe and accepted by the community. Internalized patriarchy convinces women that their fears are truths and that we must live our lives through the lens of this fear. It also teaches women not to trust—men, other women, and above all else, themselves.

THE FINAL ISOLATION TOOL: THE MEDICAL PROFESSION

Nearly a century before the witch hunts began, medicine in Europe had already become a professional field. At this time, women were excluded from universities, and female healers were being systematically marginalized and eliminated.[11] In the fifteenth century, universities taught little that we would recognize as medicine today. Lessons were not allowed to conflict with the teachings of the Church, which viewed the body, especially in relation to sexuality and health, as a source of sin and temptation. As a result, teachings about the body were severely restricted, leaving little room for the inclusion of anatomical knowledge, healing methods, or generational wisdom that might contradict or challenge the Church's doctrine. This suppression ensured that medical knowledge remained aligned with religious beliefs, further marginalizing traditional healers and their practices.

In reality, "it was witches who developed an extensive understanding of bones and muscles, herbs and drugs, while physicians were still deriving their prognosis from astrology and alchemists were trying to turn lead into gold."[12] These so-called "witches" were often skilled healers who relied on empirical knowledge and hands-on experience, building a deep understanding of the human body and natural remedies. In contrast, "doctors" at that time practiced medicine steeped in superstition rather than scientific principles.

During this period, laws were enacted to bar women from practicing medicine, with documented cases of these laws being used to prosecute women for taking part in any form of healing. "The Church saw its attack on peasant healers as an attack on magic, not medicine."[13] When the witch trials began, the Church relied on male doctors as expert witnesses to support accusations against the women on trial. It was the Church, not their medical expertise or achievements, that established the status of these male doctors.

Even as late as the 1800s, medical training for doctors was severely lacking. "Medical programs varied in length from a few months to two years; many medical schools had no clinical facilities; [and] high school diplomas were not required for admission to medical schools."[14] Over the centuries, women continued to be shut out of mainstream medical education.

In my professional opinion, one of the greatest tragedies in all of this (and there are *many*) is that women were forcibly disconnected from their reliance on their intuition, their deep connectedness with nature, their body and its cycles, and their generations of learned skills and healing knowledge. Through the legacy of persecuting and denigrating women lay-healers, witch-healers, and those who today would be considered midwives and birthers, society created a legacy where women struggle to understand their own bodies and trust their inner knowledge.

Ultimately, the rise of the male-dominated medical industry was a strategic move to support the perpetuation of capitalism, which thrives on dominance—over people, resources, and wealth. Controlling those who give birth to future laborers became crucial to maintaining this power. The exclusion of women from medicine has served to devalue them and sever their connection to Self.

MYTHS AS MAPS
Circe, Regina George, and the Trinity Wound

At first glance, Circe from Greek mythology and Regina George from *Mean Girls* might seem like an odd pairing, but they both exemplify the Trinity Wound. Their stories highlight how archetypal patterns and images reappear across time and cultures, offering valuable lessons.

In Greek mythology, Circe was a goddess of sorcery (pharmakeia), the daughter of the sun god Helios and the Oceanid nymph Perse. She resided on the island of Aiaia, often associated with Italy. By means of drugs and incantations, Circe was able to change humans into wolves, lions, and swine. Traditionally portrayed by male authors as a femme fatale and witch who seduced and doomed male heroes, Circe's story is far more complex than simple stereotypes. She embodies a rich tapestry of roles—daughter, sister, lover, mother, and spouse—providing a profound landscape for women to explore their inner selves.

Circe is best known from Homer's *Odyssey*, where she transforms Odysseus's soldiers into pigs. After a confrontation, Odysseus and Circe become lovers, and Circe provides him valuable information to navigate the underworld and aid his quest home.

Let's dig a little deeper . . . Circe's youngest brother, Aeëtes, is her father's favored heir who grows up to become a cruel and callous tyrant who tortures men for fun and despises women. Although as a child Circe is a nurturing figure to Aeëtes, he begins to despise and reject her as his desire for power and his disdain for women, especially those with innate power, grows. When Aeëtes tells their father that Circe is a witch (despite holding the same magical powers himself), Helios banishes Circe to the island of Aiaia in order to not incur the wrath of Zeus. In the world of the immortals, witchcraft is seen as a perverted power not meant for divine beings.

Thus begins Circe's exile—a woman betrayed and hated for who she is and the intuitive magical power she possesses. Yet, despite the betrayals she faces, Circe learns to protect herself, stand tall, and continue developing her gifts. She chooses to trust and love repeatedly, even after being wronged.

While many of the stories of Circe focus on her acts of vengeance as an attempt to remind us that strong-willed, intelligent, and independent women are unattractive and unworthy of love, we can instead see her as resourceful and intelligent. Circe is a goddess that symbolizes knowledge, feminine power, strength, resolve, an understanding of herbology, and femininity.

Now, let's consider Regina George in *Mean Girls*. At first glance, she appears as a self-absorbed, vicious, and power-hungry high schooler who cares only about physical looks and popularity. And yet, underneath the veneer of the social ideals of attractiveness, Regina is confident, assertive, intelligent, and unafraid to speak her mind.

The movie hints at her home life, which on the surface seems perfect and filled with material wealth but is plagued by a mother who is jealous of and competes with her, a barely there father, and their struggling marriage. While we may condemn how Regina uses her power to manipulate others, her traits—confidence, assertiveness, and intelligence—are qualities I'm sure many of us desire to embody.

SEEING OURSELVES IN THE MYTH

Circe and Regina George provide striking examples of how the Trinity Wounds play out in our lives. These figures compel us to reflect on the times we've been betrayed but chose to rise, the moments we've been ostracized for being our true selves, and the occasions we've dimmed our light out of fear of rejection. Each of us, at different times, has hidden our inner power out of fear of how it would be received by others.

These myths invite us to consider the ways in which confidence and social status may have been used to manipulate or control others—consciously or unconsciously. In reflecting on the archetypal experiences of jealousy, power dynamics, and judgment, we recognize how easy it can be to engage in similar behaviors without realizing it. They encourage us to step back and examine the moments when we have, perhaps, judged other women harshly or reduced them to their perceived "worst" qualities.

This process of reflection offers a powerful opportunity to reclaim our agency and make more conscious choices in how we relate to ourselves and others. By looking at these figures and their journeys, we can start to reimagine new ways of showing up—ways that allow for greater empathy, understanding, and connection.

GOING DEEPER

Examine the Shadow

Shadow work involves becoming aware of your unexamined internal responses to people, situations, and experiences; questioning these reactions; and consciously choosing to show up differently. When something or someone triggers or activates us, it often mirrors a part of our shadow back to us. Let's explore shadow work in relation to the Trinity Wounds.

The Witch Wound

1. Reflect on Visibility and Power:

    - When have you dimmed your light or hidden parts of yourself to fit in or avoid standing out? What were you afraid would happen if you showed your true Self?

    - Think of a time when you felt powerful or unapologetic in expressing your uniqueness. How did others react, and how did you respond to their reactions?

2. Fear of Judgment and Rejection:

   - Where have you feared being labeled as "too much"—too smart, too outspoken, too sexual? What does "too much" mean to you, and where did you learn this meaning from?

   - In what situations have you judged another woman for being bold, unconventional, or confident? What did her expression trigger in you?

3. Internalized Competition:

   - When have you found yourself competing with other women, whether in your career, friendships, or appearance? What underlying beliefs fueled that competition?

   - Think of a woman you've felt jealous of or threatened by. What qualities in her do you admire, and how might these qualities reflect what you desire for yourself?

4. Fear of Rejection for Being Different:

   - What aspects of yourself do you feel you must hide to avoid being ostracized or misunderstood? What would it feel like to embrace and embody those aspects fully?

   - How has the fear of being perceived as "weird" or "different" shaped your choices or behavior in social or professional settings?

The Sister Wound

1. Envy and Resentment:

   - Recall a time when you felt envious or resentful toward another woman. What did she represent that you felt you lacked or wanted more of in your life?

   - What qualities or behaviors in other women trigger feelings of insecurity or inadequacy in you? What does this reveal about your own self-worth or unmet needs?

2. Trust and Betrayal among Women:

   - Reflect on a time when you felt betrayed or unsupported by another woman. What happened, and how did it impact your ability to trust women afterward?

   - In what ways have you withheld support, love, or kindness from another woman? What fears or beliefs fueled that decision?

3. Projection and Judgment:

   - Where have you found yourself judging or labeling another woman for her choices, appearance, or success? What part of your own shadow might be reflected in those judgments?

   - How have you participated in gossip or negativity toward other women? What need or fear were you unconsciously addressing by doing so?

4. Reframing Relationships with Women:

    - Consider a woman in your life whom you have viewed through the lens of her "worst" qualities. What might shift if you tried to see her through a lens of empathy and shared experience?

    - How might you begin to cultivate deeper trust and support in your relationships with women? What old stories or wounds would you need to confront and release?

The Mother Wound

1. Healing from Maternal Expectations:

    - Reflect on ways your mother (or mother figure) may have shamed you for being "too much" or rewarded you for being "nice" and compliant. How have these dynamics shaped your behavior in adulthood?

    - When have you felt that your worth was tied to your achievements or ability to please others? How has this affected your sense of Self and your relationships?

2. Navigating Emotional Neglect or Over-Attachment:

    - Recall a time when you felt emotionally abandoned or misunderstood by your mother. What impact did this have on your ability to express your emotions or needs?

    - Consider ways your mother may have treated you as an emotional confidante or "friend" rather than as a child. How did this dynamic affect your understanding of boundaries, intimacy, or personal responsibility?

3. Breaking the Cycle of Internalized Patriarchy:

    - In what ways have you internalized beliefs that prioritize romantic partnerships or male approval over other forms of connection? How has this limited your ability to nurture platonic or communal relationships?

    - How have you witnessed or experienced jealousy or competition between mothers and daughters, particularly around appearance, intelligence, or independence? What steps can you take to refuse to participate in this cycle?

4. Redefining Relationships Beyond Romantic Love:

    - Reflect on your friendships and community connections. Where have you deprioritized these relationships in favor of romantic ones? How can you begin to shift your focus toward nurturing platonic and communal bonds?

    - What would it look like to cultivate self-love and inner wholeness without seeking validation from external sources, especially romantic partners?

3

the cult of busy

> "There is a pervasive form of contemporary violence to which the idealist most easily succumbs: activism and overwork. The rush and pressure of modern life are a form, perhaps the most common form, of its innate violence. To allow oneself to be carried away by a multitude of conflicting concerns, to surrender to too many demands, to commit oneself to too many projects, to want to help everyone in everything is to succumb to violence."
>
> —Thomas Merton, *Conjectures of a Guilty Bystander*[1]

I lay on the couch, crying. Not dainty tears streaming down my cheeks, but big, ugly cries. Heaving, snotty, can't-catch-your-breath cries. I could not get up. I was on day four of a fever with body-shaking coughs and barely had a voice to cry with. I was a mess.

What pushed me over the edge wasn't just the sickness. It was an email from an organization that had hired me to lead a half-day workshop on codependency recovery for women. That morning, I had regretfully written to cancel, explaining how ill I was. The response I got was curt and dismissive, suggesting that I "take some DayQuil" and speak anyway because my cancellation was making her "look bad to [her] boss." No compassion—just concern about appearances. I wasn't expecting warmth, per se, and it wasn't necessarily her harshness that made me cry; it was my shock at another woman, someone I knew also had children, planning a weekend event centered on moms (entrepreneur moms at that) and having such a complete lack of compassion.

I had been busting my ass to create a name for myself for years. This seminar was, I thought at the time, my first big "break"—a well-known and respected organization hosting a weekend seminar for women and entrepreneur mothers around self-care and work-life balance. I was sick, both physically and emotionally, over the idea that I was "ruining my career" by having to cancel this speaking gig, and this woman's response seemed to confirm it for me.

My daughter, only sixteen months old at the time, watched me cry. She stood silently by the couch, resting her tiny hand on my arm. "Mama?" Her face was filled with concern and puzzlement. In that moment, clarity hit me like a shock wave. I stopped crying and suddenly felt angry. This feeling of failing or letting someone else down, shame and disappointment in myself for not doing enough or working hard enough, fear of missing out on something or missing the boat on opportunity, was familiar. I was not going to let my daughter see me like this. It's not that I wasn't going to let her see me cry—I think it's wildly important our children see our humanity—but rather, I wasn't going to let her see me kill myself over work. Even work that I loved and felt was my calling. She needed to see that it's okay to listen to our bodies when they cry out for rest instead of pushing through the pain to avoid disappointing others or avoid the fear of there not being enough success and abundance to go around.

I could fill a book with stories of myself, colleagues, friends, and clients pushing ourselves to the brink of collapse for work. My years in corporate New York City as a creative advertising producer were filled with sixty-hour workweeks and endless meetings. Going to the office when it was dark and leaving when it was dark was par for the course. Even then, I knew this "work above all else" mentality didn't align with my values.

There was the time I had to have a serious conversation with a junior project manager about *why* it didn't look good to me, her boss, that she had just turned in her time sheet clocking *103 hours* because she had been assigned to work two pitches in one week from the executive creative director and "couldn't say no." Or the time I had to console a graphic designer by reminding her we were not doctors saving lives while she was crying over her mouse pad because she couldn't get a social post done in time for a large client's deadline (after their fifth round of the most inane and infuriatingly tedious feedback had come in . . . at 7:15 pm). Or the time I loudly expressed to a room full of team members *and my boss* that I was no longer entertaining feedback for the sake of making ourselves look smart. Or the time our senior vice president was in the office visiting for two weeks and scheduled multiple team meetings during lunch, so on the third consecutive day, I brought in my very crunchy salad and chomped loudly throughout the meeting to make a point that this was the only time most of us had to eat.

Clearly, I've always had some deep-rooted issues with the way the capitalist ethos of corporations disregards the humanity of its workers!

Even though I have always been able to access my annoyance for this type of "work above all else" mentality, I have (or had, up until the aha moment with my daughter) a tendency to only listen to my body when it shuts down, a pattern of pushing myself until I get sick. Only then do I rest, *begrudgingly*. Despite my awareness and fifteen years of mindfulness practice, I still struggle to see over-scheduling and pushing myself to the brink as a form of self-harm.

OUR VALUE AS HUMANS: DEFINED BY OUTPUT

Capitalism thrives on the exploitation and labor of workers by putting a dollar amount on people's time and energy. This cultural construct has taught us that our productivity is the most direct measure of our worth as human beings. This belief affects all, regardless of gender.

We receive so many mixed messages. On one hand, the wellness industry promotes self-care and "treating yourself," while on the other, hustle culture glorifies the mantra "I'll sleep when I'm dead." Many of us are conditioned to believe that resting or being still is wasted time—a sign of laziness. That the only way to be successful and enough is to always be running, striving, pushing forward, grinding.

How we spend our time is often characterized by feelings of shame and guilt. When we're working, we wish we had more free time to be still, then when we do have it, we feel shame and guilt around not being productive. We see others on social media on a seemingly constant beach vacation or raising five children while working and somehow maintaining a sparkling beige home, while we're just trying to figure out how to carve out time for an hour-long workout. A British coworker of mine once said that in Europe they work to live, and in the US, we live to work. The rise in burnout, or what Estés calls "*hambre del alma*, the starving soul,"[2] and chronic stress being linked to the six leading causes of death should be enough to make us pause and reevaluate, but for many of us, it isn't.

THE IMPACT ON OUR CHILDREN

Our frantic pace of living—overscheduling ourselves and our children, praising them for productivity and accomplishments, losing connectedness and community—is damaging our children's mental and emotional health. Two meta-analytic studies involving thousands of American children and college students found that anxiety levels reported in the 1990s were higher than those of child psychiatric patients in the 1950s.[3] The levels have only continued to rise. Our inability to slow down or say no is profoundly impacting future generations.

I'm not here to point fingers. I get just as caught up in the rat race as everyone else. I am a doer—a type-A, perfectionistic overachiever.

I create lists just to have something to check off. Growing up, I was praised for my achievements and reliability. I don't remember being complimented on being able to articulate my feelings, or for respecting myself by saying no, or for trusting myself enough to rest when I needed it. There is little time to reflect and be still when you are being raised by a single mother who is working herself into the ground to make sure there is food on the table. In that situation, you have to grow up fast and help the adults because if you don't, their stress and overwhelm become your stress and overwhelm.

I became very attached to the version of myself that was "good," reliable, and organized because it was the version that got the most attention from adults. According to all the adults around me, I was an "old soul" (i.e., *way* too mature for my age; i.e., a trauma response). My identity, very early, became centered around being needed, having my shit together, being calm in crisis, being able to handle a large amount of stress without showing it, and being able to compartmentalize my needs and feelings in order to focus on others' needs and feelings. All of this plagues me to this day, and I watch how it also plagues my clients.

When I was training to become a therapist, I worked in a high school counseling adolescents. On the surface, many of their problems were typical for their age—emotional regulation, questions about sex and sexuality, romantic relationships and friendships, disagreements with their parents about their budding individualism. The one consistent issue that came up time and time again was an underlying feeling of panic and overwhelm at how much they needed to do, how quickly they needed to figure out what they were going to do with their lives, and how much they needed to fill their schedules with extracurriculars and volunteer work in order to get into a good college. One day, as a sixteen-year-old female client—who had already been hospitalized twice for depression, anxiety, and suicidal thoughts—sat in my office sobbing, her entire body trembling from the sheer overwhelm of stress, I crouched down beside her and put my hand on her knee.

"None of this matters."

"What?!" She looked up at me through tears.

"Your parents and your teachers would probably be pissed at me for saying this, but NONE of this matters. It doesn't matter if you have a 3.6 or a 4.1 average. It doesn't matter what you decide to study in college. It doesn't matter if you don't get accepted into UC Berkeley because that's where your dad went. It doesn't *fucking* matter. I went back to school at thirty-one, ended an engagement even though I 'should' have been getting married and thinking about having kids, left a career where I was making six figures and was already at a director level at twenty-eight, moved across the country alone, and completely started over again. None of it matters. What matters is that you stop and listen to yourself. That you develop your intuition and a relationship to your joy. That you stop overriding your body's signals to slow down and take a break."

My client sat a little taller and wiped her face. "Thank you. No one has ever said that to me like that before."

THE LADDER ISN'T REAL

Capitalism, patriarchy, white supremacy, and colonialism are built on a belief system centered on hierarchy and marginalization—humans over the Earth and animals, certain humans over others. It is through this belief that our mistreatment of the land, animals, other humans, and even ourselves is justified. In her book *The Chalice and the Blade: Our History, Our Future*, Riane Eisler describes societies as existing on a continuum of dominator versus partnership models. Partnership societies are characterized by egalitarianism, cooperation, and a low occurrence of violence. In contrast, dominator societies are marked by hierarchy, male dominance, all-or-nothing thinking, and rigid social categories. There are very few, if any, partnership societies left within our modern globalized society.

When we buy into the hierarchies (and there are many) that a dominator model rests upon us, we become fixated on climbing above others, driven by the belief that there is only so much to go around. Having someone to blame for our suffering provides a distraction and a false sense of superiority. This endless climb keeps us focused on competition and social positioning rather than our connection to ourselves, our joy, and our community. While we fight among ourselves, those at the top continue to pillage resources for personal gain.

As I asserted in the introduction, if a group as large as women and mothers woke up and started challenging this groupthink, started going inward and reclaiming their connection to themselves and their community, our dominator systems would crumble.

"SUPERWOMAN" IS NOT A COMPLIMENT

When her third baby was only eleven months old, my client Anne, a white, thirty-four-year-old New York transplant by way of Georgia, landed in an outpatient program after a seventy-two-hour hospital hold for swallowing a few dozen pills. After ninety days, she was deemed stable and allowed to return home with a care plan that included individual therapy, peer support groups, and a regimen of mood stabilizers and antidepressants. Anne reached out to me because her oldest child's distant response upon her return home alarmed her.

When we first started working together, we talked mostly about her day-to-day life as a stay-at-home mom of three children under six. Anne's husband worked over sixty hours a week as a dentist with his own practice, usually coming home around 6:30 or 7 pm each evening and sometimes going back into the office over the weekend to manage admin work. They were comfortable financially but not enough for extra childcare or weekends away.

Anne's mother-in-law lived close by, but was seventy-eight and didn't have much energy to be a hands-on grandmother. Her parents lived three hours away by plane. Before having her first baby, she worked in advertising as an account supervisor, and during our sessions, she talked fondly about her memories of the friendships and experiences she had living in the city in her twenties. She always knew she wanted children, but assumed she would be a full-time working mother.

When she met her husband, she was twenty-seven and he was thirty-two. He had just started his dental practice and was beginning to gain some financial stability. They moved in together rather quickly and found themselves accidentally pregnant within a year of meeting. Since they both wanted children, they felt okay about it and got married. When Anne was about seven months pregnant, they moved into their first home, an hour train ride away from the city.

Fast-forward seven years and Anne was sitting across from me, telling me she didn't know how she got here. That she didn't recognize herself anymore. That she couldn't remember the last time she felt joy or was passionate about something other than things that centered around her children's school or activities.

…

Before we dive deeper into Anne's story, let's stop and ask ourselves some questions:

- What are *you* passionate about besides your partner and/or children? What *were* you passionate about before children and/or partnership?

- How many hours per week do you find yourself being the primary parent to your child/children?

- How many hours a week are you alone and untethered from all expectations?

- What about your life do you miss from before you had children or were partnered?

…

Anne expressed feeling like the past few years were a blur. She felt like a robot, completely on autopilot. Up at 6:00 am (assuming she slept, and she didn't most nights because of the baby and/or the toddler coming into their bed), she would typically feed the baby, make coffee, and wake up the other two children around 7:00 am. Then, she would mechanically move through one hour of serving breakfast, making lunches, managing fights and teeth brushing, doing hair, throwing on clothes, packing backpacks, and heading out the door by 8:00. She'd drop off both kids and feed the baby a snack in the car before getting groceries, running errands, and heading home to clean up after the morning chaos, all while managing the baby's feeding and napping schedule. She might get a few minutes here and there to flop onto the couch and scroll social media. She might schedule the occasional lunch or coffee with another equally burnt-out mom friend. School pickup was at 2:30 and 3:00 pm, then she would shuffle everyone home to work on homework, have some TV time, get into more fights, and then eat dinner and bathe. Her husband usually arrived home around 7:00, in time to read a book and give snuggles before she did the final back scratches and lullaby sings. By 8:00 pm, she was flopped back on the couch, glass of wine in hand, scrolling on her phone again as her husband did the same on the other end.

According to Anne, this was an "average" day, and not one that also included soccer, ballet, birthday parties, or other activities.

...

Pause again and ask yourself a few more questions:

- What are you feeling in your body as you read about a typical day in Anne's life?

- Can you relate to the feeling of being on autopilot as you move through life?

- Where do you build in time for rest and relaxation?

- What about connection time with your partner or yourself?

After a couple months of seeing each other weekly, Anne and I started discussing her family dynamics and childhood more in depth.

Anne's mother was a gentile southern woman with a soft accent, hair that was always salon coiffed, and a strict nightly cocktail hour routine. Anne had little memory of her mother, even presently, without a cigarette in one hand and a glass of scotch or white wine in the other. She had fond memories of her mother painting every weekend when she was small, her childhood home showcasing many of her mother's favorite artworks. When Anne was about seven, her mother began working as a real estate agent, and there was a noticeable energy and personality shift. Her mother worked long hours, entertaining clients and other agents frequently. Anne's father traveled for work often, so he wasn't around very much.

Around this point in her childhood, Anne was typically responsible for getting herself and her sister up and ready for school while their mother slept in. Occasionally, her mom would be asleep on the couch, still in her clothes from the day before, and the girls would do their best to get ready and out the door quietly. She had become "unpredictable," in Anne's words—loving and fun one minute, sullen and sad the next, and then angry and explosive at other times. Her mother was "always on the go." There was always a work or social event to go to or host at home. Anne remembers falling asleep in a pile of coats at her mother's work colleague's house on many a school night and being exhausted the next day in class.

When Anne's mother felt her worst, she would stay locked in her bedroom for a few days while Anne took charge of the house. During those stints, Anne's mother took a lot of what she called her "headache medicine." It wasn't until she was a late teen that Anne realized her headache medicine was Valium and that her mother had a serious problem.

At some point, in her own life, Anne remembered it being harder and harder to get up and get the kids out the door in time. She began to feel numb to it all, sometimes sending them to school in a pajama shirt or with unbrushed teeth because she didn't have it in her to fight them. She recognized that her disconnection might be depression, but she expressed being "too damn busy" to stop and consider getting herself help. One Saturday morning, while getting everyone ready to leave for a friend's baby shower, she had a moment of clarity. The word that flashed through her mind was: "Enough." The two older kids had been at each other's throats all morning, and she had been fighting with her husband since they woke up after expressing her fear for her daughter's well-being a week after *Roe v. Wade* had been overturned. He told her she was overreacting and to stop being so dramatic. That none of it mattered. They had enough money to make sure their daughter wouldn't be impacted. At some point, she found herself locked in her bathroom pulling multiple pill bottles out of the cabinet and shoving whatever she could down her throat.

Anne told me and anyone who would listen that she had only wanted to numb herself out, maybe take a really long nap. She insisted she didn't intend to kill herself. She was sick of being praised by everyone around her and on social media for being a "super mom." For handling it all with a smile. For not asking for help. For keeping up the front.

"Fuck the front. The front is what is actually killing me."

And *this* is where Anne's story actually begins.

BUSYNESS IS ONE HELL OF A DRUG

Anne's story exemplifies the generational and collective trauma women carry by continuing to participate in the cult of busyness. She watched her mother push herself to the brink, numbing herself with pills and alcohol to keep up with societal and financial demands. Anne learned from her mother what it meant to be a "good" wife, mother, and woman in this world.

Workaholism, overscheduled calendars, binge eating, pill popping, doom scrolling, wine drinking, gummy eating, microdosing. I have worked with women across all ages and stages who partake in one or a combination of these coping mechanisms. I am not here to judge, nor should any of us judge. Pick your poison. Most of us use something to soothe ourselves and take the edge off sometimes (refer to part 3 of this book if your drug of choice is another person or your relationships). I take sleep gummies sometimes, I have experimented with hallucinogens, I'm always busy and feel guilty when I'm not, I love wine and good food, and I spend a lot of time on social media. But when my daughter was about two, I started asking myself questions around my almost constant desire to check out: Why did I want to check out? Why was I numbing? What was I actually numbing? What was my larger strategy for managing the chaos and stress in my life? Where could I step up and take ownership or responsibility for changing the parts of my life I was numbing myself from? In what ways was I blaming my overwhelm and stress on things outside of myself, essentially disempowering myself from changing them?

Anne's mother, her mother's generation, and the generations before her had very little choice about how their lives looked and felt. This was especially true after World War II, when governments around much of the world pressured women to leave the labor force, *inventing* the nuclear family and putting a huge emphasis on the family "unit" and marriage. This time period saw younger marriages, more kids, and fewer divorces. Not coincidentally, it also saw a spike in drug use in women, and starting in the 1950s, benzodiazepines (such as Valium) and then barbiturates became commonly prescribed to women for their anxiety, stress, and "frigidity." The drugs were so commonly used by the housewives of that era that the term "mother's little helper" was coined and even used in advertisements.[4]

Anne and I began unpacking the ways in which she was self-medicating her anxiety, overwhelm, and dissatisfaction with her life. While we may feel light-years away from the lives of the 1950s housewives, we aren't too far from them emotionally. For Anne, just like for many of us, busyness is our drug of choice. If I keep myself constantly on the go, I don't have time to think or feel much of anything. If I am so exhausted from a day of nonstop running, then I can pass out at night without much time or space to ruminate on the fact that my life feels incomplete. If I buy into the stories that tell me that as long as I buy the right things, I can be happy, then I'll continue living to work so I can afford all the right things, but be too busy to notice that those things don't actually make me happy. Do you see the cycle here?

MYTHS AS MAPS
The Red Shoes and Our Loss of Freedom

The Red Shoes is a fairy tale that crosses cultures. The version European cultures are generally most familiar with was adapted by Hans Christian Andersen. However, it's also known as *The Devil's Dancing Shoes* and *The Red-Hot Shoes of the Devil*.

The Red Shoes, at first glance, is a story of a girl who becomes obsessed with a pair of magical red shoes that compel her to dance endlessly. But, as we know, myths and fairy tales are meant to connect with us on a deeper level. The metaphors used in the tales are meant to be a bridge between the body and the mind. They are the language of the unconscious, the space between.

The main character is a poor orphaned girl who uses some old rags to create a pair of shoes for herself that she is quite proud of. While out one day foraging for food, she is picked up by a wealthy old woman in a gilded carriage who proclaims that she wants to take her in and adopt her. The old woman brings her home, cleans her up, dresses her in new clothing, and burns all of her old clothing, including her handmade shoes.

The old woman not only physically cleans up the little girl but begins to teach her how to live in civilized high society—to sit still, speak only when spoken to, chew with her mouth closed, then, finally, be confirmed at the church. Prior to her confirmation, the old woman brings the girl to the shoe maker so she might have new shoes for the occasion. In a glass case, the girl sees a beautiful pair of red leather shoes, and although they are a scandalous color she knows the old woman will disapprove of, she also knows the old woman cannot see well and won't notice, so she buys them.

At church, the girl's red shoes are perceived as exactly that: scandalous. And even though the old woman scolds the girl and tells her never to wear them again, she does the following Sunday. The little girl stares at her shoes, turning them this way and that, oblivious to all of the sideways glances and whispers around her.

On their way out of the church, an old soldier standing in the doorway bows and asks to brush the dirt from the red shoes. As he does, he comments on how beautiful they are. "Those are beautiful dancing shoes!" The little girl does a twirl for him in response, but as soon as she starts to twirl, she finds she is unable to stop. She loses all control of herself and begins to dance down the street and away from the church until the old woman and her coachman are able to catch her and pry the red shoes from her feet.

Once home, the old woman locks the shoes in a box and puts them on a high shelf, forbidding the girl to ever wear them again. Not long after, the old woman becomes sick and bedridden, and the girl, who has become consumed with her obsession and desire for the red shoes, sneaks to the high shelf, picks the lock on the box, and removes them. As soon as the shoes touch her feet, she is overcome again by the uncontrollable urge to dance. She dances out of the house, down the street, and out of the town. She dances throughout days and nights, rain and snow. She is exhausted, thirsty, and hungry, yet she cannot stop dancing. There are several scenes at this part of the story, depending on the version, where the little girl dances in and out of towns and interacts with different people who she begs for help, but who are unable to help for various reasons. Finally, she meets an executioner and begs him to cut off her feet, and he does.

In some versions of the story, this is where it ends. She is disabled for the rest of her days and never again wishes for red shoes. In Hans Christian Andersen's version of the story, she finds her way back to church, and through prayer, she is forgiven and finds peace.

SEEING OURSELVES IN THE MYTH

In *Women Who Run with the Wolves*, Estés uses *The Red Shoes* to show what happens when a woman is cut off from her self-designed, instinctual life. While I agree with Estés, I believe this fairy tale also serves as a warning for anyone who falls victim to worldly distractions and the consequences of being consumed by them.

As a poor beggar, the little girl begins without many material things. However, she is proud of the shoes she has created for herself. They aren't much, but they are hers and they represent her self-made life. Some might see the old woman as the rescuer of the little girl. After all, she pulls her out of poverty and gives her beautiful clothes, food, and training on how to behave in the civilized world. However, with all of these material and physical comforts comes certain trappings. Her self-determined life and the shoes she is so proud of, that made her feel rich in her Soul, are destroyed. She must sit still and "be good." She must act and dress in a certain way to be accepted by society because outside opinion matters more than anything. As Estés says in her breakdown of the fairy tale, "this eventually leads to loss of accurate perception, which leads to excess, which leads to loss of the feet, the platform on which we stand, our basis, a deep part of our instinctual nature that supports our freedom."[5]

How many of us feel trapped by our material possessions, caught in a rat race to afford the right clothes, homes, cars, or vacations? We focus on things that ultimately don't matter as much as we've been led to believe. Patriarchy and capitalism thrive when we focus on the external rather than the internal, staying too busy trying to survive and prove our worth to connect with our souls.

When the girl sees the red shoes, she is immediately overtaken by them. She becomes obsessed. She feels something, a spark, that she has not felt since she was taken in and domesticated by the old woman. In this way, the shoes represent a potential life force and excitement that the girl longs for.

When our Souls are starved—and under our current social systems, most of ours are—we latch onto anything that seems to offer relief, be it a fancier car, bigger house, the right job, the hustle and bustle, the perfect image of what a life with kids *should* be or look like, the right religion or political party, or even the perfect partner who will rescue us from the mundane.

Ask yourself: What breadcrumbs have you or are you accepting in place of a full meal? Where and when have you sought out hustle and material goods in place of a soul-filled life? Can you see how you may have hoped that an item, substance, or even relationship (kids included) would save you, complete you, or give you purpose?

In the story, the red shoes soon overpower the girl, forcing her to dance herself to death. No matter how hard we try to conform, be good, and sit still, our wild, intuitive side—our Soul—knows it's disconnected. The more we ignore this, the more our Soul starves, and the more it clings to whatever obsession or addiction brings feeling back into our lives.

The violent way in which the executioner cuts off the little girl's feet and shoes serves as a metaphorical wake-up call. The metaphor is meant to be felt in every cell of your body. The image is a drastic, almost brutal, reminder of what it takes to reclaim a soul-based life. It's about dismantling our loyalty to a system whose sole purpose is to use us for our energy, output, and life force to keep the hamster wheel spinning and producing abundance for those very few at the top. Women's free time is a threat to patriarchy. We spend so much time being married, raising children, proving our value, and hiding behind our busyness that rest and creativity are dangerous to the dominator systems.

Now ask yourself: What are your metaphorical red shoes? What have you allowed to become your obsession-turned-anesthetizer?

How does busyness, being consumed with your red shoes, allow you to avoid caring for your Soul? Are you ready to make a radical shift to reclaim your time, space, health, Soul, and Self?

GOING DEEPER

Learning Non-Doing

Ah, meditation. It seems every therapist today tells their clients to meditate because it will improve their lives. Is it true? Sure. Is it that simple? Of course not. Within the context of our culture's Cult of Busy, however, mindfulness and meditation can teach us a lot about the practice of *non-doing*.

There's a difference between practicing non-doing and doing nothing. You're busy, I'm busy, we have to work to survive, I get it. But if we hope to break out of the Cult of Busy, we need to step back and examine the bigger picture. We have to become more conscious of what we allow to consume our time, energy, space, and peace.

Non-doing is very active, despite what it sounds like. It actually takes a lot of work to stop doing and just *be*. To be still, even for a moment, and notice what feels good, what feeds your Soul, and what triggers guilt or resentment. To get to know that part of yourself that wants to be nurtured, not pushed aside in order to nurture others. Of course, most of us can't just stop performing all of our duties and responsibilities and fly away to a deserted island somewhere or meditate in a cave all day. But if we don't create moments of stillness in our everyday lives, we rob ourselves of the joy of living, and we rob our loved ones of experiencing us when we're full rather than depleted.

For me, a key step in slowing down and prioritizing my mental and spiritual health over my checklist was to examine the "why" behind my plans. Why was I meeting that person? Why was I taking on that project? Was it fulfilling something in me, or was it out of obligation or guilt? I began to use a 50 percent me, 50 percent them rule to decide what projects or invitations to say yes to. Anything that felt like I was doing it less than 50 percent *for* me fell to the bottom of my priority list.

Not only did I start freeing up chunks of time to do things that fed my Soul (for me, this included yoga, cooking, and gardening), but I felt a lot less resentful toward the people I was spending my free time with. It no longer felt like they were taking from me; it felt like I was *choosing* to give.

I want to reiterate: I know it is a privilege to be able to say no and slow down when many of us are living paycheck to paycheck. I'm also not advocating for the continued isolation and hyperindividualism that has gotten us here as a society to begin with. Nor am I saying we can say no to everything that's essential for surviving or caring for our loved ones. I am, however, challenging you to look at your life as a whole and question the things you busy yourself with because you think you *should* or because of how it makes you look to the outside world.

Inventory

Here is an exercise I learned many years ago through my training in mindfulness-based cognitive therapy (MBCT) that I have not only used with hundreds of clients and students over the years, but that I still use for myself every year around my birthday as a yearly check-in.

Take some time to list out every single step or action you do on an average day. So, for example, you might write:

- Wake up at 6:00 am

- Scroll social media for ten minutes

- Make coffee and lunches from 6:15 to 6:45

- Shower at 6:45

- Get Little One (LO) up at 7:00 am

- Sit LO in front of the TV to eat breakfast for thirty minutes while I get ready

- Get LO dressed, hair and teeth brushed between 7:30 and 8:00

- Leave at 8:00 am, do drop-off, then head to work

- Drive to work for twenty-five minutes

- Be at work by 8:30

You get the idea, right? I'm talking minute by minute. Once you have listed out your entire typical day, I want you to go back over the list and write one of the following three letters next to each item:

P for Positive: Of the things that I do, what nourishes me and gives me a sense of aliveness and presence rather than a feeling of merely existing?

D for Depleting: Of the things that I do, what drains me and decreases my feeling of aliveness, making me feel like I am merely existing, or worse?

N for Neutral: Of the things that I do, what things neither add to my sense of aliveness or take away from it, but just *are*?

Let's label the same morning list I just created as our example:

- Wake up at 6:00 am   N

- Scroll social media for ten minutes   D

- Make coffee and lunches from 6:15 to 6:45   N

- Shower at 6:45   N

- Get LO up at 7:00 am   N

- Sit LO in front of the TV to eat breakfast for thirty
  minutes while I get ready   N

- Get LO dressed, hair and teeth brushed between
  7:30 and 8:00   D

- Leave at 8:00 am, do drop-off, then head to work   D

- Drive to work for twenty-five minutes   D

- Be at work by 8:30   N

Now, take that list, look over all of the Ps, and give yourself credit for the places in your life where you are ensuring you get moments of nourishment throughout your day. You'll notice that in this example morning, which is an honest depiction of a typical morning in my house, there are no Ps anywhere on the list.

Next, look at the Ns. During this exercise, try your best to be honest with yourself about the things, at least at this moment in time, you cannot change. Are there any Ns you might be able to shift to Ps? You don't need to stress about how many Ns there are, since they don't bring that much stress *or* that much joy; they just *are*.

Finally, look over the Ds. This is where you get to be creative (maybe after a pang of guilt or even sadness about how many are on the list). In my example, there are some Ds that I can simply hold myself accountable to remove entirely (like scrolling on social media for ten minutes when I first wake up). I can ask myself a couple questions here: How do I implement change in my routine in order to remove this D from my schedule? What might I replace it with? Maybe I can start writing a gratitude list during that time instead.

If I replaced scrolling on social media for ten minutes with naming the things and people I am grateful for each morning, is it possible that what is currently a D on my list might turn into an N, or even a P, over time?

Other Ds require more creativity to shift to an N or a P. For example, instead of listening to the news and being pissed about traffic all the way to work, I could begin a habit of listening to a spiritual podcast during my commute. I actually did this exact thing years ago when I realized this part of my morning was a D, and I felt like it could be a prime spot to squeeze in a nourishing habit. Listening to a spiritual podcast or even a guided meditation while getting ready or commuting quickly flipped this action to an N, but over time, I found myself looking forward to that thirty minutes and missing it if I didn't have it, so it flipped to a P.

What about prepping some of the lunches the night before? Would this give me more time to get the Little One ready in the morning so I could feel less rushed and challenged? Even if it gave me an extra ten or fifteen minutes in the morning, I imagine that might lend itself to a less stressful time and potentially shift the D to an N. (I don't know any mother who enjoys the morning rush . . . I bet most would label this as a D.)

It's important that we comb through the sometimes mundane parts of our lives in detail and be proactive about how we can make small changes that lead to an internal shift in our sense of aliveness. Personally, if something is labeled a D and I have at least attempted to tweak it and make it more bearable (let's be honest, not all Ds can be changed), I feel like I have taken back some control where I might have previously felt helpless and even resentful.

Rest and Revolt

In a society shaped by a capitalist ethos, rest is truly a form of revolt. Tricia Hersey's *New York Times* bestselling manifesto *Rest Is Resistance* challenges us to reclaim our bodies and spirits through rest, pushing back against capitalistic white supremacist grind culture. I remember the first time someone told me I didn't need to ask for permission or justify my need to rest, I was floored. In *Untamed*, Glennon Doyle reflects on the moment she realized how often she would see her partner Abby resting and think to herself, "Must be nice . . ." She began to notice jealousy around her partner allowing herself to rest and play. Rather than make it Abby's fault for taking care of herself, Glennon realized that societal and familial voices—not her own beliefs—were preventing her from doing the same.[6]

Now, when I catch myself thinking, "Must be nice," I stop and pay attention. When I notice a similar twinge of irritation or jealousy around others' rest or a longing to slow down, I try to pause and repeat to myself a few anti-capitalist affirmations I learned from a post on writer and poet Cole Arthur Riley's beautiful Instagram account:

> Inhale: I don't have to wait until it hurts.
>
> Exhale: I enter rest without apology.
>
> Inhale: I reclaim my body.
>
> Exhale: I can rest without shame.

Here are some more anti-capitalist grind culture affirmations I have come up with that might resonate with you. Take what works and/or create your own.

- I am allowed to spend my time creating things simply for the sake of creating.

- I do not need to monetize my hobbies; it is enough to spend time doing something I love.

- All work is valid; there is no such thing as a "real" job.

- In my home, we normalize doing less.

- I am worthy by simply existing; I do not have to accomplish anything to be worthy.

- I am not defined by what I produce.

- My Soul requires rest to be nourished.

- My loved ones are worthy of my rested Self as much as I am.

- Society does not get to define what success looks like for me.

What might you add?

4

martyrdom is not mothering

> "The greatest burden a child must bear is the unlived life of its parents."
>
> —Carl Jung, *The Development of Personality*[1]

There was always so much laughter. Music. Dancing. I have vivid memories of sitting on my mother's bed while she got ready to go work at the bar, where she worked nights to support us. I would watch her in her mirror as she did her hair and makeup, Pat Benatar or Heart turned up to full volume on the stereo, us singing together—I knew all the words. I was sad that she had to leave for work, but I was mesmerized by her beauty and radiance, and I cherished those moments together. We would dance as she held my hands while I stood on her bed, twirling past me on her way to her closet and back, perfumed and smiling. I was all of five years old; she was twenty-six.

At some point in my teen years, I stopped seeing her like that. We didn't blast music and sing the way we once had. She didn't laugh and dance while getting ready for work anymore. She was older now, and it had been many years since she embodied that vibrancy I remember so vividly. Her face was lined with age and the years of single parenting, the stress of what is required to raise children alone. I remember her as a young woman who laughed freely and loudly, who often spoke about her dreams and adventures before becoming a mom. She went back to finish her undergrad degree when I was only six, desiring a better life for herself, not just for me. But the money was always better at the bar, so that's where she stayed.

After I became an adult and moved away, she got an entry-level job in finance. She had my brother and sister to support and was determined to give them what she hadn't been able to give me—putting them through college so they wouldn't be in debt like I was. So she worked. All the time, she worked to support her children as she climbed the ladder, finally becoming financially stable in her early fifties.

During family gatherings, she still tells the same stories of her adventures before having children. Her eyes sparkle when she recounts the fun and excitement of her youth, and as her eldest daughter, I feel a deep sadness. She used to talk about all of the dreams she had for herself as if they were bound to happen. At some point, the way she talked about them changed from present tense to past tense.

What I didn't realize then, but see so clearly now, is that my mother's light didn't dim because she aged; it dimmed because of the relentless demands placed on her as a single mother trying to balance work, parenting, and her own unrealized dreams. Like many mothers, she gave all of herself to her children and work, leaving little for her own fulfillment. This self-sacrificing role is one that society applauds, but what does it cost our mothers, their children, and the community as a whole when their lives become synonymous with martyrdom? How many of us have witnessed this dimming and internalized it as our fault or just the way things must be? This chapter explores the myth of the self-sacrificing mother—how it has been shaped by history, culture, and religion, and why it may not be the most nurturing path for either mothers or their children.

WE ARE WEIRD PARENTS

My mother's transformation from a vibrant, dream-filled woman to someone whose life revolved solely around the demands of others reflects a cultural script that many mothers follow, often unconsciously. This script is deeply rooted in our societal norms and expectations around motherhood, which are shaped by historical, psychological, and cultural forces that promote self-sacrifice over self-realization.

I have come to understand that the way we parent in a patriarchal, capitalistic, and white supremacist culture creates and then fosters much of the stress and dissatisfaction experienced by parents, specifically mothers. Anthropological studies show that many of our common modern parenting practices are unique to Western culture, including having infants sleep alone in separate rooms, fearing spoiling babies by picking them up too much, scheduling breastfeeding sessions instead of relying on on-demand breastfeeding, and sleep training.[2] Let me be crystal clear, this isn't about shaming anyone for using these techniques. I sleep-trained and schedule-fed my daughter. My intention is to highlight how different, and sometimes WEIRD (an acronym I'll discuss in a moment), our practices are compared to the rest of the world—and yet many of us don't realize there are other ways because of the systems of supremacy in which we were raised.

In her work *Mothers and Others*, anthropologist Sarah Blaffer Hrdy highlights that in early human history, and even today in many non-Western societies, cooperative caregiving (or alloparenting) is a central feature of child-rearing. She points out that humans are evolutionarily wired for communal caregiving, which stands in stark contrast to the isolated nuclear family structure that is so common in Western societies.[3] Similarly, Suzanne Gaskins's research on Mayan child-rearing practices shows how caregiving is shared not just by family members, but by the entire community, providing emotional and physical support for mothers and children alike.[4]

The first time I saw the acronym WEIRD was in Michaeleen Doucleff's book *Hunt, Gather, Parent*. I became obsessed with understanding more about this way of living and parenting and the impact it has had on us. The acronym WEIRD stands for Western, Educated, Industrialized (or Individualistic), Rich, Democratic, and it came from the research of psychologists Joseph Henrich, Steven Heine, and Ara Norenzayan. They found that while 96 percent of psychological research is conducted on people of European descent, Europeans make up only about 12 percent of the global population.[5] This highlights a significant limitation in the scope of psychological research, as much of the data reflects a narrow subset of humanity. Despite this, many psychologists and authors present these findings as if they are universally applicable.

The same issue extends to parenting books, which often draw from this limited research base. Given that the US is one of the largest book markets and many major publishing houses are based in the US and Europe, a substantial portion of published parenting advice reflects Western sensibilities, which may not be relevant or applicable to much of the world.

WEIRD parenting practices, however, do not exist in a vacuum; they are informed by deeper cultural and religious beliefs that have shaped Western notions of child-rearing for centuries. If we view modern parenting through the puritanical lens that shaped the US, another layer of understanding emerges. The concept of Original Sin, for instance, though complex and not universally accepted, deeply influences parenting, schooling, mental health policies, and even criminal justice in the West. It suggests that humans are born with a proclivity for sin, needing lifelong correction. This cultural undercurrent affects how we view children, often leading to the belief that they are inherently bad and must be shaped into "good" people. Whether you subscribe to the idea of Original Sin or not, it's important to look at how threads of the doctrine permeate the social context of the US and thus impact how we see and rear our children.

The belief that children are inherently sinful has historically justified strict, obedience-based parenting models that prioritize control over emotional connection and nurturing. Calvinist and puritanical traditions, in particular, have promoted the idea that a child's will must be broken to ensure moral goodness. In his book *Spare the Child*, historian Philip Greven critiques how these religious doctrines have perpetuated authoritarian parenting styles, shaping generational beliefs about discipline, compliance, and punishment. Greven's analysis aligns with other critiques of Christian doctrine, such as those found in *The Family Crucible*, which examines how religious teachings have influenced family dynamics and child-rearing practices.[6]

If there is an underlying cultural narrative that children are born bad and need to be forever trained and molded into "good" people, that belief then becomes supporting evidence, justification for, and thus a motivator behind many Western ways of parenting. In the late 1800s and early 1900s, publications advised mothers not to kiss and hug their children and to strictly schedule their bowel movements.[7] Freud then claimed, around 1923, that all people are born driven by instinctual and selfish urges for immediate gratification.[8] Freud and his early followers even believed babies bonded with their mothers solely for milk, and that love and touch were not of importance.[9] This thinking laid the foundation for a rigid, emotionally distant approach to child-rearing.

It wasn't until 1946 that change began to emerge, when Dr. Benjamin Spock published *The Common Sense Book of Baby and Child Care*. As a pediatrician who became trained in psychoanalysis, he was one of the first to begin pushing back on rigid behavioral approaches to parenting, telling parents to listen to their "common sense" instincts and provide their children with "natural loving care." By 1958, British developmental psychologist, psychiatrist, and psychoanalyst John Bowlby (largely responsible for attachment theory) began to talk about the "original goodness" of babies and children in an attempt to mitigate Western enthusiasm for punishing children (and adults), stemming partly from the puritanical belief in Original Sin.

Research shows that people who believe that children are bad, selfish, manipulative, and sinful are more likely to abuse them than those who think they are good and innocent.[10] This belief also places an unrealistic burden on parents—especially mothers—who feel solely responsible for shaping their children into moral adults, a heavy load in a society increasingly disconnected from community support.

Ultimately, the WEIRD framework highlights how Western parenting norms are shaped by historical doctrines, psychological theories, and cultural narratives that prioritize control, independence, and punishment. These norms stand in stark contrast to many other cultures around the world, which focus on community, cooperation, and nurturing. Recognizing that our approach is not the only way, and perhaps not always the best way, opens the door to rethinking how we parent in a manner that fosters more connection, more well-being, and less stress for both parents and children.

What I have presented so far is a simplification of what impacts the way we parent in the West. In the United States alone, we are comprised of a vast number of cultures and heritages that also influence how we raise our children. However, whether through the melting pot theory of multiculturalism, cultural assimilation, or cultural acculturation theory, most immigrants will eventually begin to adopt aspects of the dominant culture within which they live. And many of the WEIRD ways of parenting—along with the puritanical belief that we are not born inherently good and need to be *taught* how to be good—are among those adopted practices.

REVISITING PENDULUM THEORY IN OUR PARENTING STYLES

If we trace the generations and their parenting style back to the Greatest Generation (we could go further, but for the sake of brevity, a little over a century feels far enough to prove my point), we can see the Pendulum Theory at work, which helps us understand more of how and why we got to where we are now. Let me give you a quick (and overly generalized) takeaway.

The Greatest Generation (born approximately 1900–1927), shaped by the Great Depression, raised their children using authoritarian methods: strict obedience, unquestioned compliance, and conformity, with little regard for autonomy. Children should be seen and not heard. Their children, the Silent Generation (born approximately 1928–1945), mimicked this authoritarian approach, but because they experienced post-war prosperity during their coming of age, they had more wealth and more children at a younger age than any previous generation. The Silent Generation then raised their children, the Baby Boomers (born approximately 1946–1964), who experienced economic prosperity at an even younger age and were able to focus on things their parents could not, like education, pleasure and travel, hoarding wealth, and purchasing for convenience. They, in turn, raised Generation X (1965–1980) and older Millennials (1981–1996) with a more permissive, often uninvolved parenting style, leading their children to be highly self-sufficient with a lot less parental involvement or emotional nurturance—hence the term "latchkey kids."

Now, Gen X and older Millennials are raising their children with an overcorrected approach as overly involved helicopter parents who fill their children's free time with activities and extracurriculars and put so much attention on their emotional development that some consider it suffocating. This generation of parents (myself and likely many of you reading this book) seem to be living with social media experts constantly telling them what they are doing wrong, leading them to continuously strive to "get it right." Shunning the authoritarian and uninvolved methods of past generations, they now hover somewhere between authoritative (a balance between clear boundaries, independence, respect, and love), gentle, permissive, or what we call attachment parenting methods.

While attachment parenting is often praised, it's exhausting in a detached society. Yes, babies want to be held and we want to hold them, they want to be breastfed and we want to breastfeed them, they want to sleep with us and we want to sleep with them, they want us to wear them and we want to wear them. These are all intuitive ancestral practices that have kept our species alive. Attachment parenting is actually just *parenting*. But in an individualistic capitalist society, we are isolated within nuclear families. Where there were once aunties, sisters, uncles, grandmas, cousins, and neighbors around to help, now it's often just us. I frequently repeat to my friends and clients who are struggling with the demands of attachment parenting that in some current non-Western or collectivistic societies, such as Mayan, Inuit, or Hadzabe communities, biological mothers perform about 20 to 25 percent of the direct childcare. In contrast, in Western societies, biological mothers are responsible for up to 80 percent or more of the childcare, with much less support from extended family or community members.[11]

The final rub for many Gen X and Millennial parents is that their preferred parenting styles (aside from permissive) require parenting from a place of patience, emotional regulation, and behavior modeling. But since these generations were mostly raised with hands-off, emotionally distant parenting, they often feel like they're raising themselves while also raising their children. This is draining and a recipe for burnout. We need to find balance and work toward the center of the pendulum. Neither extreme is healthy.

MARTYRDOM IS NOT MOTHERHOOD

> "What if love is not the process of disappearing for the beloved but of *emerging* for the beloved? What if a mother's responsibility is teaching her children that love does not lock the lover away but *frees* her? What if a responsible mother is not one who shows her children how to slowly die but how to stay wildly alive until the day she dies? What if the call of motherhood is not to be a martyr but to be a *model?*"
>
> —Glennon Doyle, *Untamed*[12]

Candace, a thirty-six-year-old Asian American woman, came to me to work on feelings of burnout, stress, and a general dissatisfaction with her life.

"You don't understand. I can't leave them for an entire weekend with their dad. He won't feed them right, they'll fight all weekend or get sat in front of the television, and they probably won't even get proper baths or brush their teeth."

"Candace, your kids are eight and eleven. Don't you think they're old enough to know when they're hungry? And so what if they eat a little extra junk food or don't get the best baths? Will they die?"

"No, they won't die. But they are so used to me being home with them on the weekends and with their routine. They're going to have a really hard time, and I just know my husband can't handle it."

I sighed and leaned in a little closer before speaking again.

"Candace, I think you are struggling to leave them for two days more than they will actually struggle. I think you are hiding behind your perceived incompetence of your husband and kids. I think you're worried about not being as needed as you think you are." I could tell she was a little hurt by what I just said. "You have wanted to be a stylist your entire life. You put your career on hold to have kids and be a present mother. You came to me a year ago because you were struggling with depression, anxiety, unhappiness in your life and relationship, and not knowing who the hell you were. The universe has begun to present you with opportunities to lean into what lights you up, what you find joy in, your passion and interests, and yet all you keep talking about are the reasons you can't take the opportunities. You're seeking out reasons to sacrifice yourself. To *martyr* yourself.

"Let's talk about the real fears. If you take a risk and do something that makes you uncomfortable, you might fail and have to feel hurt and maybe embarrassed. You're used to blaming your husband, and honestly your kids, for your stress, burnout, and unhappiness, and if you start to take back some responsibility for your own happiness and it doesn't change anything, you won't have anyone else to blame. If you stop doing everything for your kids and let them develop some self-agency, you won't be the sole giver of all of their joy and comfort . . . they may even find that in others, including their father, and you might get left behind. If you aren't an overworked and all-consumed mother anymore . . . then who the hell are you?"

Candace had begun to cry but maintained eye contact with me. "I'm terrified that I have no clue what I'm doing and that I'm going to look like a complete fool. I KNOW how to be an amazing mother. I don't know if I know how to actually be anything else. But I want to take this weekend styling gig so fucking bad I feel like I could scream."

Candace's struggle to reclaim her identity outside of motherhood mirrors a broader societal expectation that mothers must sacrifice themselves to be seen as "good" or "lovable," a belief deeply rooted in both cultural narratives and historical conditioning. The natural discomfort and pain of pregnancy, labor, and child-rearing often lead discussions of motherhood to be intertwined with themes of pain and sacrifice. Coupled with our tendency to equate caring and self-sacrifice with morality and perfection and goodness with lovability, it's no wonder so many of us lose ourselves in parenting, partnership, or both.

In *Mary, Mother of Martyrs*, Kathleen Gallagher Elkins notes that "feminist scholars and activists . . . often find themselves in a double bind; leaving the connections between motherhood and self-sacrifice unchallenged means that mothers (and, by extension, all women) will be expected to gladly sacrifice for their children and for others, yet critiquing the 'natural' association . . . can lead to charges that feminists are antifamily or antimother."[13] Elkins's research explores how Western religion and politics have long used the image of the self-sacrificing mother to control women. To be clear, neither Elkins nor I argue that caregiving and sacrifice are inherently negative. On the contrary, we are interconnected beings who depend on one another, and caregiving can be a commendable life path, provided it stems from an internal desire and not an externally imposed standard of lovability.

Feminist theorist Adrienne Rich argued that the institution of motherhood has been used to control and suppress women's autonomy, turning them into martyrs for the sake of maintaining the family unit.[14] Psychological studies also show that mothers who internalize this martyr role are more likely to experience burnout, depression, and a sense of worthlessness, as their own needs are continually suppressed.[15] Mothers are told not to reach too high, expect too much, or be too big, but instead, we're allowed to experience those things through our children. The problem arises when we lose ourselves in our children, when our lives become consumed by theirs, and when our passions are subsumed by their interests.

Contrary to our conditioned belief that martyrdom is a selfless way to mother, it actually creates more anxiety and stress in our children than if we were fully alive and passionate about our own lives. Children don't learn by what they hear; they learn by what they see. If they see us putting everyone else ahead of ourselves, losing our lives and identities to parenthood or partnership, and hiding behind them because we lack the courage to stand up and out on behalf of ourselves, they'll believe this is what a good life looks like, what healthy partnership and parenting looks like. They'll emulate us, internalizing the belief that to be loved, they too must sacrifice their dreams, desires, autonomy, passion, and zest for life.

Candace did take that weekend styling job, and her children and husband managed just fine. She now freelances on weekends semi-regularly, sometimes leaving the kids with her husband and sometimes arranging for them to stay with friends one of the nights she is gone. While her anxiety about leaving them has improved, it hasn't disappeared entirely. Prioritizing herself remains one of her greatest struggles, and she often slips back into her old patterns. However, she has become more protective of her time and energy and regularly challenges herself to focus more on her own needs and fulfillment.

As with all of my clients, I learned as much from Candace as she learned from me. When I find myself putting my self-care, joy, or creativity last on my list of priorities and resenting my partner and kiddo for it, I think of Candace and pause. I want to walk my walk as a therapist, not just talk my talk. It isn't easy, even for me, to put my dreams and desires on equal footing with everyone else's. Sometimes they can't be the priority, and that's as it should be—but not always.

And when I struggle to choose myself for my own sake, I do it for my daughter. I remind myself that her best chance of growing up to become a passionate, embodied, risk-taking, self-loving woman is to see her mom actively working to be the same.

MYTHS AS MAPS
The Virgin Mary, from Goddess to Martyr

The Virgin Mary, as we know her today, is a complex and multifaceted figure whose narrative has been shaped, molded, and constrained by the theological, cultural, and social forces of early Christianity and beyond. The early Christian Church Fathers initially opposed the worship of Mary, aware that she was not an original figure but rather a composite of multiple ancient mother goddesses revered across different cultures. Scholars such as Joseph Campbell and Marina Warner have noted that Mary's image was influenced by goddesses like Isis, Cybele, and Artemis, revered in various parts of the ancient world for their maternal and protective qualities.[16] These goddesses, often associated with fertility and nurturing, were venerated long before Christianity, and elements of their mythology were later incorporated into the evolving image of Mary. Over the first few centuries of the Christian era, despite initial opposition, Mary's image gradually developed, borrowing from these ancient deities who were known for conceiving "sons of God" and saviors in temples around the world.

Despite these attempts to diminish her, Mary's figure grew in significance. In Catholic traditions, she was elevated to a status where her mercy and intercession were considered even superior to that of God or Jesus, as seen in the veneration of her as Mediatrix[17] and Mother of Mercy.[18] This highlights a profound and perhaps unconscious need within Christianity for a maternal, compassionate counterbalance to a more patriarchal and justice-focused deity. Carl Jung, a practicing Christian who analyzed religious symbols throughout his career, proposed that Mary represented Christianity's response to the need for a feminine aspect of God. She introduced principles of humility, tenderness, and understanding into a faith that had become increasingly obsessed with rigid justice and patriarchy.

While the Church worked to portray Mary as a symbol of submission and humility, her image also took on a deep association with suffering and sacrifice. Over the centuries, Mary has been cast as the Mater Dolorosa, or "Mother of Sorrows," enduring profound pain as she witnessed her son's crucifixion and accepted her role as a silent sufferer. The Church Fathers gradually shaped a narrative where her motherhood was intertwined with martyrdom, embodying ideals of piety, purity, submissiveness, and self-sacrifice. As Kathleen Gallagher Elkins notes, "Pain and loss are key features of nearly every interpretation of Marian texts, even explanations of the Immaculate Conception."[19] Elkins further explores how interpretations of Mary often idealize submissiveness and martyrdom as cornerstones of femininity, womanhood, and motherhood.

This theological construction aligns with the modern idea of a "martyr," someone who is always suffering in some way, always sacrificing themselves for others. In many ways, Mary has become the archetypal martyr of the Christian tradition, not because of a single defining moment of suffering, but because her narrative continuously reinforces her willingness to endure pain and loss for a higher purpose. Her presence at the crucifixion alongside other women, like Mary Magdalene and her sister Mary of Clopas, offers an alternative vision of motherhood—one that connects to communal solidarity and care in response to violent loss rather than an exclusive association with individual suffering and sacrifice. "It is not, then, an intimate moment between mother and son, even though the artistic tradition stemming from this text might suggest such a scene . . . If Mary is not alone at the crucifixion but is one of many women who experience loss and yet remain present, this presents an alternate vision of motherhood."[20]

Yet this more nuanced view of Mary has often been overshadowed by the narrative that idealizes her as a solitary figure, silently bearing the weight of her son's suffering. This distortion of her role has led to an oversimplified understanding of the feminine as being inherently tied to martyrdom and sacrifice. The archetype of the Great Mother, by contrast, embraces duality—both creation and destruction, light and dark. This duality, present in many myths and cultures that celebrate virgin births and resurrections—from the Egyptian sun god Ra to the Indian god Krishna and the Mesopotamian fertility god Tammuz—has been largely stripped away in the sanitized, patriarchal portrayal of Mary.

The current cultural understanding of Mary does not represent the full spectrum of feminine power, but instead serves as a tool to dictate womanhood and motherhood. In modern contexts, we see the concept of the "martyr mother" play out in everyday life: where women are expected to self-sacrifice, be everything to everyone, and erase their desires and needs in the name of family or duty. Clarissa Pinkola Estés, in *Women Who Run with the Wolves*, encapsulates this cultural expectation: "Women's 'heal everything, fix everything' compulsion is a major entrapment constructed by the requirements placed upon us by our own cultures, mainly pressures to prove that we are not just standing around taking up space and enjoying ourselves, but that we have redeemable value."[21]

The cultural and theological construction of Mary as the archetypal martyr has profoundly shaped Western notions of motherhood, womanhood, and femininity. By emphasizing her purity, submissiveness, and willingness to suffer, her image has been used to dictate what is expected of women and mothers. This portrayal has stripped away the complexity of the feminine, reducing it to a one-dimensional narrative that prioritizes sacrifice and martyrdom over completeness and empowerment. It is a narrative that has been constructed to control and suppress the vast potential of feminine identity, keeping it confined within the limits of patriarchal ideology.

SEEING OURSELVES IN THE MYTH

The myth of Mary as the eternal martyr has been leveraged as a blueprint for female behavior, one that is both deeply flawed and profoundly damaging. Yet recognizing this truth is only the first step. To truly free ourselves from this external narrative, we must confront how this blueprint has shaped our lives and begin to rewrite the script.

As we peel back the layers of Mary's story, we can ask ourselves: What does her myth mean for us today? Where have we internalized the image of the "martyr mother"? Where have we felt compelled to sacrifice our needs, silence our voices, or endure suffering in silence in the name of being a "good" woman or mother? These are not relics of an outdated religious tradition; they are living myths that continue to shape our daily experiences as women, particularly as mothers, in modern society.

While researching the Virgin Mary, I repeatedly encountered works pointing to the global celebrations and cathedrals dedicated to her, as if to say, "See! Women and mothers are important! We're celebrating them!" But what exactly are we celebrating? Many of the great Gothic cathedrals in Europe, including those named Notre Dame—meaning "Our Lady"—were not dedicated to God or Jesus, but to Mary, the Queen of Heaven. These "palaces of the Queen of Heaven" were often built over ancient pagan shrines dedicated to the Great Goddess, symbolizing a continuation of feminine worship—but with a significant shift toward prioritizing purity, submission, and sacrifice over the full spectrum of feminine strength and complexity. Similarly, in our own lives, we may find ourselves celebrated for our selflessness, while our deeper needs and desires go unacknowledged.

Ask yourself: Where in my life have the idealized qualities of piety, virginity, purity, dutifulness, discipleship, goodness, faithfulness, submissiveness, and martyrdom made me feel less than? Where have these qualities compelled me to compare myself to others or trapped me on a hamster wheel of trying to prove myself and keep everyone happy at the expense of myself? Have you ever caught yourself thinking, *Must be nice*, about your partner, friends, colleagues, or kids?

As mothers, we don't burn out because we're doing too much; we burn out because of *why* we're doing too much. Here's a harsh truth: If your "why" is rooted in proving your worth—whether it's worthiness of love, of your motherhood, or of acceptance—it's based on the unhealthy masculine ideal of perfectionism. Your "overdoing" isn't about them (the ones you claim to do it all for); it's actually about you (*ouch, I know*). Martyrdom in motherhood is about being seen a certain way or as a certain type of person, not about the act of giving itself. We can pretend that we do it all for "them," but if we're walking around depleted, angry, and resentful, I can assure you it's not. We often use "them" as a way to hide from the deeper work of setting boundaries, slowing down, speaking up, making hard changes, and challenging societal norms—the deeper work of prioritizing the Self.

These questions and challenges are not meant to provoke guilt, but to spark awareness. By naming and questioning the pressures we've internalized, we can begin to break free from the roles that have been prescribed for us. This is not about rejecting caregiving or motherhood, but reclaiming it on our own terms—grounded in authenticity, connection, and self-compassion. This is also not to say that caregiving or sacrifice is inherently wrong. Rather, it is the *compulsion* to sacrifice—the belief that our worth is tied to how much we endure—that we must question. When we examine the myth of Mary, we see how her narrative has been used to idealize suffering and silence. But we also see glimpses of an alternative: Mary at the crucifixion, not alone but surrounded by her sister and friend, embodies communal solidarity and care. This image invites us to redefine motherhood—and womanhood—not as solitary martyrdom, but as a shared journey of connection and support.

The myth of Mary reminds us that the feminine is not a one-dimensional archetype defined by pain and passivity. It is a vast, dynamic force, one that encompasses creation and destruction, light and shadow, strength and vulnerability. By embracing this complexity within ourselves, we can move beyond the limiting roles imposed on us and create a more expansive, authentic expression of womanhood and motherhood.

GOING DEEPER

Reconsider

If you are already a parent, do you ever feel frustrated that you no longer have control over your life? Do you feel responsible for constantly entertaining your children, filling their time, making sure they are stimulated, learning, and engaged? We just took some time to plot an average day in chapter 4, but consider: What gives you joy throughout your day?

Our current child-centered world is a recent development in the grand timeline of our species. Until very recently, children's lives were folded into their parents' lives. In *Hunt, Gather, Parent*, Michaeleen Doucleff shares a question she asks herself before agreeing to any child-centric activity: "If my daughter were sick, would I still go without her?" If the answer is no, she passes on the activity.[22] When I first read this, it blew my mind and made me uncomfortable. Wasn't that . . . mean? Wasn't it my job to ensure my daughter was learning, stimulated, and entertained? To run from sports practice to birthday parties to museums all weekend? No. No, it wasn't. I began implementing this rule (with some exceptions) and started reminding my daughter that her boredom is not my responsibility (yes, I tell her that exactly). She doesn't always like it, but I feel a lot less pressure to be her main source of fun.

So what about the things on your activities list that are for your (and only your) joy? A workout class, pottery, dance lesson, gardening, coffee or dinner date with a friend, massage, reading, writing, or simply a solo walk? Remember, we don't burn out because we're doing too much; we burn out because we're doing too little of what makes us come alive.

Are you ensuring you get this time? Are you protective of your joy? Let's explore that further.

Prioritize

Prioritizing yourself can bring feelings of guilt, overwhelm, and even sadness, especially if you've forgotten what brings you joy. The societal programming that a mother must prove her love by burying her dreams, ambitions, feelings, desires, and ultimately herself is patriarchal nonsense. As we've discussed, motherhood is about modeling, not martyrdom. Children learn by what they see, not by what they hear. If we show them that being a woman and mother means sacrificing yourself for others, that's what they'll grow up to do. Our daughters will replicate it, and our sons won't truly respect women with strong desires and convictions.

Many of my clients and workshop attendees over the years look at me like I have two heads when I emphasize the importance of prioritizing themselves. In an overly scheduled world where many are struggling, it can seem privileged to tell a parent to prioritize themselves, but it doesn't have to mean a week-long retreat or spa day. It can be done in small moments. For me, it looks like maintaining my workout routine, even if my daughter is upset that I'm leaving for the gym. I don't lie and tell her I have to work. I tell her, "Mommy is going to work out, to move her body. It makes me happy, keeps me healthy, and makes me a better person and mommy." If she cries, I hug her, validate her feelings, and then go anyway. I also schedule nights out with my friends and explain it to her the same way.

"I want to come with you!" she cries.

"Honey, it's important that mommy gets to spend time alone with her friends. Just like you have your friends, I have mine. I love you, and I will see you in the morning!"

Can you practice doing the same? Can you carve out even twenty minutes a day for yourself? Communicate to your children that this time is important for your well-being and that it helps you be a better parent. Consistently showing them that self-care is a priority teaches them to value their own needs and passions.

Our children will only live as fully as we do. When you prioritize yourself, when you do things just for you, it's not selfish; it's love. It's modeling. It's parenting.

Part 2

the myths of sex

> "Whereas sex should be a symbol of union, it becomes a symbol of power. Total union is not possible when the ego is afraid to give up. And where the ego is not firmly grounded in the instincts, it dare not surrender to the transpersonal power."
>
> —Marion Woodman, *Addiction to Perfection*[1]

For most new parents, especially mothers, sex often becomes the farthest thing from our minds. And yet it remains the number one issue couples come into my practice to discuss—more than money. And even more interesting, the conversation about sex is rarely about *sex*. It's about desire, longing, acceptance, and connection (or, rather, disconnection). It's also often tangled with control, dominance, belonging, being chosen, trying to please, and unearthing the way a culture of supremacy (i.e., patriarchy, patriarchal capitalism, colonialism, and misogyny) has severed our connection to the parts of us that are wild, primal, feminine, dark, soft, caged, untapped, longed for, and even feared.

When I work with clients on sex, we work with Eros—life force, the drive for love and creativity. In our hypermasculine culture, we often lose touch with this force in favor of doing, achieving, and seeking control. This disconnection, often rooted in childhood wounds like the Mother Wound, shapes how we seek intimacy and healing in adulthood. So what happens when these unresolved wounds show up in our closest relationships?

5

the mother wound

> "When men feel the wound that cannot heal, they either bury themselves in a woman's arms and ask her for healing which she cannot provide, or they hide themselves in macho pride and enforced loneliness."
>
> —James Hollis, *Under Saturn's Shadow*[1]

I can either mother you or I can want to have sex with you, but I can't do both."

We were sitting in couples therapy talking *again* about the difference in our sex drives. Talking *again* about him feeling undesired. *Again* about him not feeling like we were connecting enough or connecting in the way that *he* wanted.

Two days earlier, I found myself in a full-blown meltdown, rocking back and forth on the floor, sobbing harder than I had in years. My daughter was crying in my room, and John was standing in the doorway watching me silently. Just moments before this scene, I had been standing in the kitchen making breakfast, still in my pajamas, messy bun and cozy socks, whisking an egg while sipping my coffee.

My then three-year-old appeared at my side, asking for a snack despite the fact that I was making breakfast.

"Honey, I told you I'm making breakfast. Just give me one minute, it's almost ready."

"Moooooom. I want a snaaaaack. I don't want eeeeeggggggsssss."

The whining immediately started to agitate me, as it usually did. I inhaled deeply. "I hear that you are hungry. I need you to go into the other room. Breakfast will be ready in a minute. I will give you fruit and toast with your eggs."

"Mooooooooooooom." She stayed put, now pulling on my pant leg.

"Hey, so today, I have this meeting with my editor at 11:00, and I'm going to tell her that I want to talk about my next book idea."

"What?" I said, turning to my right to see John, now standing in the kitchen, holding his coffee.

"I'm ready to get moving on my next idea. I'm just worried that they aren't going to give me the type of deal I had before, and then we are going to struggle financially this next year."

"Mooooooooom. I WANT A POPSICLE!"

I could suddenly hear my heartbeat in my ears. I put down the whisk and started walking into the living room. My daughter and partner both followed me.

"Mooooooooom. I WANT A POPSICLE! Mooooooooooooom!"

"I'm just worried that since the ad sales from the podcast aren't as high as they were and then if this deal isn't the same, or more than the last one, we are going to . . ."

"Moooooooom!"

"OH MY GOD! EVERYONE, SHUT UP! EVERYONE, PLEASE JUST SHUT UP!" My hands covered my ears as I screamed out loud the thoughts that were meant only for the inside of my head.

My daughter immediately burst into tears, startled. I then burst into tears when I saw her tears. Scooping her into my arms, I brought her into her bedroom and rocked her, crying along with her.

"I'm sorry, I'm so sorry. Mommy was overwhelmed. Mommy didn't mean to yell at you. I'm so sorry. I know that was scary. I'm sorry."

I was sobbing. She was sobbing. I kept rocking her. After a few moments, she began to calm down. I placed her in my bed with her tablet. "Let's watch something while I finish breakfast, okay?"

"Okay." She sniffed, her face red and blotchy.

I stumbled into the back office, slumping to the floor. The sobs were deep, raw, and relentless, my body heaving and choking. I remember John standing over me. I remember him saying something that I didn't register. I remember asking him to leave me alone. I remember crying for what felt like an hour. And then, when my body had worked through my nervous system's complete overwhelm and the absolute crippling shame that came from yelling at my daughter, I slowly stood up, went back out to the kitchen, and finished making breakfast.

It was Wednesday after all, and we still had to get out the door for school in twenty minutes.

UNDERSTANDING THE MOTHER WOUND

The scene I described—a moment of overwhelming frustration, guilt, and emotional collapse—is not just a personal anecdote, but a reflection of the deeper psychological struggles tied to the Mother Wound. This wound, often rooted in the complex dynamics of maternal relationships, extends beyond individual experiences and permeates the way women navigate motherhood, partnership, and self-identity.

Motherhood, as transformative as it is, strains partnerships and affects how women are seen and valued within their relationships. Research on maternal roles and relational dynamics shows that societal expectations placed on mothers can exacerbate feelings of competition and resentment within partnerships.[2] Many women report experiencing a competitive energy from their partners after a child enters the couple's dynamic, as the partner begins to vie for the mother's attention. This tension can deepen over time, with the baby and the partner both competing for her care, affection, and focus, revealing underlying challenges in how attention is redistributed within the family.

Regardless of our actual relationship with our mother, it is the most impactful relational experience in our lives. Whether mother was present or absent. Whether mother was loving or cruel. Whether mother was emotionally attuned or indifferent or sick. These dynamics shape us at a profound level and influence the rest of our relationships.

Beyond our individual mothers lies the archetypal Mother, a universal symbol rooted in the collective unconscious, as described by Carl Jung. The archetypal Mother represents the nurturing, life-giving energy found within all individuals, regardless of gender.[3] She embodies qualities like compassion, warmth, and unconditional care, but also encompasses the shadow aspects of motherhood, such as smothering or emotional absence. This archetype, often explored in depth psychology, influences how we connect with ourselves, our communities, and the natural world, shaping our capacity for empathy, vulnerability, and belonging.[4]

While the Mother Wound can be viewed tangibly—for example, an injury to a child's psyche caused by dysfunction or disturbance in their relationship with their *actual* mother—it also encompasses a broader disconnection from the relationship to the archetypal Mother. This distinction is crucial because, for too long, the actual mother has been blamed for the bad behaviors of her grown children, and while some of this can hold true, we are *all* acting out of our disconnection to the archetypal Mother—especially in a patriarchal system that devalues everything about the feminine.

We have all longed for warmth and connection, felt a desire to be nurtured and held. We have wished to be taken care of and embraced, to return "home" or feel at home. *This* is the yearning for the archetypal Mother, and it is universal. While none of us want to leave the metaphorical comfort of home (and for some of us, the physical comfort), if we do not differentiate and establish our own emotional and spiritual autonomy, we remain trapped in a childlike state, even as we grow into adulthood. The Mother Wound is both deeply personal and profoundly collective, reflecting our struggle to reconcile these internal and external dynamics in a patriarchal world.

> **DEPTH 101**
>
> *Differentiation:* A foundational concept in depth psychology. A natural and necessary process of growth that supports individuation. It involves distinguishing individual parts from a unified whole, untangling and separating what was once unconsciously fused. Differentiation allows us to identify and establish our own sense of Self, distinct from others, such as separating our identity from that of our mother or partner. According to Jung, differentiation allows for the integration of unconscious thoughts, feelings, and patterns into conscious awareness, ultimately enabling individuals to cultivate an authentic and autonomous sense of Self.[5]

THE GREAT MOTHER: IN BALANCE AND BECOMING

The archetype of the Great Mother, or the inner feminine, symbolizes the nurturing and life-giving aspects of the psyche that guide individuals toward authentic connections with themselves, their communities, and the natural world. It embodies emotional and spiritual intelligence, craves Soul fulfillment, ignites creativity, allows for vulnerability, and fosters compassion, intimacy, and sensuality.[6] It is our intuition embodied.

Carl Jung was the first Western psychoanalyst to discuss the masculine and feminine energies within all of us, drawing on universal themes from diverse cultural traditions. He expanded on the terms "Anima" (feminine) and "Animus" (masculine), originally coined by Johann Wolfgang von Goethe in *Faust*, formalizing them as archetypes in the human psyche and emphasizing that everyone embodies both of these energies. While the language of masculine and feminine can be limiting and sometimes confusing, Jung's insight remains relevant: an overemphasis on either energy creates imbalance within individuals, communities, and society.

Both men and women have emotionally and spiritually suffered at the hands of our modern patriarchal, capitalistic structures that dismiss and devalue feminine traits. As a therapist, I avoid terms like "toxic masculinity," which suggest that masculine traits are inherently negative. In my opinion, this is a common trap in today's discussions around the rise of the feminine. It is not to replace the masculine; it is to reclaim and balance the energies within us.

OUR FEAR OF LIFE'S CYCLES

Archetypally, the Great Mother is symbolized by and felt through the circle or cycles—the natural rhythms of beginnings, endings, and renewals. Yet these cycles are often absent in our upbringing, as many of our caregivers, too, are shaped by a culture disconnected from the instinctual, numinous, symbolic, and metaphorical world of the psyche (the Soul) and the universe's cyclical design. This disconnection breeds fear and resistance against life's natural flow. We fear and resist cycles because they inherently include endings, suffering, symbolic deaths, and loss—aspects of ourselves and life that we struggle to accept. By resisting these cycles, we resist the archetypal Mother herself—the source of security and comfort—and hinder our growth into a sovereign, differentiated, emotionally mature adult capable of embracing life's inherent challenges. Instead, we often spend a lifetime looking outside of ourselves for something or someone to make us feel like the Great Mother did (or how we imagined the Great Mother should), forever striving to feel secure, seen, and adequate.

Tangibly speaking, this fear of cycles manifests in parent-child dynamics, such as:

- Parents who shut down, distract from, or dismiss their child's big emotions, disrupting the natural cycle of feeling, expressing, and integrating emotions as teachers instead of something to be feared.

- Overprotective parents who shield their children from struggle and discomfort, preventing them from learning self-reliance and resilience.

- Enabling parents who never hold their children accountable, disrupting the natural cycle of healthy shame, social learning, and the development of skills like attunement and empathy.

This distrust of life's natural cycles—expansion/contraction/expansion, life/death/life, light/dark/light—keeps us in a constant state of fear and control. We try to control that which ultimately cannot be controlled: other people and life itself. We fight to find ways to not feel the anxiety and discomfort that being in a state of contraction, death, or darkness bring (and require), and we struggle with emotional regulation, trust, and intimacy.

WOUNDED BY OUR EXPECTATIONS

The psychic need for nurturing is universal, and as a depth psychotherapist, I've seen unexplored and unhealed Mother Wounds in nearly all my clients. The negative impact of this wound manifests differently based on gender, due to our society's arbitrary gender rules and stereotypes.

For women, the Mother Wound often appears as low self-esteem, poor boundaries, fear of rejection, perfectionism, difficulty expressing themselves and their emotions, a harsh inner critic, and a reliance on external validation. This stems from societal messaging that women must be subservient, that they need to be chosen to be of value and that having a solid sense of Self will impact their ability to be chosen, that they must be small and not have a strong voice or presence, and that physical beauty is the price they pay to exist in this world.

For men, their wounding is centered on the idea that their worth lies in providing, not relating. Vulnerability and care are seen as weak, and attunement and emotional intelligence are of little importance. Emotional detachment is the price *they* pay to exist in this world. In *Under Saturn's Shadow*, James Hollis describes how an unhealed Mother Wound manifests in men as jealousy, emotional ambivalence, obsessive and controlling behaviors, putting women down, homophobia, cheating, and anger at a woman for not providing the nurturing and attention, whether emotionally or sexually, that they crave.[7]

These unhealed dynamics often find their counterparts in relationships: the partner who fears rejection may attract someone who obsesses and controls, even subtly, while the partner who craves constant validation may pair with someone who has poor boundaries. Because the Mother Wound hinders the development of a differentiated sense of Self on which to rely, trust in, and draw stability from, many adults remain stuck in an infantile longing for mothering and nurturance that even the most codependent partner cannot fulfill.

This explains why so many of us need our romantic partner to make us feel lovable, worthy, seen, understood, desirable, or strong. Of course, we want to feel desired and valued by our partner, but when we need them to constantly affirm these aspects of ourselves because we can't see or source them from within, we unconsciously force them into a parental role. Before children, these dynamics may seem manageable and maybe even a little intoxicating, but once a child enters the picture, the complexity increases, especially for mothers.

If I *need* my partner to make me feel sexy and desirable, and my partner is now consumed with keeping a tiny human alive and is disconnected from their own body and sexuality for a period of time, I will personalize it and make it about me. If I *need* my partner to make me feel worthy and seen, and suddenly they have shifted a lot of their praise and validation over to our child, I will personalize it and make it about me. If I *need* my partner to make me feel stable and safe, and they are now focused on the safety of our child, I will personalize it and make it about me. Time and again, I see this play out in the couples in therapy, where mothers express some variation of "I feel like I have another child at home, not a partner."

I CAN'T BE YOUR EVERYTHING

Many of my heterosexual female clients report an energetic shift in their male partners when a child is added to the family dynamic. This observation aligns with research on gender roles within the family system, which shows that men often experience a sense of displacement or loss of primary attention when a child is born.[8] In a patriarchal and mononormative culture, men are accustomed to being the center of their partner's attention. The arrival of a child—a new "planet" that not only orbits the mother, but also pulls her orbit away from the father—can feel deeply unsettling, leading to feelings of insecurity or emotional withdrawal.[9] You were once each other's sun, and now, a third presence disrupts that balance.

While research shows both genders undergo psychological changes with parenthood, societal gender norms often make this transition more impactful for women's identity and self-conception. Motherhood demands an immediate shift in priorities; there's simply less time, energy, and mental space to devote to anything else, including oneself. It creates an ongoing tug of war, where a mother feels caught in the middle, unable to be everything for everyone. The energy competition may vary, but the result is the same: someone feels neglected or disappointed, and you can't win.

WHO'S THE BABY HERE?

Robert, a fifty-two-year-old white man, sought couples therapy with his wife, Rachel, a forty-one-year-old Black woman, to understand why she had become increasingly distant, angry, and critical since the birth of their daughter two years prior.

"All I ever hear is what I'm doing wrong and how I could be helping more. Rachel tells me to stop being so needy. Our daughter is glued to her all day, and by the time 8:00 pm rolls around, Rachel is exhausted. We barely talk about anything besides the next day's schedule. She scrolls her phone, watches TV, and hardly touches me. She doesn't text me flirty things anymore; when I reach for her, I feel her go cold. Honestly? I'm lonely."

As Robert talked, I watched Rachel's face. I caught what I interpreted as a flash of anger. I asked her about it.

"Yes. I'm annoyed and fed up," Rachel said. "I'm doing my best to just keep my head above water, and all Robert talks about is how I'm not paying enough attention to him. Of course I want to know how work is going, I want to connect, but I can't be his total support system like I used to be. I'm too tired to have deep conversations at 8:00 pm. He gets upset when I forget to text him back during the day. I'm constantly doing mental gymnastics around what I say or do or don't say or do and how he will respond, how upset or sulky or annoyed he will be by it. I just can't be his everything anymore."

This dynamic isn't unique to Robert and Rachel; it is emblematic of a broader issue where women, conditioned to be emotional care takers, often feel overburdened. The woman is expected to maintain her role as a nurturing figure while also managing her own emotional needs and identity—a nearly impossible balancing act that can lead to feelings of resentment and emotional depletion.

Robert looked hurt. I asked Robert about his other intimate relationships outside of Rachel. Rachel raised her eyebrows.

He hesitated. "Um, I have a few guy friends. I see them at the gym and we text. Sometimes we go out for some beers."

"They text about cars and workouts," Rachel interjected.

"Do you talk about fatherhood, your relationship, or work anxieties with them?" I asked.

"Not really. I mostly talked to Rachel about that stuff—or at least I did . . . before our daughter was born."

Over the next few months, we explored how a patriarchal, misogynistic society positions women as the "natural-born" caretakers, despite evidence that both men and women are capable of being emotionally attuned caregivers. Our species simply would not have survived if women were truly the only gender born to be caretakers. This societal belief manifests in adult heterosexual dynamics, where women are often expected to fulfill all the emotional needs of the family, leaving them exhausted, touched out, and feeling inadequate. Meanwhile, men become disconnected from their own nurturing capacities, questioning their self-worth and seeking emotional reassurance and validation primarily through their romantic and sexual relationships.

We also discussed societal expectations like mononormativity and amatonormativity, which center two-party romantic relationships as the sole source of deep emotional fulfillment, ignoring the human need for a diverse web of intimate connections. As James Hollis wisely notes, "The purpose of a committed relationship, of marriage, as but one example, is not to take care of each other to reinforce the parent-child complexes, but to grow through and with each other."[10] It is imperative that couples work to move beyond traditional roles of dependency and toward a partnership grounded in mutual growth, individuation, and a shared commitment to challenging the societal norms that confine them.

EMOTIONAL DIVERSITY IS A MISSING KEY

Our culture largely discourages men from being vulnerable or nurturing with others, and they often have fewer emotionally intimate friendships compared to women, leaving them reliant on their romantic partners for emotional support and to fulfill needs that should be met through multiple relationships.[11] This lack of emotional diversity can strain the relationship, especially in times of conflict or change, as it places a disproportionate emotional burden on one partner.

I gently challenged the belief that Rachel should be Robert's best friend, confidant, lover, advisor, and emotional stabilizer, all while being a good mother and maintaining her own identity, work, and self-care. Similarly, women are often socialized to believe their value is tied to their ability to care for and support others, leading them to overextend themselves emotionally. This not only depletes their resources, but also reinforces codependent patterns that can be difficult to break.

Understanding and working with differentiation offers a crucial way out of these patterns. By supporting individuation, differentiation enables individuals to distinguish themselves as independent entities, separate from their partners. Developing emotional diversity and differentiation go hand in hand; when individuals cultivate a range of supportive relationships outside of their primary partnership, they also strengthen their sense of Self. As seen in the case of Robert and Rachel, a lack of differentiation—where personal identity is overly fused with a partner—can lead to emotional dependency and conflict. Through therapy, they began the process of differentiation, recognizing their distinct needs and emotional boundaries. This process allowed them to engage more authentically with one another and reduce the emotional over-reliance that strained their relationship.

BUILDING EMOTIONAL INDEPENDENCE: ROBERT'S JOURNEY

Step one for Robert was recognizing the societal myth that his partner should be his everything and grieving this false expectation. Step two was beginning to take a critical look at his friendships and take the uncomfortable steps to try and deepen these relationships and cultivate others. He reached out to each of the four men closest to him to schedule one-on-one time. I challenged him to discuss deeper topics with them—what his hopes for the future were, what his greatest challenges were, his fears. Pretty quickly, he saw that three of the four friends were uncomfortable and closed off when he started going deeper, but one really leaned in. He listened to Robert and also shared similar struggles and concerns of his own. I encouraged Robert to nurture this friendship, and I pointed him in the direction of a few male mental health content creators and men's groups that had been instrumental in the budding emotional lives of other male clients of mine.

These efforts were not just about expanding his support network, but also about shifting his expectations within his marriage. Robert began to see how his reliance on Rachel for all his emotional needs placed an unfair burden on her. By developing a more emotionally diverse circle of connections, he could reduce this dependency and foster healthier, more balanced dynamics at home.

We also examined the restrictive belief that opposite-sex friendships must involve sexual tension, a narrative rooted in patriarchal ownership models. This opened the door for Robert (and Rachel) to consider healthier boundaries and broader support systems. The ability to engage in friendships with people of different genders without the expectation of romance or sexual tension further supported Robert's journey of differentiation and individuation.

By challenging these myths, Robert was able to recognize the importance of emotional diversity—not just in his friendships, but in all areas of his life. This shift was hard but essential for moving toward a partnership with Rachel that was based on mutual respect, growth, and support rather than emotional dependency.

WHEN PARENTAL DYNAMICS CREEP IN

During a couples retreat I led, a couple with two young kids at home, he a military officer and she a stay-at-home mom, attended. She had recently asked for a divorce, exhausted by her husband's inability to emotionally regulate and support her, especially given one of their son's special needs. She shared how, during conflicts or overwhelm, he would withdraw for hours, leaving her alone to manage not only her emotions, which she knew were her responsibility, but also their children's, with one struggling immensely with emotional regulation due to his autism.

At that point, he jumped in to defend himself, quoting back to me . . . me!

"Aren't we supposed to take care of *ourselves*? To emotionally regulate ourselves? To not expect the other person to do that for us? That's why I walk away and go be by myself. I am calming myself down."

I responded, "That's fair, to a certain extent. But then you get to walk away to regulate yourself and she's left by herself with two kids that don't actually have the capacity to regulate themselves. So you're essentially saying to her, 'It's not only your job to regulate you, it's your job to regulate them too. Because I come first.'" I clarified that while this wasn't his conscious intention, he was acting out of a fight-or-flight response.

I finished by saying to him, "So as a partner, you get to a place where you ask, 'What am I doing here? What is the point of or purpose to this relationship?'"

This exchange resonated widely when I posted my part of it on social media, garnering over one million views. Why did it strike such a nerve? Because it highlighted a common issue: in our culture, men often lack the tools to manage their emotions and soothe themselves due to societal norms that suppress the development of emotional intelligence. This can manifest in three ways:

1. They become defensive and withdrawn, leaving their partner alone in the conflict.

2. They lean on women to co-regulate them.

3. They explode and get aggressive or even violent. This is just another way of forcing co-regulation.

As children, we rely on our caregivers' regulated nervous systems to help calm and guide our own emotional responses. Through their attunement and ability to sense into our dysregulation, they use their voice, body, and breath as a safe anchor until we are able to calm down. However, in a society that discourages emotional expression, many of us—especially men—were told to suppress our feelings rather than be guided through them by attuned caregivers. We grew up hearing, "Stop crying," "Stop being so dramatic," "Knock it off," or "It's not a big deal" rather than having a caretaker with the capacity to allow our emotions to be felt and expressed without personalizing them. Instead of learning that emotions are manageable and instructive, we were taught that they are to be controlled or dismissed.

These dynamics, combined with misogynistic views of women being seen as the natural caretakers whose role it is to regulate everyone, set the stage for adult romantic relationships where men do not have the tools to regulate their emotions and so look to their female partners for the co-regulation they did not receive in childhood. This isn't exclusive to men; women can also exhibit these behaviors, as can partners in same-sex relationships. In fact, one of the fundamental issues I see in the relational struggles of my clients is the expectation that our partners will co-regulate and reparent us, acting as the "Positive Mother" we never had. This expectation actually perpetuates a lot of our childhood wounds by keeping us in a dependent position, continually seeking unconditional love and acceptance from someone who, as another flawed human, cannot fulfill that need. As a result, we remain trapped in a cycle of disappointment, perpetually unsatisfied with their inability to make us feel "okay."

> ### DEPTH 101
>
> *Reparent/Reparenting:* A therapeutic process rooted in Jung's work on the inner child, where the therapist assumes the role of an ideal parent, allowing the client's inner child to feel seen, heard, and validated. Therapists can also teach clients to reparent themselves in order to provide themself the loving and containing experience of an ideal parent. In couples therapy, reparenting often appears when one partner unconsciously provides the other the reparenting needed for growth and emotional safety.

YOUR PAST, IN YOUR PRESENT

Once a child enters the picture, a mother, now focused on co-regulating with her child, often struggles to do the same for her adult partner without resentment and anger. She may begin viewing him as another child who "needs" her. Biologically, we are hardwired to avoid sexual attraction to our offspring (or parent) to maintain healthy boundaries for strong genetic lines, so the second a parental dynamic enters a romantic relationship, we stop seeing our partner as what Jung would call "the erotic other." Centering their comfort and tending to their emotional state is what we naturally do for our children, but when it extends to a partner, it blurs the lines between parental and romantic feelings, making it difficult to separate the two.

Adults co-regulate their nervous systems constantly—with people, nature, and even animals. Even self-regulation is a form of co-regulation between mind and body. The issue isn't co-regulation itself, but the expectation that it is a partner's duty to regulate the other.

Through our continued sessions, I helped Robert recognize when his desire for Rachel to make him feel better led him to act out through withdrawal, coldness, and "pouting" (as Rachel put it) when his needs weren't met. It was crucial for him to understand that his reliance on Rachel for emotional stability reflected an imbalanced dynamic, where he unconsciously expected her to fulfill the role of emotional caregiver, mirroring unmet needs from his developmental years. We worked on self-soothing techniques and explored alternative sources of co-regulation, like nature and friendships, to reduce his dependence on Rachel. We also expanded attunement practices and developed consent language, helping Robert practice being more aware of Rachel's emotional state and checking in with her verbally before allowing his expectations to dictate his behavior.

We were also able to identify and make conscious the resentment and anger Robert harbored toward his own mother for not tending to his emotional needs in the way his inner child felt he deserved. As Robert came to understand how these unmet childhood needs shaped his relational patterns with Rachel, he realized the necessity of addressing these unresolved feelings. This led him to begin his own individual therapy, where he could explore the deeper roots of his resentment and anger toward his mother and how these emotions continued to impact his behavior as an adult. As Hollis notes: "If men are to heal, they must activate within what they did not receive without."[12]

MYTHS AS MAPS
Cinderella and Rescuing Ourselves

Many fairy tales represent the process of individuation, highlighting the struggles and lessons we might face along the path of self-development. *Cinderella* is one such archetypal story, with variations found across cultures and eras. Many believe the earliest known version, the story of Rhodopis, tells of a Greek slave girl who marries the king of Egypt, recorded sometime around 7 BC.

The familiar versions—whether through the 1940 ballet, Disney's 1950 film, or the 1965 musical starring Lesley Ann Warren—focus on themes of enduring mistreatment, dreaming of rescue, and ultimately being saved by a man, Prince Charming. While these popular retellings emphasize external validation and rescue, they miss the deeper psychological message of the original tale: the journey of individuation, self-discovery, and self-agency that follows the loss of a primary nurturing figure.

Cinderella's journey begins with the loss of her mother and the emotional abandonment by her father, leaving her in servitude to her cruel stepmother and stepsisters. She becomes the household servant—cooking, cleaning, sewing, and tending to everyone's needs without complaint, all while maintaining her kindness. This is more than mere labor; symbolically, the tasks of cleaning and cooking represent the inner work of excavating the unconscious, bringing to light the shadow elements and ingrained patterns that keep us stuck and uninitiated.

In some versions of the tale, Cinderella requests that her father bring her a hazel branch from the fair to lay on her mother's grave. Watered by her tears, it grows into a beautiful tree. The tree is an archetypal image of the individuation process itself—a source of life and a symbol of resurrection and rebirth. Depending on the version, a magical bird nesting in the tree or a fairy godmother appears to help her attend a ball thrown by the prince. The bird or fairy godmother represents the Great Mother or inner Goddess—the nurturing aspect of the Self that empowers transformation and performs the magic of creating our own reality, even in adversity.

The magical items given to Cinderella—dress, slippers, carriage, horses, and coachmen—symbolize different facets of the Soul, or the Self, such as enlightenment, resilience, and the capacity to transcend suffering. The midnight limit imposed on the magic reminds us of life's inherent limits and the necessity of balance. At the ball, Cinderella meets the prince, who represents the Great Masculine aspect of the Soul, a force that seeks true connection rather than abiding only by tradition and structure. They dance for hours, forgetting all others, symbolizing the union of masculine and feminine energies within the Self, an integration crucial for wholeness.

After leaving in a rush at midnight, Cinderella loses her slipper. The prince's search through the kingdom and ultimate discovery of Cinderella back in her servant clothes reflects the journey of reclaiming the true Self. When she tries on the slipper, it fits perfectly, symbolizing the integration of her new, now whole identity. Their union represents the harmonious merging of masculine and feminine aspects within, marking the emergence of a transformed and individuated Self.

SEEING OURSELVES IN THE MYTH

Cinderella's story illustrates the journey of discovering one's Self after the loss of the mother (whether actual or metaphorical) and navigating the challenges of individuation. The tale captures the psychological process of separating from external caretaking roles and reconnecting with inner resources, symbolized by the Great Mother—resources that provide the emotional nourishment we often seek outside ourselves.

Cinderella teaches us the importance of stillness, inner strength, and perseverance. Despite her mistreatment, she does not complain, expect others to save her, or seek validation from external sources. Instead, she faces her hardships head-on and with integrity, using them as fuel on her path. Most importantly, Cinderella shows us that through *inner* transformation, a life of integration and fulfillment is born.

Like Cinderella, many women feel burdened by expectations that they must make others feel secure and valued, losing touch with their own needs in the process. This dynamic perpetuates the belief that women are the default source of comfort, mirroring Cinderella's servitude and loss of Self.

How often do we believe circumstances and people need to be different for our dreams to come true? Or that we need something or someone outside of ourselves to nurture and love us into feeling whole? The lesson of Cinderella is that we don't need external validation; we have everything we need within ourselves. Her transformation begins when she connects with the inner Goddess or Great Mother—the part of her that symbolizes the strength and guidance needed to reshape her life. Women, too, must undertake this journey: stepping back from the roles of caretaking those who are capable of taking care of themselves and recognizing that we often find a false sense of worth in providing this care.

What we don't yet have access to or recognize within ourselves can be found and developed through a committed path of inner evolution. It is in this continuous journey of self-discovery and integration that we find our true power and potential.

GOING DEEPER

Take Ownership

Throughout this chapter, I've explored how Robert took ownership of his Mother Wound and began examining its impact on his relationship with Rachel. But it's important to note that Rachel, too, had her own inner journey to undertake. In our dominator culture, with its deeply embedded assumptions of mononormativity, men often have more work to do to develop the emotional and relational skills that women have been cultivating, whether by choice or societal expectation. However, women cannot do this work for men, nor should they. Women have their own work to do.

The struggles I see most frequently in my female clients revolve around trying to drag their partner along by the ear—attempting to change, mold, and teach them who and how to be. This is a huge indicator of where women need to focus their own healing.

For many women, healing around the Mother Wound involves:

- Recognizing their tendency to try and rescue their partner, friends, or family members from themselves and their own struggles.

- Examining how they may martyr themselves and self-abandon to make sure everyone else around them is okay.

- Working through their feelings of inadequacy for their partner and the fear that arises from this belief.

- Building tolerance for the wildly uncomfortable feelings that come from prioritizing themselves and stepping back from caretaking behaviors.

The conversation around the division of household labor and the mental load has been gaining traction, but less attention is given to the emotional labor that women often carry in relationships with uninitiated cis-heterosexual men. I have deep empathy for men within a patriarchal structure—they are in a terrible bind. They face shame from women or violence from other men when they embody so-called "feminine" traits, yet these are the very traits and skills *required* to have a fulfilling partnership. Developing skills that have atrophied from shame or have been cut off through cultural conditioning is hard work, but I trust in men's capacity to do this work. For women, the focus should be not on enabling or propping up their partners, but on cultivating stillness and an ability to not act out of our own discomfort and fear.

Assess Your Role

So begin to suss out what is your responsibility and what is your partner's:

- Where do you enable them to avoid discomfort?

- How do you prevent things from upsetting them?

- Where and how do you help regulate them?

It's important to recognize that an unregulated person can be unsettling and even frightening. You may have good reason to do these things based on your story or personal safety, but it is still important to notice your role in maintaining this dynamic. Reflect on how much of your time and energy are spent worrying about what might upset or irritate your partner. Pay attention to the physical sensations in your body when you find yourself "mothering" your partner. Become aware of how often you prioritize their needs over your own or even your children's.

Regulate

When we have children, our capacity to manage other people's needs dwindles. There's less tolerance for drama, selfishness, a lack of reciprocity, or even noise (hello, whining). This is because motherhood is especially hard on our nervous systems. Prior to having children, we were more in control of our basic needs—when we ate, when we slept, when we peed, when we showered. Part of learning to soothe

the nervous system is learning about your own emotional barometer, meaning your capacity at any given moment for one more thing to enter into your already filled-to-the-brim nervous system.

For the past few years, part of my personal practice has been around developing my barometer. I use a scale of 1 to 10. "1" means I'm basically sleeping, while a "10" means I'm in full-blown meltdown mode. "10" is seeing red, losing my mind, shutting down, yelling, sobbing, etc. I try not to get to a 10 if I can help it. I'm not ashamed of my humanness, but I am actively working on implementing healthier ways of expressing overwhelm and tending to myself before I potentially hurt others around me. For many women, the sheer overstimulation of motherhood pushes us down a very slippery slope—once we are at a 7 or 8, it takes very little to get to 10. So the practice here is to establish a personal range that can be your indicator to push pause and reset.

Throughout the day, pause and check in with yourself. Whatever you are doing, close your eyes, take three slow inhales and exhales, and ask:

- What's happening in your body? Aches, pains, tightness? Or maybe expansiveness and calm?

- What's happening with your breath? Tight, shallow, quick? Or maybe slow, steady, and deep?

- What emotions are swirling around? Do you feel like you're holding back tears? Or do you feel happy and content?

- What thoughts surface in the moment of pause? Are they frenetic, full of to-do lists, trying to convince you that there's no time in the day to get everything done? Or are they easy and grounded in the moment?

Now, rank your current state from 1 to 10. This regular practice will help you gauge and establish your baseline and recognize what activities, times of day, or interactions upshift or downshift your nervous system.

Here's the hard part. When you feel yourself creeping toward your slippery slope number, you have to speak up, ask for what you need, and actually act on it. So for me, when I creep into the 6 range, I say out loud to whoever is around me (usually my partner and my four-year-old), "There's too much going on right now!" It's almost like a safe word or phrase. I had a client once say when she hits that point, she loudly proclaims, "Candy corn!" At this point, after lots of teamwork on this topic, my partner and kiddo usually both pause. That's the point of the safe word or phrase. But I do not and cannot expect them to always do this. I also have to take care of me, and I have to model to my little one what that looks like. I may need to remove myself from the situation for a brief period.

The key difference here from the earlier example of a male partner withdrawing in conflict is the intention and communication behind the action. This is not about abandoning the situation or avoiding discomfort, but rather taking a moment to recalibrate so you can return more grounded and fully present. It's about taking a brief, intentional pause—knowing that you will return—rather than creating emotional distance. For example, you might say, "I need five minutes to calm myself down so I can be fully here with you," rather than storming off or leaving without explanation. By setting this expectation, you help maintain connection, even during moments of overwhelm.

Remember, your work is not to keep others comfortable; discomfort can be an opportunity for growth. When you feel yourself reaching capacity, prioritize your self-regulation and take the necessary steps to care for your emotional well-being. This allows you to reenter the situation more centered and capable of responding rather than reacting.

Examine

If you felt discomfort when I suggested that Robert examine his female friendships and deepen his relationships outside his marriage, that's great! As a therapist, I love jealousy—it's fertile ground for self-examination. Part of my life's work is to get all of us to reexamine the way in which our (here we go again . . .) patriarchal, misogynistic, white supremacist, colonial societal messaging has created a template of ownership in our relationships. And not just our romantic relationships. When we believe we should be the only important person in someone else's life, we are not only severely limiting *their* capacity for joy, fulfillment, and spiritual development, but we are also setting ourselves and the relationship up to fail from the strain and pressure. Instead of seeing love as a finite resource, recognize it as infinite. Deep connections with others help heal these wounds.

Sometimes, jealousy stems from past experiences of broken trust. Yes, it's painful when trust is broken, but a lot of the work I do with clients, and that I offer in this book, is meant to help you establish a deeper sense of and trust in Self and an inherent feeling of safety within, so when someone else breaks trust, you are able to see it is about them, not about you. It doesn't mean you're defective or that others are always untrustworthy. It means people are flawed, and your security doesn't depend on their actions. It doesn't give us permission to demand another person act or not act a certain way in order for us to feel a false sense of safety in the world. Women, too, need to examine their part in perpetuating these wounds through our jealousy and possessiveness.

Mantras

These are great reminders as you do this work. I repeat these to myself often:

- I will not teach, I will not lead, I will not manage others.

- My Soul's path is my Soul's path, and theirs is theirs.

- I do not have to teach others how to be their best selves; that is for them to discover and for me to simply mirror back to them.

- I am okay even if others are not.

- I am responsible for me and my nervous system.

Are there others you can create that feel resonant or supportive for you?

6

the father wound

"Where love reigns, there is no will to power, and where the will to power is paramount, love is lacking."

—Carl Jung, *The Collected Works of C. G. Jung*[1]

In the span of one week, I had cried four times about the same topic. As I sat in front of my therapist, working with a very distressing dream I had that week and crying for the third time (the fourth would happen the next day, during our couples counseling session), I tried to articulate the cause of my tears.

"I don't believe he is discerning. That he is looking out for our best interest. That he has our safety at the forefront of his mind the way I do. And I know this is so much bigger than just John; I know this goes back to my dad. My distrust of the masculine as a whole."

This feeling of not being safe and protected had been a constant undercurrent since the inception of my relationship with John, but something had shifted in me that was allowing what was once unconscious to come to the surface and make itself known. I began to realize that I may never have felt truly safe in any relationship with a man. This realization emerged only as I started to unpack and deconstruct my patriarchal and supremacy-based views of intimate relationships. I saw how deeply these societal narratives had shaped my expectations—that John should be the one to make me feel safe and at ease, contained and protected. I expected him to prioritize me and my comfort, to show up for me in specific ways or face my rejection.

These expectations were not just about John; they were reflections of a broader patriarchal script that equates masculinity with control and provision rather than emotional attunement and genuine partnership. As I continued this journey of self-reflection, I began to see how guarded and protected I had become from men as a whole, and how, in my relationship with John, I was projecting my unresolved Father Wound—my deep-seated distrust of the masculine—onto him.

The next afternoon, we sat over Zoom with our intimacy coach, and I opened up again about the feelings and revelations around not feeling safe that were coming up for me. John looked hurt and also slightly confused.

He repeated, as he had multiple times over the past six-plus years of our relationship, "I work so hard to make sure you don't have to worry about anything. You can make money, you can *not* make money. It doesn't matter. But I've got us."

"It's not about providing financially, John." I reminded him that the time I was able to pinpoint feeling the most safe and protected by him was when I was on the back of his motorcycle. "You are grounded when you are on the bike. Present. You feel safe, and I know that you are protecting me, us. I have no choice but to surrender control. I find myself more aroused and attracted to you when I'm on the bike. It isn't logical. I feel it in my body."

He continued asking questions and bringing up how much he had grown and changed since we had a child four years prior. "In this relationship, I am the most responsible that I have ever been in my life. I do more around the house and try so hard to notice and work on sharing the mental load with you."

"John, stop." Our coach intervened gently. "You are trying to put logic on something that is emotional. You are trying to check off to-do items and prove to her that providing for her in this way is protection. She's not minimizing the help and work you do; she is asking you to drop into your body and feel into the centuries of pain and distrust of men and the masculine that are inside her."

I burst into tears (the fourth time) and choked out, "I have spent my entire life being the one to scan for danger. To look out for everyone and make sure they are all safe. My whole life has been spent putting other people's needs and safety above my own. I'm exhausted, and I don't want to do it anymore. I know I've got my own back. But I want to feel in this partnership like we both have each other. That I can soften, and you've got me when I do."

UNTANGLING THE FATHER WOUND

As I reflected on the deep-rooted feelings of mistrust and self-protection surfacing in my relationship, I realized that these emotions were not unique to me. In my work with clients, I've often seen similar patterns—this pervasive sense of having to guard oneself, of not being able to fully trust the masculine. These feelings are part of a much larger, deeply ingrained wound: the Father Wound.

DEPTH 101

The Father Wound: A form of cultural and generational trauma passed down through fathers, rooted in patriarchal expectations, emotional unavailability, and rigid masculinity norms. It often leads to feelings of inadequacy, abandonment, or disconnection, perpetuating harmful patterns of control and power.

The Father Wound, much like the Mother Wound, is both a personal and a collective experience shaped by patriarchal structures. At its core, it reflects the unmet need for a guiding, protective, and steadying presence. This wound is not just about our direct relationships with our fathers, but also about the distorted relationship with the masculine itself—within us, in our partners, and in our culture.

Beyond our individual fathers lies the archetypal Father, another universal symbol rooted in the collective unconscious. This archetype embodies the guiding, protective, and authoritative energies present within all individuals, regardless of gender. It represents qualities like structure, wisdom, and strength, but also includes the shadow aspects of fatherhood, such as rigidity, domination, or emotional detachment. The archetypal Father shapes how we relate to authority, establish boundaries, and cultivate a sense of purpose and autonomy in our lives.

The Father Wound operates on both tangible and archetypal levels. It can arise from direct negative paternal interactions, such as verbal abuse, physical violence, or a persistently hostile emotional environment.[2] Indirectly, it can manifest through a father's emotional absence, indifference, or lack of relational skills, which deeply impacts a child's ability to form intimate, trusting connections.[3] These experiences lay the groundwork for how both men and women navigate their relationships with the masculine—both externally in partners and internally within themselves.

The Father Wound is also deeply embedded in the patriarchal construction of masculinity, which equates emotional detachment and control with strength. Historically, this wound has been shaped by shifting social currents. For example, some psychologists and historians point to the Industrial Revolution as a pivotal moment when fathers and sons stopped working side by side in fields or trades and instead began working long hours in factories. This shift disrupted the village and tribal relationships that once fostered close, nurturing bonds between fathers and sons, creating a model of fatherhood characterized by absence and emotional distance.

Others look even further back to ancient myths and fairy tales that often depict fathers as distant or disconnected figures—away at war or emotionally unavailable—leaving their children solely in the care of their mothers. These narratives have reinforced a cultural model of masculinity that disconnects men from their vulnerability and emotional expression. As a result, these inherited patterns continue to shape the lives of many men today, leading to a profound disconnection not only from their own emotions, but also from their capacity for genuine intimacy and connection in relationships.

THE QUEST FOR WHOLENESS

The Father Wound extends beyond personal dynamics; it is a collective, cultural issue that spans generations. Throughout recorded history, men have been asked to kill in the name of defense and honor, disconnecting from their vulnerability and humanness to perform horrific acts. This form of "performing masculinity" often necessitated severing the deeply connected aspects of the feminine within their souls. Just as the Witch Wound manifests in modern women through generational trauma, the deep distrust of the masculine is passed down through generations.

This wound is visible in the lives of my female clients, friends, family members, and even in my own experience. For centuries, men have been the single largest threat to the safety and well-being of women (and themselves). While most women love and respect the men in their lives, there is a residual suspicion at play in our relational dynamics—not only with men, but also within our relationship to our own inner masculine.

Metaphorically speaking, the Father Wound represents a rupture in our relationship to the archetypal Father or internal masculine within all of us. This wound reflects our longing and unmet need for protection, guidance, and a steadying presence—qualities often associated with the positive masculine archetype. When these needs go unmet, whether through personal relationships or broader patriarchal dynamics, we experience a profound disconnection that impacts our sense of safety and autonomy.

Because the driving force in a patriarchal system is domination and power, there will always be a tenuous relationship between the masculine and feminine—an inherent conflict between a longing for protection and a fear of control, a yearning for love and respect and a fear of domination. Like the inner yearning for the archetypal Mother, these desires and longings are natural. However, if we do not work toward emotional maturity, we risk remaining in a state of emotional dependency, forever looking to be saved by an external representation of the Great Father and unwittingly accepting the control and power that come with patriarchy.

RECLAIMING THE INNER MASCULINE

Unlike the process of initiation from the Great Mother, which comes through leaving the warm hearth and creating a rich emotional, relational, and spiritual life, the initiation from the Great Father requires leaving the metaphorical father's house. The journey involves setting out on our life's quest, where we will encounter and slay our dragons, discover and ultimately become grounded in our purpose, and develop an ability to, in our own way, fight for a better world.

The Great Father, or the inner masculine, represents an essential internal Soul energy that provides a grounding presence and a sense of protection for ourselves and those we love. This energy is not about dominance or control, but about guiding us with clarity and discipline to hear and act on the deeper callings of our hearts. It helps us navigate our life's mission along the path of individuation, encouraging us to serve others, live with integrity, and remain in awe of the greater mystery of life.

As James Hollis explains, if the mythology of the Great Mother is the circle, nurturing and containing, then the mythology of the Great Father is the quest, symbolizing the journey toward purpose, direction, and self-realization.[4] However, when this inner masculine energy is wounded or overshadowed by societal distortions, it can manifest across all genders as a lack of purpose, a disconnection from one's inner guidance, and patterns of seeking external validation to prove our worth. Reconnecting with the positive aspects of the inner masculine means embracing this quest not as a pursuit of power, but as a journey toward wholeness, balance, and a deeper understanding of the Self and the world.

WE'RE ALL WOUNDED

The Father Wound manifests differently in women and men. In women, it can show up as falling into patterns of relationships with emotionally unavailable men, being emotionally unavailable themselves, fearing intimacy, viewing other women (including daughters) as competition, and feeling unsafe within themselves and in their relationships with men and the masculine. Because patriarchal gender norms have often denied many women the ability to live their true purpose, some women may live out their unlived life through their sons or make their sons their emotional husbands (insert all of the mother-in-law jokes and horror stories here).

In men, the Father Wound is often expressed through fear and rage against women as well as difficulty forming warm bonds with other men, which leads to isolation. Studies on masculinity and emotional suppression suggest that these dynamics are often rooted in early relational experiences with paternal figures that discourage vulnerability and emotional expression.[5] This wounding can result in an inability or lack of desire to emotionally attune to others, engage in inner healing, or pursue growth and self-development. It may also manifest as an aversion to "powerful women" or women who are outspoken and self-assured, instead seeing dependence as a means of feeling valued and important, leading to behaviors rooted in control, dominance, and jealousy.

These different expressions of the Father Wound, whether in women or men, often stem from a deeper unmet need that goes beyond mere survival or relationship dynamics. At its core, it reflects an archetypal longing for something more fundamental: empowerment. As James Hollis insightfully puts it, "If nurturance is the archetypal need behind the boy's relationship to his mother, so we might say that empowerment is the archetypal need that seeks fulfillment from the father world."[6] When this need for empowerment and purpose is unmet or distorted, it leaves wounds that ripple across both individual lives and society as a whole.

BEING NEEDED IS NOT A SUBSTITUTE FOR PURPOSE

"I don't *need* you; I want you. I don't want you to *need* me; I want you to want me."

This was the first sentence out of Sarah's mouth to her husband Brad during our couples session one morning. Brad turned toward her, not replying, and stared. Sarah, thirty-four, and Brad, thirty-nine, both second-generation Korean Americans, had sought out couples therapy about a year prior to work on communication issues, but over the course of the year, as so often happens, we had gone to depths neither one expected. For the past few months, we had been focusing on Sarah's lack of desire for Brad and his subsequent feelings of inadequacy.

Not surprisingly to me, the pattern in their relationship had begun many years ago. Brad pinpointed it to when the first of their two children was born, and Sarah pinpointed it to right before she got pregnant. As an outsider aware of this specific and typical pattern, I saw the shift occurring even earlier, before they started their family.

When Sarah met Brad, he had just published his second novel, was actively researching his PhD program, and was deeply involved in running the nonprofit organization he had founded, which led men's healing workshops, groups, and retreats. Sarah was in grad school herself, in a career transition, and full of excitement, feeling like she had finally found her direction and purpose. They stayed up late talking about their desire to change the way people loved themselves and loved each other. They took long motorcycle rides to and from the beach, and they sat side by side, writing and working on new ways they could be of service in the world.

Somewhere in their first two years together, Sarah expressed watching Brad "lose his spark." He became more focused on money and notoriety and no longer seemed to find the same passion in the work he was doing. He sold his nonprofit and started focusing on media pursuits. Sarah still felt very connected to her mission, and the moments where they would reconnect over their shared passions were times she valued. These moments almost inevitably led to a night of passionate sex between them. Yet it was also around this time—when Brad's interest in his life and career shifted—that Sarah noticed he was seemingly never satisfied with their sex life. They began fighting about it frequently. He pouted, talked about not feeling desired, and expressed a desire for more adventurous sexual play.

Four years and two children later, not much had changed in their relationship from the start of their "sexual disconnection," as Brad labeled it—except there was now a bigger rift, more resentment, and less emotional and sexual connection. Brad had withdrawn more into his work, taking on a strategist role at an ad agency for the stability and benefits. Meanwhile, Sarah had become consumed with parenting and her expanding career, in which she had found a niche that felt fulfilling. While we worked on more tangible relational tools like developing communication skills, working through resentment, and addressing attachment style activation, we also engaged in deeper conversations about the ways in which both Brad and Sarah were acting out deeply ingrained heteronormative patterns and how their unresolved Father Wounds were manifesting in their relationship.

The Father Wound, whether developed through direct negative interactions or indirect emotional absence, significantly impacts one's capacity for intimacy and connection in adulthood. This concept was reflected in Brad's story, where his unresolved Father Wound manifested as emotional ambivalence and withdrawal in his relationship with Sarah. His journey in therapy involved recognizing this pattern and learning to develop healthier relational dynamics that did not replicate the neglect or hostility experienced in his early life.

Sarah's ability to pinpoint when her perception of Brad's passion shifted provided a crucial entry point for us. Around the same time Brad's sense of purpose started feeling shaky, Sarah's became more clear. Within my practice, I have seen that when a woman is self-sufficient and capable of taking care of herself, regardless of her relationship status, men with an unexamined Father Wound can feel inadequate because they rely on her dependency to feel valued and important. When a man is disconnected from his purpose and mission, he may begin to feel childlike and emotionally dependent on his female partner. Conversely, when a man begins to examine his patterns and embraces evolution, this emotional maturation and independence can trigger a woman's unhealed Father Wound, especially if she is reliant on his emotional dependency for *her* sense of worth and purpose. To move through this wounding, both partners need to work on their desire to be needed and relied upon in order to feel this sense of purpose and validation.

As Clarissa Pinkola Estés writes in *Women Who Run with the Wolves*:

> We all have made the mistake of thinking someone else can be our healer, our thriller, our filling. It takes a long time to find it is not so, mostly because we project the wound outside ourselves instead of ministering to it within. There is probably nothing a woman wants more from a man than for him to dissolve his projections and face his own wound. When a man faces his wound, the tear comes naturally, and his loyalties within and without are made clearer and stronger. He becomes his own healer; he is no longer lonely for the deeper Self. He no longer applies to the woman to be his analgesic.[7]

Estés captures the essence of the healing journey for both men and women—the need to dissolve projections and face our wounds head-on.

For Brad, this meant finding a sense of purpose and empowerment that did not rely on Sarah's dependency or desire. For Sarah, it meant embracing a relationship dynamic that wasn't about compensating for Brad's lost sense of purpose, but about genuinely wanting each other without the weight of need.

WE CONTROL WHAT WE FEAR

Since starting personal therapy and joining a men's group a few months prior, Brad had been showing up to our couples therapy work with more self-awareness and accountability.

"I think I am finally realizing that I have always tried to get the women in my life to give me the love I believed they were withholding. When that didn't work, I would become pouty, angry, and demanding, and then I'd withdraw into hurtful silence. Sarah is the first woman I've ever been with who I feel truly doesn't need me, and while it was the thing that I was drawn to most, it's now the thing that also terrifies me and triggers me the most." Both Sarah and I listened, somewhat wide-eyed.

"That's a pretty profound insight, Brad. Tell us more," I implored.

"I like feeling like I am the center of my partner's world, and if I'm not, I get jealous and, I guess, pout, as Sarah calls it. I also get upset when they don't initiate sex. I can be really defensive, and I see how I've always relied on them to bring up hard conversations, even though I know I don't make those conversations very easy."

"Interesting. So we're circling around emotional labor—like scanning for tension in relationships and being the one to step in and smooth things over. Or monitoring someone else's moods to make sure the rest of the family isn't affected. Even things like keeping track of family birthdays, remembering events, and making sure everyone feels connected. It's a lot, right? Here's something that's tough to hear: emotional labor inequality is actually about power. The one doing the emotional labor often ends up in a 'one-down' position, like their role is less valued. And this isn't just about romantic relationships. We see it with women and people of color in the workforce too, always expected to manage the emotional tone or take on the invisible work."

The fear and misunderstanding of the feminine—which represents qualities like empathy, humility, patience, and communication, but also intuition, passion, chaos, sensuality, assertiveness, fluidity, and all that cannot be named (such as spirit, the transpersonal, or the numinous)— are the reason societies, religions, and men have historically sought to control women. It's why we attempt to cut off these aspects from the Self, and it's why women sometimes undermine and keep other women small, ensuring they stay "in their place."

If we are to heal our collective and personal Father Wounds, we must examine where this fear manifests as control in all our relationships, including the one with our planet. We must notice how, due to this fear of and disconnection from the feminine, the divine, and the unknown, we look outside ourselves for the authority, strength, and boldness we feel we lack within. This is how we lose ourselves in what Jung called false goals and idols—whether they be fancy cars, big houses, celebrities, politicians, or imbalanced romantic relationships.

Part of our healing process requires moving from uninitiated, youthful ignorance—where we seek external validation and guidance because we feel shaky in our purpose—to an initiated mature outlook—where we trust in our own resilience and inner compass. Archetypes can guide us through this process of initiation, serving as symbolic maps. While the Hero archetype is one of the most recognized in our culture, often symbolizing the journey toward self-discovery and external achievement, it can also keep us trapped in immature, patriarchal notions of worth, driven by the need for recognition and conquest.

As Michael Gurian points out, "Killing a lot of men (or at least beating them up), sleeping with a lot of women, making a lot of money . . . these are the qualities of an adolescent hero, a Prince disguised as a King. These are also the qualities of most popular-culture heroes. Most of us, no matter how 'developed' we are, we feel a tug of glory at the end of *Rocky* or *Top Gun*. Most of us have been primed to want endless youth, money, conquest."[8]

To heal the Father Wound and transcend outdated models of masculinity, we must move beyond the Hero archetype and instead embrace the Conscious Warrior. Unlike the Hero, who seeks external achievement and the validation of others, the Conscious Warrior operates from a place of internal strength, self-awareness, and a deeper connection to both masculine and feminine energies. This archetype guides us not toward external victories, but toward a more integrated, mature version of ourselves—one capable of true resilience, emotional depth, and genuine connection.

A NEW PATH FOR HEALING WITH THE CONSCIOUS WARRIOR

The Conscious Warrior represents a different kind of strength—one that does not rely on conquest, dominance, or external affirmation. It embodies a masculinity secure enough to seek connection without control, to be vulnerable without fear of being perceived as weak. This approach can transform not just our relationships, but also our sexual dynamics, fostering equality and mutual respect that are often lacking under patriarchal conditioning. When we confront fear, pain, and our inner wounds without seeking approval, we are embodying the Conscious Warrior archetype. When we take a risk in therapy, coaching, or support groups by examining our patterns and challenging how we self-abandon in relationships without seeking congratulations, we are embodying the Conscious Warrior. Even the curiosity or internal nudge to pick up this book is the psyche prodding us to grow, to find our purpose, our mission. The Conscious Warrior is at the helm of all of this, reminding us to face discomfort head-on as we forge ahead.

As Sophie Strand discusses in *The Flowering Wand*, the masculine is often reduced to a rigid set of archetypes—like the Hero or Warrior—that emphasize conquest, control, and linear progression.[9] But the masculine is not a singular force; it is a web of relationships, interactions, and expressions. Strand encourages us to think of the masculine as a constellation of archetypes, allowing for a fuller, more nuanced exploration of qualities like collaboration, creativity, and ecological empathy. By moving beyond the traditional Hero archetype, we can embrace a more holistic, relational form of masculinity, much like the Conscious Warrior, who embodies both strength and emotional attunement.

Let us also reimagine the Warrior archetype not as a killer wielding a sword, but as a protector wielding wisdom, emotional attunement, and a deep connection to the world. This warrior fights not to dominate, but to protect and nurture, embodying strength through compassion rather than violence. By embracing the Conscious Warrior, we can cultivate a masculinity that is relational, ecological, and rooted in inner resilience.

Throughout history, both men and women have demonstrated the power of the Conscious Warrior. Women, too, have ruled empires, led armies, advanced science and medicine, written books, protested injustice, and loved fiercely. The Conscious Warrior archetype exists within us all, guiding us to transcend fear and embody a mature, balanced strength.

MYTHS AS MAPS
The Girl Without Hands, Leaving the Father's House

The fairy tale we know as *The Girl Without Hands*, published in 1812 by the Brothers Grimm, repackages countless myths that came before it. Here, I will recount several versions of this story, omitting discussions of purity, sin, and other Christian ideals that were added to align with the values of the time.

Most versions of this fairy tale begin with either a young girl promised to a stranger—often the devil in disguise—or pursued for marriage or sex by her father or brother. In each version, the man (father, brother, or stranger) holds the power, attempting to dominate the girl. This man, disconnected from his inner feminine and trapped by his Mother

Wound, desires the "perfect" patriarchal womanhood as a way to save himself by suppressing the child's own psychological growth.

In response to this threat of being "taken," the girl's hands (or arms) are cut off. In some versions, this is an offering to the devil (the stranger); in others, it is a way to repulse the father or brother's advances, or serves as punishment for denying those advances. Regardless of the version, we see a common theme: a young, innocent maiden is subjected to attempts by patriarchal figures and forces to own and control her, resulting in disfigurement that renders her helpless.

Yet, in all versions of the story, the girl devises a plan to save herself and ultimately find her true Self. She escapes—sometimes to the forest, withdrawing and going inward; other times she finds work as a servant, enduring many trials. We witness her move from dependence to independence. She liberates her inner feminine from patriarchy by discovering her own values, learning to relate to and deeply know herself, and protecting herself by outwitting those who seek to control her.

While the details vary across versions, the lesson is the same: to discover our true selves, we must leave the Father's house and embark on a quest for purpose. Only after the ego has been broken down and we are reborn can we return, transformed and mature, the masculine and feminine within us integrated.

SEEING OURSELVES IN THE MYTH

At some time in our lives, all of us will reach a point of crisis, a moment when we must choose between rolling over and accepting our fate, playing along, and conforming to what we have been told we "should" be, or facing our fears, striking out on our own, and searching for our true identity. The motif of "leaving the Father's house" is not gendered. A man, too, will face his own crisis and must decide whether to remain controlled by the patriarchal system in which we are all raised or challenge it in order to find himself.

For many heterosexual women, however, "leaving the Father's house" often means moving directly into a husband's house, without ever striking out on their own to discover the Self. They remain the helpless maiden, blown along by the winds of culture, society, familial expectations, and the "shoulds." Many of these helpless maidens find their way into my office and retreats—some at thirty, some at forty-five, some at sixty and beyond—gnashing their teeth, restless with their longing for the process of finding and ultimately knowing themselves.

This excerpt from Marion Woodman's *Leaving My Father's House: A Journey to Conscious Femininity* forced me to pause the first time I read it, as I hope it does for you too:

> What does it feel like to leave your father's house? Or your father-husband's house? How does it feel to look into his eyes and see yourself as the betrayer of the one man who has always trusted you? How does it feel to leave the security of his love even if he never cared who you were? How does it feel to say no to a man to whom you have always said yes? What happens in your body when you stand up to a beloved and reject all the standards that he has never questioned? And when he calls your feminine approach rambling, lacking in clarity, coherence, and emphasis, do you wonder if you are stupid? And when you find yourself alone in your empty apartment, hearing voices inside you previously thought were outside, do you wonder if finding yourself is all it was cracked up to be? Can you be the person you have always denied?[10]

GOING DEEPER

Look Inward

In my clinical experience, I've often observed that women can unintentionally stand in the way of the men in their lives healing.

When men show up in a vulnerable way, women sometimes respond with disgust or fear, shutting down the very emotional expression they claim to desire. This reaction points to a deeper issue: the need for women to unpack their own internalized patriarchy. We cannot, on one hand, say we want the men in our lives to be vulnerable, express their emotions, and become more attuned, and then, on the other hand, shame them when they do because of the discomfort their vulnerability creates in us.

As noted earlier, bell hooks examines this issue in *The Will to Change*:

> It stands to reason, then, that the masses of women committed to the sexist principle that men who express their feelings are weak really do not want to hear men speak, especially if what they say is that they hurt, that they feel unloved. Many women cannot hear male pain about love because it sounds like an indictment of female failure. Since sexist norms have taught us that loving is our task whether in our role as mothers or lovers or friends, if men say they are not loved, then we are at fault; we are to blame.[11]

This contradiction is difficult to face, but it's a crucial realization. How do we begin to dismantle this bind and provide safety and space for the emotional qualities we desire in men, whether they are our partners, friends, or members of our society? Start by paying attention to your responses, both internally and externally, when the men in your life speak about their pain and fear, especially when it involves you or their relationships with the other women in their lives. Do you get defensive, shut down, or become confrontational? Do you offer space for their hurts and fears without trying to fix them? As you grow, continue to notice these behaviors and habits and work toward creating a more open and accepting emotional environment.

Cultivate Safety

While many women feel physically unsafe in the world, many men report feeling emotionally unsafe. Without a sense of internal safety, we often seek control externally to attempt to create this safety, making others responsible for our feelings of insecurity. This can hold us back from taking risks, being vulnerable, or speaking our truth. Yet safety, both emotional and physical, is essential for collaboration, growth, and meaningful change in our personal lives and relationships.

Henrik Bresman and Amy C. Edmondson's research is focused on psychological safety in corporate settings, but I absolutely feel these can be applied to our home environments as well. Reflect on these questions with your partner or loved ones to assess the level of safety and trust you feel:

- If you make a mistake, is it held against you?

- Are members of your family or relationship able to bring up problems and tough issues?

- Do people in your circle accept others for being different?

- Is it safe to take risks in your relationships?

- Is it easy to ask for help from those close to you?

- Would anyone deliberately act in a way that undermines your efforts?

- Are your unique skills and talents valued and utilized by those around you?[12]

How you and your partner answer these questions can reveal the degree of psychological safety that exists in your relationship. This awareness can be the starting point for creating a more emotionally secure environment.

Get in Your Body

Cultivating a sense of internal safety is a process that develops over time, much like any aspect of personal growth. Embodiment practices, such as breathwork, somatic movement, and trauma release exercises, help us cultivate safety within by reminding us that we have the inner resources to face difficult challenges. By developing a relationship to the body, we connect to one of the most essential tools for inner safety. Disconnection from the body often means disconnection from the Self.

Working with a practitioner trained in Somatic Experiencing® or Integral Somatic Psychology™ or even participating in trauma-informed yoga classes can be transformative. These practices help ground us in our physical selves and foster a sense of safety that goes beyond what we might initially imagine. Remember, the body holds wisdom and insight that the mind may not fully grasp; connecting with it can guide us to deeper healing and understanding.

7

sex was never about me

> "Craving and addiction is not desire. It's pain. Desire arises from the place in you that is full. Craving arises from the place in you that is empty. A moment of craving is a moment of feeling incomplete. It's an externalized attempt to feel whole again. There is no amount of fulfilling your cravings that will make you feel whole. Temporarily, maybe. But you will always come back to the hole in your bucket. Eventually, you need to fix your container."
>
> —Cory Muscara[1]

"I wanted to tell you something."

I had just walked in from Pilates and was on my way back to my office to get some work done when John stopped me. I sat down on the chair across from him in the living room.

"I took care of myself this afternoon."

"I'm sorry?" I was confused by what felt like an out-of-context confession.

"Well, I realized that I was really wanting to have sex today, and I was trying not to pressure you, so I took care of myself." He smiled, looking proud.

"Okay," I said slowly, feeling anger bubbling quickly to the surface. "Did you want a cookie?" I said calmly and slowly.

"What?"

"Did you want me to give you a cookie?" I repeated. I was now seething. Without waiting for a response, I got up and walked back into my office. John followed me. I stopped and looked him in the eyes. "You don't get it. *I don't care*. I don't need to know. It's not my job or responsibility to ensure you are sexually satisfied, and you telling me that makes me furious. It's like you're saying it to make sure I know that you're a good boy who didn't bug mommy today, like you want an award for having some self-awareness."

John got heated in response. "I feel like I have been trying for the past six months to change my behavior. To pull back and stop being so needy. To give you more space because you're 'touched out.' To take care of myself more. And yes, sometimes I want some acknowledgment! What are *you* even doing? Where is *your* part? What changes have you made to make us better and more connected? All I see is me backing off and not asking for sex all the time and you not doing anything in return."

My eyes narrowed. "Your desire to have sex with me in order to *feel something* or release stress and anxiety is not about me. It's about you. You don't want to connect with *me*. You want to connect to yourself, to something, *anything*. You want to feel good, and you're using me to do it."

CRAVING AND DESIRE ARE NOT THE SAME

John's attempt to share his efforts at "self-care" reveals a common misconception that many of us carry about intimacy and sex. For him, the act of telling me about him "taking care of himself" was not just a gesture of self-awareness but an attempt to manage his underlying feelings of anxiety and need for validation. This moment underscores a critical misunderstanding that often surfaces in relationships: the conflation of desire with craving. Desire, when rooted in a genuine connection and appreciation of the other, comes from a place of fullness. In contrast, craving arises from a sense of lack, a need to fill a void within oneself.

Research in neurobiology shows that craving and desire activate different parts of the brain. Desire, associated with connection and genuine intimacy, often engages areas related to reward and positive emotional states. In contrast, craving—particularly when it stems from unmet emotional needs—activates brain regions associated with addiction and compulsive behaviors.[2] Understanding these differences helps us see how these dynamics affect our relationships. When sex is driven by craving, it often leads to a cycle of dissatisfaction, as the underlying emotional needs remain unaddressed.

HARMFUL FICTION TURNED MYTH

In my retreats, individual and couple clients, the online communities I am involved in, and myself personally, I have seen a swell of women rejecting the notion that it is our job to keep men sexually satisfied, rejecting all of the absolute nonsensical and outright false messaging that was shoved down our throats since before we were even sexually active:

- Men are more sexual than women (i.e., it's biological).

- Women need to cover up so as not to get a man worked up (i.e., men can't control themselves).

- Blue balls for a man is *so* incredibly painful (i.e., it's our job to always make sure they get off if they get excited in the slightest way).

- Women who are virgins are more pure and lovable (i.e., slut shaming and purity culture).

- Men's body count can be/should be high, but a woman's shouldn't be (i.e., there is no male equivalent for slut shaming).

- Women who cannot have orgasms during penetration and/or do not want to have sex with their partners are frigid and need psychological help (thank you, Freud, for this wildly sexist and entirely false belief that still plagues us to this day).

These myths not only burden women, but also perpetuate harmful expectations for men. From a young age, boys and girls are socialized into different roles around sex and emotional expression. Boys are often taught that their worth is tied to conquest, strength, and sexual prowess, while girls learn that they must be the gatekeepers of sex, responsible for saying no and maintaining purity. This dichotomy is reflected in everything, from locker room talk to romantic comedies, and it creates a gap in understanding between partners. Men come to believe that their desirability is proven through sexual persistence, while women internalize the belief that their value lies in their ability to please or regulate a man's sexual appetite. These scripts limit authentic connection and foster environments of guilt, shame, and miscommunication. This is not a neutral dynamic; it actively shapes the way we relate to one another and perceive our own value in relationships.

Consider the common script that men are expected to be the initiators of sex and the ones who are always "in the mood." This belief is not just a neutral observation about differences in libido; it reinforces a power dynamic where men feel pressured to perform, and women may feel like their sexual needs are secondary. In therapy sessions, I often see couples where men express feeling rejected when their advances are turned down, which isn't about a lack of desire from their partners, but stems from this cultural script that positions male sexuality as a constant, driving force. This creates a cycle where men feel unwanted unless their partners are always receptive, and women feel guilty or inadequate for not meeting this expectation. Similarly, when women take on the role of initiators and find their advances rejected, they often report feeling undesirable, unworthy, or insecure. This is not necessarily a reflection of their partner's lack of desire, but rather the internalized belief that being sexually desired is a validation of one's worth. Whether it is men or women in this role, the underlying issue often revolves around seeking validation rather than pursuing a genuine connection. This dynamic can lead to a cycle of miscommunication and unmet needs, where both partners feel unsatisfied.

Largely, women are not taught how to pleasure ourselves, or that our pleasure is even something worthy of being spoken about, explored, or prioritized. What both women and men are not taught about women's pleasure is made obvious through multiple research studies over the past decade, which have shown over 50 percent of women cannot accurately label their own anatomy or know where the vagina is. It's no wonder so many of my female clients have spent many, if not all, of their sexually active years not having regular (or any) orgasms when having sex with men, while convincing their sexual partners they have through faking it.

Research on sex education has consistently shown that discussions around female pleasure are often absent or minimized, contributing to widespread misinformation and misunderstanding about women's bodies and needs.[3] The orgasm gap is a direct result of this lack of education and open dialogue, revealing the broader cultural neglect of female sexual autonomy. Multiple studies conducted since 2015 deemed the orgasm gap a social problem (not a biological one),[4] telling us that:

- Lesbian women have significantly more orgasms than straight women.

- 39 percent of women said they always orgasm during masturbation, while 6 percent said they always orgasm during sex with a partner.

- 30 percent of men said they thought the best way to help a woman orgasm is through penetrative sexual acts, while over 50 percent of women say they require clitoral stimulation to orgasm.

Many of my female clients, even those who have been in long-term relationships, express not being able to articulate what turns them on. This difficulty often stems from years of social conditioning that teaches women to prioritize their partner's desires over their own. Through my work with clients and in my own life—especially after becoming a mother and experiencing being so overstimulated and "touched out" that the very thought of my partner making a sexual advance made me cringe—I have come to understand many aspects about this prevalent issue in heterosexual couples:

- This is not the sole fault of men. We are all byproducts of our patriarchal and sexist culture, and we have all been fed the same misogynistic lies about men, women, biology, and sex.

- Just like everything else I have laid out in this book, the brainwashing always serves a larger purpose (i.e., keeping dominator systems like patriarchy and capitalism in play) and always hurts all individuals who are swept up in it.

MOVING FROM CRAVING TO CONNECTION

While men may sexually "benefit" from patriarchy, they do not benefit emotionally and spiritually. My hope is that this chapter will both enrage you and create more space for empathy for the men in your life. Patriarchal norms disconnect men from a massive part of their humanity, pushing their emotional and feeling parts of their Soul into the shadow and branding them as something shameful.

Cutting off a boy's emotional Self does not lead to men who don't feel. All it does is create men who have two socially acceptable ways to feel: through anger or through sex. When sex becomes the primary conduit for emotional expression, immense pressure is placed on their partner(s) to serve as this outlet. In my practice, I often see resentment explode in my heterosexual female clients after a child is born. The expectation for the woman to be the man's conduit to his emotional Self, while she simultaneously grapples with needing to be that for her developing child and herself, all while navigating her massive initiation, is an impossible burden.

This dynamic reflects a broader systemic issue of emotional disconnection perpetuated by patriarchal structures. When men are socialized to suppress their emotional needs and vulnerability through sex, they unknowingly place an enormous emotional burden on their partners. Women, already stretched thin by the demands of motherhood and their own emotional needs, find themselves in a double bind: expected to be the nurturer of both their child and their partner. This imbalance breeds resentment and deepens disconnection between partners, creating a wedge that can feel insurmountable.

True intimacy requires dismantling these deeply ingrained scripts and beliefs about sex, gender, and emotional expression. For both men and women, reclaiming their full humanity involves challenging narratives that have been imposed on them since childhood and embracing a more authentic and balanced approach to relationships. Genuine connection is built on mutual respect, understanding, and the freedom to express one's true desires and needs, not on fulfilling societal expectations.

By reframing our understanding of sex—not as a tool for validation, but as an opportunity for deeper connection and emotional intimacy—we can begin to heal these wounds. This requires empathy, not just for ourselves and our experiences, but for our partners, who are equally trapped in these cycles of expectation and misunderstanding. Only then can we break free from patriarchy's damaging legacies and build a more equitable, emotionally connected future.

IT FEELS LIKE I'M SIGNING A CONTRACT

Let's revisit Brad and Sarah from the previous chapter. While our exploration of Brad's Mother Wound brought awareness to some of their relational patterns, it did not resolve the issue of Brad feeling "sexually disconnected." Sarah continued to express frustration with how Brad's behavior shifted drastically based on whether they were able to connect sexually.

"When Brad is overwhelmed at work or home, he becomes more sexually needy. When he's feeling low or I can sense his energy is off, that is when he comes to me for sex. He's more touchy. He sends me more dirty texts or whispers things in my ear. What I've noticed is if we are able to have sex, his entire attitude changes. He is happier, kinder, and more engaged with both me and the kids. But if we don't, for whatever reason, his mood gets worse. He withdraws, gets cold and short with all of us."

Brad saw it differently: "I fail to see what is wrong with wanting to have sex with my wife, and I don't see why it's so bad that when I'm not feeling great, I want to connect with her more. Sarah has always made me feel better. She's my light! She turns my mood around. I feel like that's a compliment."

Sarah visibly cringed at hearing this.

"Brad, I'm glad I make you happy, but I cannot be the only thing in your life that makes you happy. It's too much responsibility. And honestly, it doesn't feel like you want to connect with *me*. At all. It feels like you are using me as some sort of pacifier. I've got a rambunctious four-year-old who climbs all over me and is a lot emotionally and energetically, and an eighteen-month-old still breastfeeding. I just want to not be touched or needed all the time. It's like my body doesn't even belong to me anymore. It belongs to the three of you and is just used for your own personal means. You get mad at me when you come up behind me in the kitchen and put your arms around me and I pull away. But you aren't doing that to hug me or hold me. You go for my breasts. Or you put my hand on your crotch. It's like I'm not even a human being. Here. Inside this body. If your desire was to connect with me, Sarah, you would notice and see what's happening with me."

Sarah began to weep softly. Brad didn't say anything.

Sarah wiped her face and spoke again. "I can't even allow myself to get close to you. I would love to lay with you on the couch or snuggle you in the bed. I would love to even make out or kiss you deeply. But it's like any physical contact feels like I'm signing some sort of contract that it has to lead to sex. And if it doesn't, you get pouty and pissed. It's never enough for you."

Brad replied softly, "I just feel like if you loved me, you would want to physically connect with me, have sex with me. It's like there have to be all these conditions met for you to want to be intimate with me. You have to be in the right mindset, mood, you need to have had enough sleep. I want to have sex with you all the time. Even now, all these years later, I'm still so attracted to you. I guess I wished you felt the same way about me."

At this point, I interjected gently. "Unconditional love does not mean unlimited access, Brad. Not even with our children. We are all autonomous beings with our own needs, cycles, and nervous systems, wants, likes, and dislikes. And when we feel like we aren't being seen or considered, we shut down. The number of men in my practice who use sexual coercion to get their partners to be intimate with them is . . . kind of astonishing."

Brad's head snapped up. "Jesus, Vanessa! I'm not a monster! It's not like I'm forcing Sarah to have sex with me!"

"I hear you, Brad, but coercion is common, and it's very often covert in relationships. Many men in our society think these behaviors are normal because of what we are *all* taught about sex. When men hold the belief, even if it's unconscious, that sex is how we show love or get connection, that they are owed sex, or that sex is guaranteed in a partnership or just in life in general, they get upset when it's withheld. Constantly bringing up how long it's been since you had sex, emotionally withdrawing or being cold or angry with Sarah or the kids when you don't get sex, bringing up the fact that you work all day and just want to connect when you get home, telling her she's being uptight or that she clearly doesn't love you because she doesn't want to have sex—these are all coercive tactics. Somewhere deep down, you know if you push enough, she'll give in."

HUNGRY GHOSTS

The dynamics in Brad and Sarah's relationship reveal another larger, deeper societal problem. As bell hooks explains, "Sex becomes, for most men, a way of self-solacing . . . Patriarchal men have no outlet for their pain, so they simply seek release."[5]

Men in our society are struggling—with loneliness; a lack of purpose; disconnection from Self, others, and something larger than themselves; and the pressure to conform to ideals of strength and invulnerability. These struggles are often compounded by societal expectations that discourage men from expressing vulnerability or seeking emotional support. Because we have not equipped our boys with the tools to sit with and process emotions or to cultivate deep intimate friendships that provide emotional nurturance, many men turn to their partners as their primary source of comfort and emotional regulation. But this need for comfort often doesn't manifest as nonsexual intimacy, gentle connection, deep attunement, conversation, or spiritual depth. Instead, it emerges as a hunger for physical touch and sex.

In a patriarchal culture, sex often becomes an act of emotional reassurance—a way for men to reconnect to Self, their bodies, the numinous, and the archetypal Mother, rather than an experience of mutual intimacy with another sovereign being. bell hooks continues in *The Will to Change*, "The more intense the pain of fear, unworthiness, and feeling unlovable becomes, the more obsessive becomes the need to have a sexual interaction."[6] In this context, male sexual obsession is normalized, rarely questioned, and often misunderstood. Instead of examining the deeper motivations or needs behind such behaviors, our culture labels them as "biological" and places the burden on women to manage men's unmet emotional needs.

From a depth psychological perspective, what I observe both in my practice and in society at large is that many men view sex symbolically as a form of religion or salvation. For some, sex is the closest they come to a transcendent experience. The issue is that when sex is approached this way, it objectifies women, turning them into tools for men's emotional regulation. This dynamic mirrors addiction, where dependency on a single outlet for alleviating discomfort creates a vicious cycle of emotional highs and lows.

The addiction cycle manifests in several ways:

1. Craving and Withdrawal: Intense cravings and withdrawal symptoms drive a man's desire to use sexual intimacy to alleviate discomfort rather than as a means to connect to the Soul of their partner.

2. Tolerance Increase: Over time, they build tolerance for what they are addicted to, requiring more—both in quantity and frequency—to achieve the desired emotional effects.

3. Negative Consequences: This cycle damages relationships, work, and health, exacerbating feelings of guilt, shame, and hopelessness, which may then further fuel the addictive behavior.

4. Further Isolation: As women engage in personal, relational, and spiritual work that includes ending self-abandoning behaviors—such as having sex to placate their partners—this contributes to an exacerbated sense of loneliness and despair among men, perpetuating the cycle of addiction.

IT ISN'T CONSENT IF YOU CAN'T SAY NO

In working with Brad and Sarah, this pattern of sex as self-solacing became a central theme. Brad often pushed back against our conversations about sex in couples therapy, continually struggling to understand why his needs for sexual intimacy were not being met. There came a point, about a year into our work together, where a separation between him and Sarah seemed imminent.

During that time, I focused much of my work with them on two strategies:

1. **Building Awareness and Emotional Regulation:** Developing the capacity to recognize and sit with hard feelings like anxiety, frustration, and discomfort and tracking how they managed the feelings in the moment. Noticing how often they used other people as an outlet or a distraction versus sitting with and processing the hard emotions themselves.

2. **Using Consent Language to Build Emotional Safety:** Introducing consent language not only around physical intimacy, but also around emotional expression. This strategy aimed to build emotional language, trust in oneself, and trust in the other person, creating a more equitable emotional environment where both partners could feel safe and respected.

By reframing the role of sex in their relationship and helping Brad and Sarah cultivate new forms of emotional intimacy and understanding, they began to navigate their challenges with more compassion and awareness.

Using consent language as a therapeutic tool for couples is a fairly new technique for me in my practice. Unlike Gen Z and especially Gen Alpha, consent language is not something many Millennials and Gen Xers grew up practicing or hearing in their everyday lives. While my four-year-old daughter has been practicing this language in preschool since day one—"May I give you a hug?" or "Excuse me, you are too close to my body and I need some space"—many adults are still recovering from experiences where we were forced to sit on *that* uncle's lap we didn't feel comfortable with because our parents said we had to in order to be polite. It's no wonder why using explicit consent language within our partnerships can feel so awkward and uncomfortable; it's a mostly unused muscle.

I'm almost embarrassed to admit that the first time I realized how powerful consent language was as a relational tool was when my own couples intimacy coach suggested John and I start practicing it. Over the years of struggling with many of the issues covered in this chapter, my resentment around the unspoken expectations of access to my physical space and body, and a perceived inability to speak up about it, had built up. I was confused during the first few years of my daughter's life because I genuinely do love physical touch—I crave it. But I came to realize that after having a child, we are constantly being touched without asking, our physical and emotional boundaries are compromised constantly, and we lose much of our bodily and emotional autonomy in early parenthood. It became clear why, when my partner "intruded" on my physical space, I became almost irrationally angry.

CONSENT AS A PATH TO INTIMACY

Consent is not only something practiced in the bedroom or around sex and sexuality; it's a practice that can be used all of the time. Here are some of the examples our couples coach gave us for practicing consent in everyday situations:

- I am standing in the kitchen in the morning making my daughter's lunch. John comes in to get his coffee and says, "Can I grab your butt?"

- I am on my way into a meeting, and as I am rushing around getting my computer set up, John might say, "Are you available for a hug right now?"

- I am lying on the couch after putting my daughter to bed, mindlessly scrolling social media. John leans over me and asks, "May I give you a kiss?"

- John is sitting at the kitchen table, going through bills and finances. I come up behind him and ask, "Can I rub your shoulders?"

As you can see, the practice goes both ways, as I would do my best to practice the same language when I wanted to touch John. Here's the most important question to ask yourself if you are partnered: Do you feel like you could say no in any of those moments? While these questions may sound a little silly, that's actually the problem. Why does asking someone—or being asked—for permission before touching our bodies feel silly? Because in our culture, where we are taught that love and intimate relationships equate to some level of ownership and loss of autonomy, we have often experienced that when we have listened to our internal system and actually said no or drawn a boundary, the other person personalized it and responded with guilt or shame, effectively punishing us. To avoid the discomfort of guilt or shame, we do the thing our system actually didn't want, such as allowing an unwanted physical touch. Our bodies are not anyone else's but ours. I can say this with absolute certainty to my daughter about her body, so why do I struggle to feel the same way about my own?

Two of the most valuable tools this practice has helped me hone further are the ability to even *know* if my body is desiring touch or not and the ability to actually open my mouth and say the words "yes" or "no." Neither of these are easy for me, and most of my female clients agree. The first part—knowing if we actually desire touch or not—requires slowing down and inquiring within. So if you are going to start practicing this with a partner, let them know that it needs to be done slowly and with some pauses built in. For me, a "no" in my body feels like tightness, agitation, and heat. The hardest part is then saying something like, "No, not in this moment" or "I appreciate you asking, but right now, I don't want a kiss. What I would like, though, is X." If John is hurt by my no, the practice for me is in noticing my desire to go against it to make him feel better (i.e., to make *me* feel better in the short term) and resisting that temptation to self-abandon.

This practice is equally important to instill with our children. It should go without saying that if our child says they do not want a hug or a kiss, we respect their wishes. But what about us? Do we practice checking in with ourselves and expressing if touch from our kids feels okay? This is important because, as we have established, kids learn by what they see, not by what they hear. If they see me not respecting my own physical boundaries, they will internalize that it is not important for them to do the same for themselves. What might this sound like?

- My little one loves to pull on my arm and my clothes when she wants something. I know this agitates me and my nervous system. I don't need to feel guilty for this response or even dig into the "why" in the moment; it just is. So I practice repeating (because we know kids do not listen the first or even the one hundredth time they hear something): "Mommy doesn't like to be pulled on. Can you hold my hand instead?"

- She also loves to come behind me on the couch and wrap her arms around my neck and pull. Again, I do not like this. So I might say something like, "That isn't comfortable for me. Can you sit in my lap instead?"

- I am feeling overwhelmed or stressed about something with work, and she wants me to pick her up and hold her. I might say, "Mommy loves you, but I don't actually want to be hugged right now. Can we sit on the floor and play a game together instead?"

These are examples of how we might clearly express when we don't like or want touch and offer an alternative instead. For some, this might be difficult to read, as feelings of guilt may arise when imagining how your child might respond to your words. But even in their discomfort, there is learning for *both of you*. Doing something you don't want to do to avoid making somebody else feel uncomfortable is about you—not them.

RECLAIMING OUR SOVEREIGNTY

Reconnecting to the Self and our bodies, including our sexuality, is essential to reclaiming our sovereignty. But this requires access to our inner knowing, the ability to discern when we do or do not want to be touched, and then the courage to speak up. As Jungian counselor Sheryl Lisa Finn shared on her Instagram, "Every time you override your no and ignore your voice, you shut down the pathway to desire. Every time you speak your truth and the truth is honored, you open the channel to desire, for there is a direct line between the throat and the genitals."

Our journey toward reclaiming autonomy over our bodies is deeply intertwined with our ability to listen to and honor our own "yes" and "no." This practice of consent, both with our partners and with ourselves, becomes a vital pathway to genuine intimacy—where sex is not a tool for self-solacing or validation, but an expression of mutual respect and connection.

MYTHS AS MAPS
Lilith as Demon or Symbol of Sovereignty

Lilith is a highly controversial figure within Mesopotamian and Jewish folklore and mystical traditions, with origins that are both fascinating and widely debated. She is most commonly known as the first wife of Adam, both created from the same dust or clay. According to *Alphabet of Ben Sira* (also known as *Alphabet of Sirach*), an anonymous text from the eighth to tenth centuries, Adam and Lilith frequently argued, with Adam insisting that Lilith be submissive to him in all ways, including sexually. Lilith, however, is said to have declared, "We are equal because we are both created from the earth," refusing to "lay beneath Adam."[7]

Frustrated by these power struggles, Lilith eventually reaches a breaking point. In a bold act of defiance, she utters the Lord's name—a name considered (and in some traditions still considered) so sacred that it was unspeakable. This transgression symbolizes her ultimate rejection of divine and patriarchal authority. She then flies away from the Garden of Eden, leaving Adam alone and finding her independence in the desert or by the Red Sea, depending on the version of the story. Here, we see her first association with a winged demonic character.

In response to Lilith's departure, God commands three angels—Senoi, Sansenoi, and Sammangelof—to bring her back to Adam, by force if necessary. God threatens that if Lilith fails to return, one hundred of her children will die each day. Lilith refuses to obey and experiences the loss of her children. As retaliation for God's punishment, she is said to rob children of life, becoming associated with the deaths of stillborn infants and crib deaths (what we now know as SIDS). Eventually, Lilith negotiates a deal with the angels, agreeing not to harm newborn children if they are protected by an amulet bearing the angels' names.

Alphabet of Ben Sira (or *Sirach*) appears to merge older Sumerian and Mesopotamian legends of female demons with the idea of a "first Eve." The result is a tale featuring Lilith, an assertive and bold wife who defies both God and her husband's desire for control and subjugation, is replaced by a more compliant partner (Eve), and Lilith is subsequently vilified in Jewish folklore as a dangerous killer of babies.

Over the centuries, through different cultures, languages, and translations of ancient texts, Lilith has been associated with a variety of symbols, including a night bird, screech owl, serpent, wind spirit, hag, and a demon. She often embodies chaos, temptation, and defiance against divine order, and is typically portrayed as a promiscuous breeder of evil spirits and a carrier of disease. Later texts claim that Lilith instills lust in men, suggesting that this lust is responsible for exiles and wars.

The story of Lilith evolves and takes on different forms across various mystical texts and traditions. After leaving the Garden of Eden and her life with Adam, Lilith's narrative continues in later Jewish mystical traditions, such as the fundamental Kabbalistic text, the Zohar. Here, Lilith is no longer associated with Adam but becomes paired with Samael, a male personification of evil often associated with Satan, the leader of the fallen angels. God fears that their union will spawn a legion of demons capable of overwhelming the world with evil. To prevent this catastrophe, God intervenes by ordering Samael's castration, effectively neutralizing the threat of their offspring. Deprived of her partner, Lilith is said to seek fulfillment through other men, supposedly inducing their nocturnal emissions (i.e., wet dreams) to conceive offspring.

SEEING OURSELVES IN THE MYTH

As with most myths, it's crucial not to interpret the story of Lilith literally or concretize the characters as absolutes. Lilith, who represents the feminine opposite to the masculine order, is banished from the fertile territory of the Garden of Eden and exiled to a barren wasteland for her refusal to be controlled. The conflict between Lilith and Adam symbolizes the tension between patriarchal authority versus the feminine desire for autonomy. In this myth, man grapples with his struggle to reconcile woman's longing for independence, while woman remains steadfast in her refusal to accept anything less than freedom.

No sooner was it obvious that Lilith would not return to the Garden of Eden than God created a second wife for Adam. Adam is portrayed not only as lonely and in need of companionship, but as needing someone who would conform to his expectations of subservience. This myth, like many others, reflects a longstanding patriarchal belief system: the notion that a woman's voice, opinions, and allegiance to her independence are inherently threatening or even evil. Such ideas are not unique to Western religions; they echo through ancient texts from Mesopotamia, a culture deeply rooted in patriarchal values.

While many of the myths and archetypes explored in this book serve as guides for women on the path of individuation—the journey of the development of the Self—Lilith's story takes a different turn. It was crafted not as a model for empowerment, but as a cautionary tale designed to frighten women into subservience. Rather than following it as a literal guide, I invite you to see Lilith's story as a spark that ignites a fire in the belly, a call to challenge patriarchal narratives that have long cast feminine figures as warnings against seeking sovereignty. To see Lilith not has a demonic figure, but as a symbol of a woman who spoke up, forged her own path, and not only survived but thrived.

GOING DEEPER

Attunement and Accountability

I want you to reflect on this question: Where do I focus more intently on what I want to get from my relationships than who I want to be in them? Bonus points if you invite your partner to sit and answer this question as well. When we are overly focused on the other person, what they are doing wrong, what they are not providing, or how we wish they would change, we are missing the entire point. It's not that we can't have needs and desires, but so long as we point the finger at others, we evade taking responsibility for our own work and, ultimately, growth.

We absolve ourselves from our own work so long as we say yes when we really want to say no, stay silent about things we should be speaking up about, or focus more on what the other person is doing than on our own inner work. When we do this, we place the control of our lives, emotional stability, and peace in someone else's hands. While much of what I've shared about my work with Sarah and Brad has centered on Brad, Sarah had her own deep work to do as well. She needed to learn to be radically honest with herself and with Brad and to be comfortable with Brad being upset without feeling the need to rescue him from his feelings.

This process of self-reflection is an essential and ongoing practice in any self-development work. So ask yourself again: Where do I focus more on what I want to get from my relationships than on who I want to be in them? This question invites you to shift the focus inward and take ownership of your actions, boundaries, and desires.

Play
Because women are often conditioned to view sex as something we do in service to others, reclaiming sexuality as something that belongs to us and centers our pleasure can be a profound and transformative journey. If sex is something we are doing begrudgingly, is approached with resentment or reluctance, or is an activity where coercion is involved, it's not about us or for us. There is a lifetime of work here in unpacking centuries of inherited beliefs about sex and pleasure that have shaped our understanding.

One practice that has helped me transform my relationship with sensuality and sex (whether with myself or another person) is to view it as part of my self-care routine or as a form of play. Life can be demanding and overwhelming, full of stress, bills, and endless responsibilities. We, as adults, need a playground too—a space to escape, explore, and have fun. Sensual play can serve as that playground. If you're already incorporating body-oriented practices like yoga, breathwork, mindful movement, dance, or body scan meditations into your routine, and you're working on reclaiming your relationship to your body, I encourage you to tap into your sensual side as well.

I am not advocating for you to have sex when you don't want to; rather, I am advocating for you to either reconnect with or, for the first time, discover your sensual side and honor it as an essential part of the Self. What feels good, and what doesn't? What sparks that life force inside of you, even just a little? Is it a massage? Cuddling? Eye gazing? The warmth of a hot shower? Find things that feel good when you're by yourself, then explore what feels good with another person. Speak up. Advocate for yourself. Honor your boundaries and be clear about your wants. Practice consent language in all aspects of your interactions.

If you're in the very early stages of parenthood, there may not be much of a spark there right now. You might still be deep in the spit-up and dirty diapers stage, and a lack of sensuality is entirely normal. Honor this as part of a cycle, and remember that, like all cycles, this stage is not forever. Continue the work of connecting with and listening to your body; this practice will serve you well, no matter the phase of life. Notice, feel, and honor the ways in which your body is working hard to keep a tiny being alive so when the focus can shift back to yourself, you will be attuned and ready for it.

8

the wild woman's role in our evolving feminism

"Feminists are made, not born."

—bell hooks, *Feminism Is for Everybody*[1]

You have a deeply held belief that men are useless and can't be trusted. *And* that they always leave."

I felt my face grow hot as I sat across from John on the couch. "That's not true. I don't believe that about men," I snapped back.

"Maybe not consciously, but I think unconsciously it's true, and I think it's an underlying factor in the way you show up in our relationship. I think the women in your family have been hurt by men and have had to rally around each other, finding strength in their ability to do it all on their own, and I think that belief was passed to you."

John and I were sitting on the couch discussing a fight we had had earlier that morning while going somewhere as a family. We had been attempting to understand and break a cycle we found ourselves in over and over since our daughter was born. It was a cycle where I became hyperfixated on doing everything, and then grew frustrated with John for not doing enough—or, rather, not doing things the way I wanted them done. In his words, this pattern resulted in me "mothering" him.

As we dug deeper into these recurring conflicts, we began to realize that our default roles—mine of overfunctioning and his of underfunctioning—were not merely reactive behaviors, but rather deeply rooted in more profound historical patterns. We recognized that the intergenerational trauma shaped by sexism and patriarchy was influencing both of our behaviors, especially during moments of stress. When I slowed down and asked myself where my quickness to jump in and take over, my distrust of John's ability to be careful or aware of danger, or my belief that he was not doing things "right" began, I realized it started far before ever meeting him, so they weren't entirely connected to . . . him.

My family leaned heavily toward the female gender. More aunts than uncles, more girl cousins than boy cousins. The women were fiery, opinionated, strong-willed, quick-witted, and sharp-tongued. Growing up I would hear them bash men, sometimes outright and verbally, but often in the rolled eyes, deep sighs, and knowing looks they gave each other. From childhood through today, I've been exposed to conflicting messages. While my mother was openly pro-choice, was pro–gay marriage, and always told me women were capable, strong, and could do anything, I still heard sexist jokes about Monica Lewinsky (who was barely twenty-two during that infamous time) and remarks about "just not trusting Hillary Clinton." During the #MeToo movement, they made comments about how the women speaking out should have just "been stronger and said something," or that what they experienced was just part of being a woman in the workplace and they should "suck it up" and stop ruining those poor men's lives.

These confusing messages from the women in my family reflected a broader cultural ambivalence about feminism and the roles of men and women. This ambivalence isn't unique to me; many women in my practice have shared similar experiences of internalized confusion. Can men truly be trusted, or are they inherently unreliable? Are men mentally and emotionally inferior to women, or is this a stereotype rooted in pain and mistrust? Is it okay to be an outspoken woman, or does it come with the risk of being labeled difficult or aggressive? Is it acceptable to be unpartnered and independent, or does that make a woman undesirable or lonely? Is it okay to be a sexually embodied woman, or does embracing one's sexuality lead to being shamed or dismissed? Is feminism empowering and necessary, or is it divisive and threatening to traditional family dynamics? And, perhaps most confusing of all: can a woman be both strong and vulnerable, both self-sufficient and open to receiving support?

THE ENEMY WITHIN

> "There are countless women of the '60s and '70s, who so deeply resented the patriarchy, which had destroyed their femininity, and that of their mothers, that they lashed out against that patriarchy. But in doing so they identified with the masculine side of their own psyches. In some cases, they turned into the very thing they most feared."
>
> —Marion Woodman, *Addiction to Perfection*[2]

Why does the word "feminism" stir such an array of differing feelings in people? Why does it conjure up the term "man hater" for some, create the idea that being a feminist means not being loved by men for others, or lead to the belief that feminism is destroying the traditional family? The answer is complicated, but the true definition of the word is not. bell hooks used this simple definition throughout her work: "Feminism is a movement to end sexism, sexist exploitation, and oppression."[3]

In my therapeutic work with women, a foundational component is examining and unearthing our, *women's*, internalized sexism and patriarchy. Women, like men, are socialized to internalize the same sexist thinking and values. Feminism isn't women against men; it's about recognizing that we all, regardless of gender, participate in perpetuating these cycles and upholding patriarchal values.

When women internalize patriarchal beliefs, it creates a cycle that reinforces the very structures feminism aims to dismantle. For instance, when women view other women through a competitive or judgmental lens rather than one of solidarity and support, it upholds the patriarchal myth that women cannot trust each other, stoking the fires of the Sister Wound. This "divide and conquer" mentality weakens feminist movements by keeping women focused on competing against one another rather than working together for collective liberation. The myth of sex, discussed in chapter 7, thrives when women, consciously or unconsciously, absorb and perpetuate these beliefs, undermining the progress feminism seeks to achieve by dividing its forces from within.

Since its inception, the feminist movement has undergone many iterations and evolutions, some of which have diluted and fractured its original message, mission, and core tenet of examining internalized sexism. It is only in the past few decades that mainstream modern feminism (often led by white voices) has begun to fully embrace the intersectionality of gender, race, and sexuality, integrating the ideals of longstanding Black and queer feminist theories. This shift is what we call fourth-wave feminism, a pendulum swing from the third-wave feminism of the early 1990s that many of us watched our mothers and grandmothers navigate.

During the late 1980s and into the 1990s, two core tenets of feminism—excavating internalized sexism and eradicating all forms of sexual oppression—were lost as focal points to what became known as "lifestyle feminism." This shift emphasized a woman's personal choice, even when those choices didn't benefit all women or limited another woman's ability to choose. This thinking undermined the traditional ideals of feminism, which called for the liberation of all women from sexist ideals and oppression. The comfortable allure of lifestyle feminism deepened divisions among women, as many white women with class privilege took their newly gained economic status (fought for and won by second-wave feminists) and stopped advocating for women of other classes and races. This move away from a sisterhood mentality of feminism toward individualism mirrored patriarchal values, effectively stopping the process of examining internalized sexism.

While this chapter is not intended to be a robust history lesson on the feminist movement, understanding these shifts is crucial for those of us currently navigating motherhood with younger, or dependent-age, children. The feminism of the late 1970s through the mid-1990s influences how we approach feminist ideals, family dynamics, and our roles as mothers today.

Third-wave feminism, in particular, fueled a deeper distrust and distaste for the feminine in all of us. This has manifested in various harmful ways, including, but not limited to:

- A dominator model of society still being prized and pedestalized.

- Women not trusting other women.

- The belief that women must be more like men to be respected.

- Women not respecting and/or infantilizing men.

- Women deepening their skills of covert control in their relationships because, under patriarchy, overt control is reserved for men.

- The social media "tradwife" phenomenon.

- The rollback of *Roe v. Wade* and affirmative action.

If we, the mothers of today, are to continue dismantling white supremacist, colonial, misogynistic, and patriarchal societal structures in favor of creating (or reviving) a more collaborative and egalitarian model, we must return to the hard work of uncovering and challenging our internal sexist beliefs and behaviors. While I will continue to champion examining the history and structures in which we live so we can speak up and act out against how they impact *all* of us (remember, without intersectionality, it is not feminism), I will also bring the focus back to ourselves and the role we play in betraying our own cause by avoiding the discomfort of personal accountability and internal change. Collective change starts with individual change—not in a hyper-individualistic way, but in a way that understands that collective liberation is the ultimate goal.

RIGHTEOUSNESS IS NOT OUR DOOR PRIZE

Clarissa, a forty-year-old white woman, was unhappy in her relationship with Marcus, a forty-nine-year-old Black man, and came to her therapy session with an actual list of the reasons why she thought she should leave.

"I do love him. He's sensitive, kind, and generous. But he's been struggling with depression on and off for years. He's barely working right now, and I've had to pick up more clients to cover it all. When it comes to our infant son, I doubt Marcus and his choices constantly, so I feel like I'm always hovering and checking everything he is doing. It's exhausting. I keep trying to be more 'in my feminine.' I've asked him to go to therapy, but he won't. I know he needs to do some work on himself; he has a ton of childhood trauma, low self-esteem, and he's defensive. When I bring this all up, he talks about how unappreciated and unvalued *he* feels! I'm stuck. He just won't do the work."

"Clarissa, I know you aren't going to love my response . . . where are you in all of this?"

"What do you mean?" she asked.

"For the past few weeks, we have listed out in detail all of the ways Marcus isn't doing his part in the relationship. But we haven't spent much time talking about you. Not only your role in all of this, but also just YOU. What lights you up? What inspires you? What are you passionate about right now in your life and work?"

Clarissa looked at me, clearly offended. "My part is that I am juggling everything, alone. And who has time for fun when you are the only one responsible for everything running smoothly."

"Right, and I hear that, but I want to know more about *why* you don't trust him to manage the basic things around the house or with your son. *Why* you resent Marcus so much for not making more money when the dynamic between you two has always been that he is a freelance artist and you are the breadwinner with the big-wig corporate job. *Why* you get so upset with him when he takes an hour between his clients to go sit at the coffee shop alone and read. I'm not blaming you, I'm not attacking you; I'm just wondering if we might look more closely at where *you* are in all of this. What the motivation might be behind the feelings that are now bubbling on the surface."

I was trying to help Clarissa see where and how she was giving Marcus all the power in the relationship by making him responsible for her contentment and peace. Clarissa is not an anomaly. She actually represents the most common relational complaints I hear from women in my retreats, groups, and individual therapy practice. Often, clients come to me to lament about what their partner isn't doing and the ways they wish they would change. They often hold the belief that once their partner changes this or that, they will feel happier in life and more fulfilled in their relationship. This is simply untrue. Our society has operated for centuries within a dominator model of power and control—power over other people, over our earth, and even over ourselves. This model convinces us that our happiness, success, fulfillment, and even our identity depend on someone else behaving or becoming what *we* want them to be.

In this next great evolution of consciousness, the one I believe we are standing on the precipice of, we will remember and return to the partnership model—not just in our social structures but within our homes and within ourselves. The partnership model emphasizes mutual respect, shared responsibility, emotional equality, and a shift from codependency to interdependence. Instead of relying on a partner to fulfill all our emotional needs or blaming them for our personal unhappiness, each person in an interdependent relationship takes accountability for their own well-being while also supporting their partner's growth. This involves fostering open communication where both partners express their needs and vulnerabilities without fear of judgment or dismissal. Rather than assigning blame or expecting one person to change to make the other happy, both partners work together to understand each other's experiences and co-create solutions to challenges.

In practice, this could mean moving away from rigid gender roles and embracing flexibility, where both partners feel empowered to explore their full range of emotions and capabilities. It looks like recognizing each other's strengths, valuing the different ways each contributes to the relationship, and creating space for individual pursuits and self-care. The focus shifts from control, competition, and dependency to collaboration, support, and mutual growth—where both individuals thrive together rather than struggle against each other. By moving from codependency to interdependence, we can cultivate relationships that honor both individuality and connection, recognizing that true partnership is about being whole within ourselves while remaining deeply connected to one another.

I pushed Clarissa to become more curious, to think of curiosity as a muscle that needed to be worked out as much as, if not more than, her physical body that she took great care of. Here are some of the things she noticed during this practice of curiosity:

- How often she was in a state of judgment, annoyance, and disappointment toward Marcus and how it felt connected to the moments when she felt like she wasn't enough—as a mother, partner, or person.

- How often her group of mom friends seemed to complain about their husbands and kids, speaking about their husbands in demeaning and minimizing ways, and how easily and often she joined in.

- That when she was feeling bad about not doing enough or being enough, she found herself jealous and resentful of Marcus when he would read, rest, or be in his studio working on his art.

- The way she became angry when Marcus wanted to talk about himself—his sadness, struggles, or self-doubts—and either shut the conversation down by changing the subject to herself or the baby or by feeling victimized and getting defensive.

- How her feelings of unhappiness became more prevalent after her best friend went through a divorce. While the divorce itself was hard and Clarissa felt good in her capacity to be a supportive friend through it all, she found herself jealous of her friend now that she was on the other side. The friend had expressed how, as a co-parent with 50 percent custody, she felt she was a far better mother than when she was with her kids all of the time. The friend had gone back to school, was dating, had picked up dancing, and overall was the happiest Clarissa had ever seen her.

Focusing on Clarissa's role in the relationship dynamic was not meant to blame her for all her struggles or let Marcus off the hook for not stepping up, but rather to begin to notice how often he was the focus of her emotional turmoil, how much energy she spent being upset with him, and how little she was actually focusing on herself. Most of us do this. We lose ourselves to the hard realities of kids, work, and running a household, and we tend to make all of our stress and resentment someone else's fault. It feels a lot easier to blame others in the moment than own our part in our unhappiness.

THE TRUE COST OF "HAVING IT ALL"

Another consequence of that third wave of feminism: many women of our generation grew up hearing—whether explicitly or implicitly—that this was our lot in life. That we could "have it all." We could be a wife, mother, *and* a career woman, or choose to be a stay-at-home mom. But this promise of "having it all" came with a heavy price: a lot of stress, struggle, control, bitterness, discontentment, and a big ol' dash of self-righteousness. For women, part of the deal within the heteronormative, mononormative, nuclear family model—the so-called "American Dream"—was partnering with men who often couldn't pull their weight and were untrustworthy, incompetent, or a "man child" who needed to be treated as such, on condition that they could provide financially. So long as we (especially white women) took the little economic gains that were given to us in the 1980s and 1990s, kept our heads down, and played our societal roles without too much pushback or desire to challenge the larger structure, we were permitted to hold onto our anger and righteousness. And hold onto it we did (and still do).

This sneaky inner misogyny shows up in the way we view women who dare to reject the trap of righteous bitterness and the way our grandmothers, mothers, and now we look with jealousy at other women who are free from the shackles of bitterness and control. "How dare you take up space, love yourself, and expect more!" our deeply unconscious beliefs say. "We are supposed to be angry. Yes, we live in a sexist, patriarchal society that treats women as inferior, but at least we know we're smarter, more evolved, and better than men."

This chapter may upset you. It may feel like I am asking you to excuse men from accountability. But this isn't meant to let men off the hook for the work they need to do, but it does give us, as women, a choice. We do not have to be beholden to the war of the sexes. We do not have to participate in the man-bashing rhetoric that continually puts the focus on *them*, allowing us to avoid looking at ourselves. Constantly fixating on what others need to do, stop doing, or change so we can be happy is a symptom of our internalized misogyny that keeps us stuck forever in the one-down, powerless, victimhood role that patriarchy relies on to sustain itself.

MYTHS AS MAPS
Baba Yaga and the Wild Woman: Feed the Soul or Face Devourment

As a character, Baba Yaga is both heroine and villain. She originates in Slavic folklore, with some disagreement on the exact time and location of her first appearance in stories. Baba Yaga is most notably featured in the Russian fairy tale *Vasilisa the Beautiful*, but she appears in other tales as well. Her character may have inspired the Fairy Godmother in *Cinderella* and the witch in *Hansel and Gretel*. Baba Yaga is the crone personification of the Wild Woman—the old wild hag, the wise teacher whom we consult in matters of the Soul. She rebukes the passive female nurturing role, instead representing the relationship between women and the wild (both natural and instinctual). She reminds us that freedom and connection to the great wildish powers of the feminine psyche, including intuition, lie a little beyond the border of social norms and require challenge and grit to access. She is a model for being true to the Self, encouraging transformation and teaching us the importance and wisdom of the natural cycle of death and renewal.

In the story of *Vasilisa the Beautiful*, Baba Yaga lives in a hut that stands on chicken legs in the middle of the forest, surrounded by a fence made of human bones, with skulls that glow in the dark. She is known for her fierce, unpredictable nature—both a nurturing guide and a terrifying adversary. Vasilisa, a young girl who is mistreated by her wicked stepmother and stepsisters, is sent to Baba Yaga's hut on a seemingly impossible task: to retrieve light for their darkened home. Along her journey, Vasilisa carries a magical doll that her dying mother had given her, a doll that represents her inner intuition and guidance.

When Vasilisa arrives, Baba Yaga does not welcome her with kindness; instead, she demands that Vasilisa complete a series of grueling tasks in exchange for her help. Baba Yaga tests Vasilisa's patience, strength, and resourcefulness. If she fails, Vasilisa knows she could be devoured by the witch. However, with the help of her intuitive doll, Vasilisa completes each task with diligence, humility, and cleverness, proving herself worthy of Baba Yaga's wisdom. Vasilisa does not wallow in self-pity or wish her circumstances were different. She does not blame her stepmother or stepsisters for her hardships. Instead, she takes charge of her own fate. Satisfied, Baba Yaga gives her a skull lantern that contains a powerful light. When Vasilisa returns home with it, the light incinerates her wicked stepfamily, allowing her to be reborn into a life of freedom and authenticity.

Baba Yaga, the wild soul, not only serves as a guide for those on their journey of initiation, but also teaches that "developing a relationship with the wildish nature is an essential part of women's individuation."[4] She tests the unsure, making them prove their worthiness and commitment to returning with and living out the wisdom found on the path. She needs to be nourished through a feverish devotion to our Soul growth, our passion, our creativity, our life's work. If she is not nourished, she will devour you, as represented in her appetite for the children who stumble upon her in fairy tales, asking only for her assistance without anything to offer in return.

SEEING OURSELVES IN THE MYTH

> "The Wild Woman archetype sheaths the alpha matrilineal being. There are times when we experience her, even if only fleetingly, and it makes us mad with wanting to continue. For some women, this vitalizing 'taste of the wild' comes during pregnancy, during nursing their young, during the miracle of change in oneself as one raises a child, during attending to a love relationship as one would attend to a beloved garden."
>
> —Clarissa Pinkola Estés, *Women Who Run with the Wolves*[5]

I feel strongly that Baba Yaga can teach us important lessons to guide us on a path toward individual and collective liberation. In my work with female clients, as in my own personal work, I see a reclamation of the wildish force within the female psyche, the Wild Woman archetype, as being in service to the continued dissolution of not only patriarchal mothering, but to patriarchal thinking and living.

Many clients and women in my groups come to me with a desire to discuss ideas and terms like "goddess culture" or "the divine feminine" in connection to their liberation and the evolution of consciousness we seem to be witnessing in the world. While these conversations and movements can have huge impacts on the creation of a sense of Self, our reconnection to our sexuality, the balance of our internal masculine and feminine energies, and even the strengthening of our relationships with men and the masculine, I ask you, just as I ask my clients, to proceed with caution as you take in some of the content and ideas being put forth.

If we only look to these archetypes as a means to reconnect with our individual selves without also addressing the internalized patriarchal beliefs we may still hold, we risk falling into the same traps that have hindered feminist progress. The Wild Woman's strength is in her ability to see beyond societal conditioning, take radical responsibility for her life, and live in her truth. If more women embraced this archetype not only to empower themselves, but also to challenge their internalized beliefs about power, worth, and gender roles, we could dismantle the myths that keep feminism from reaching its full potential.

Much of what I see being espoused as a part of the rise of the feminine is, in many ways, anti-feminist ideals wrapped in beautiful flowing dresses draped on thin white bodies. If there is shame, a lack of inclusion, or othering involved in the message, be suspicious. If there is a lack of nuance and a prescriptive or preachy tone about the "right way" to look, feel, or be a good woman, wife, or mother, be suspicious. If there is a "power over" message in any way, be suspicious. If there is a lack of personal accountability and a critical look at your role in the collective liberation of all women, be suspicious. Many of these well-curated, beautifully adorned messages feed on our disconnection from each other, ourselves, and our intuition, and I see many an inner Wild Woman—a Baba Yaga—gnashing her teeth in response. Always come back to the importance of *finding your own inner truth.*

In therapy sessions, over coffee with friends, or via social media, women grapple with their feelings of fatigue, depression, lack of inspiration or meaning, anger, suffocation, self-doubt and self-consciousness, sexual disconnection or dissatisfaction, overwhelm, underwhelm, uncertainty, fear, anxiety, frustration, rage, and stuckness. I work with women and couples from all ages and walks of life who are not able to put their finger on a specific "issue," but rather complain of some combination of these symptoms and a desire to make them go away. And to that I say, you (we) have lost touch with the Wild Woman, and by bringing her into our consciousness and nourishing her, these challenges begin to recede. No, this acknowledgment of the Wild Woman does not in and of itself dissolve sexism, misogyny, white supremacy, or patriarchy, but I see the next evolution of our work in reconnecting with her.

According to Estés, the Wild Woman is the "permanent and internal watcher, a knower, a visionary, an oracle, an inspiratrice, an intuitive, a maker, a creator, an inventor, and a listener who guide(s), suggest(s), and urge(s) vibrant life in the inner and outer worlds."[6] The dominator culture we live in has, in so many ways and through so many avenues, cut us off from this deep intuitive knowing, our inner visionary and creator. Part of the work for all of us is revivifying the nourishment of the Yaga so she might grant us the wisdom we need to initiate from the child-mother to the Queen, then to the Wise Woman and the Crone—personally and collectively. Reconnecting with and nourishing the creative aspects of the feminine Soul are elements of therapeutic work I engage all of my female clients in.

You may think you don't have time to be creative, but creativity comes to us and is expressed through more ways than are possible to list. We may think of writing, painting, music, and dance when we consider creativity, but Estés reminds us that we can also find creativity in loving someone well, raising a child, arranging flowers, and cooking a good meal. Creativity is what flows through us when we are connected to our intuitive selves. "It is the love of something, having so much love for something—whether a person, a word, an image, an idea, the land, or humanity—that all that can be done with the overflow is to create. It is not a matter of wanting to, not a singular act of will; one solely must."[7] Creativity is not only about us; it is about everyone. It is the vital energy that feeds *everything*.

There are many avenues we can take in order to discover what our Soul longs to create, but connecting with our Wild Woman is not a cognitive exercise. As we do the work of reconnecting to the wild intuitive feminine Self, we might ask ourselves some questions. Estés suggests these: "What am I hungry for? What do I long for? What do I wish for now?" Alternate phrases are "What do I crave? What do I desire? For what do I yearn?" And the answer usually arrives rapidly, "Oh, I think I want . . . you know what would be really good is some of this or that . . . ah, yes, that's what I really want."[8]

Remember, the more we honor and nourish Baba Yaga, the wise and wild woman, the more she provides us the strength, wisdom, and clarity needed to move forward on this path of inner reclamation and outer transformation. Feeding her, feeding us, is not a luxury; it is a necessity. Baba Yaga represents the Wild Woman archetype's fierceness, who refuses to be placated or tamed. She embodies the wild feminine energy that insists on growth through challenge, reminding us that we must feed our inner fire, intuition, and creativity—our "wildish nature"—or risk being devoured by stagnation, complacency, bitterness, or a life lived for others. She invites us to see our own initiation journeys mirrored in her story, the moments when we must step into the unknown, confront our fears, and trust our inner guidance. Baba Yaga's myth teaches us that the path to true empowerment and authenticity often lies in the dark woods of our psyche, where we must confront not just our outer oppressors but our inner ones as well.

GOING DEEPER

Be Curious

It is impossible to be in a state of judgment and control when you are in a state of curiosity and imagination. Plus these states develop and maintain our connection to the Self. The Wild Woman archetype resides below the intellectual level, in the imagination, and manifests *through* creativity. She is our life force, the energy that allows us to feel like we are thriving, not just surviving.

When you make it a practice to pay more attention to yourself, your creativity, and your passions, you find that eventually you are no longer interested in controlling anyone else. You are living through your Soul and allowing others to do the same. This practice of curiosity followed by creativity isn't going to solve your real-world relational problems, obviously. There is still the hard work of improving our communication skills, tackling how our attachment wounds are activated in our intimate relationships, and working out the domestic and emotional load in a household. But a woman who has not examined her own internal misogyny is more of a threat to the advancement of feminism than a man who is committed to his anti-sexist principals but is still fumbling in his daily work as an ally.

Here are some reflection questions for curiosity and creativity that build on those of Estés:

- What brings you alive and makes you feel connected to your Self? How often are you making time for those things?

- In what areas of your life are you more focused on others than on nurturing your own growth?

- When you think about your creative expressions (whether in art, work, or daily life), where do you feel most restricted? What might happen if you gave yourself permission to explore those areas more freely?

Become Boundaried

There it is, the "B" word! Were you wondering at what point in the book I would bring up the word that has become a buzzy focal point in therapy and wellness? I could write a whole book on boundaries, as many therapists can and have, but I won't. Instead, I will discuss boundaries and their importance in conjunction with reclaiming this wildish, instinctual feminine nature. Boundaries can be your springboard to further development of the Self.

First, let's clear something up about boundaries. I hear the word being misused so often. Boundaries are not a demand or request you put on someone else. They are not an ultimatum. They are not something you use to control others. Boundaries are *your* internal guidelines, rules, or limits on what you are willing or not willing to tolerate in terms of treatment by others and what action(s) you will take if that line is crossed. In order to have healthy boundaries, you have to believe that your needs, wants, and health deserve to take priority. For many of us, we discover and develop our boundaries through the process of discovering and developing our relationship to, respect for, and trust in the Self.

As you begin to develop a relationship to your inner knowing—the intuitive part of the Self that knows what your boundaries are—and then, through practice, artfully communicate and uphold your standards, space will begin to develop in your life, heart, mind, and psyche. A patriarchal structure exists on the backs of overworked, overcommitted, burnt-out women who doubt their knowing and feel guilty and selfish for taking up time and space for themselves. We spend a lot of time being partnered and raising children. The luxury of free time to think, rest, be creative, and consider our position is dangerous to the system. If we are consumed by trying to perform for our belonging and love, we won't have time to feed Baba Yaga, our Wild Woman.

Here are some reflection questions for setting boundaries:

- What are the areas in your life where you feel most depleted or overwhelmed? What boundaries could you set to protect your energy and well-being?

- Are there places where you are afraid to set boundaries because you fear the response from others? What are those fears, and how might they reflect deeper beliefs about your worthiness or role?

- If setting a boundary feels too difficult right now, what would setting a "50 percent boundary" look like? What is a smaller step you could take to claim space for yourself?

As you begin to put more attention on yourself, your creativity, and your spiritual and emotional fulfillment, you will notice pushback. I have never once worked with a client who began experimenting with boundaries and prioritizing themselves who did not experience some upset in those around them. But remember, the only people who don't like your boundaries are those who benefit from you not having them. Even knowing that, the fear of the pushback alone is sometimes enough to make us not hold firm. So, in the face of potential pushback, replace the question "How do I set this boundary?" with "What are my fears around setting it?" This points to a deeper layer of understanding around certain relationships. Another thing to ask yourself when fear creeps in is if setting a specific boundary feels like too much, and not doing anything is staying the same (i.e., no growth, no feeding of your Soul), then what would 50 percent (i.e., a middle ground) feel like? How can you claim something for yourself without feeling too bad about it? Any progress is progress.

> "A woman must be careful to not allow over-responsibility (or over-respectability) to steal her necessary creative rests, riffs, and raptures. She simply must put her foot down and say no to half of what she believes she 'should' be doing. Art is not meant to be created in stolen moments only."
>
> —Clarissa Pinkola Estés, *Women Who Run with the Wolves*[9]

Part 3

the myths of relationships

> "The most dangerous phrase in the English language is: We've always done it this way. It raises the question, 'Are we doing this because we always have, or because it's the right thing to do?'"
>
> —Grace Hopper, *ComputerWorld*[1]

Disconnection, discontentment, and fear often rule our relationships. We twist ourselves in knots trying to avoid discomfort, believing that, with enough control, we can keep life calm and untroubled. But nature, in its wisdom, shows us a different truth: Where there is contraction, there will be expansion. Where there is darkness, there will be light. An initiated woman knows that discomfort and endings are not to be feared, but embraced as part of the natural cycle of life, death, and rebirth.

In our spiritually immature society, we fear emotional discomfort and the natural cycles of life, leading us to contort ourselves in relationships—silencing our truths and clinging to codependent patterns that inhibit intimacy. The feelings we fear are not barriers but portals, gateways to deeper understanding and connection.

Codependency, rooted in the fear of discomfort, shapes how we form attachments, express our needs, and navigate conflict. It creates a dynamic where we seek to control others rather than embrace the natural ebb and flow of relationships. As a therapist, and someone who has walked this path, I've seen how fear drives manipulation, emotional suppression, and self-abandonment, keeping us from true connection. This section peels back those layers, unraveling the fear and control that block the deep, authentic connections we seek.

9

liberation through responsibility

> "Codependency is externalized power.
> Interdependence is internalized power."
>
> —Vanessa Bennett (me!)

"I don't feel safe in this relationship. I don't believe that you are being honest with me. That you aren't secretly upset about something and just carrying it around while, on the surface, pretending we are totally fine."

This was one of the last texts I received from my then best friend of ten years before our relationship ended. She had done something that hurt my feelings, and it had taken me about a week to express it to her. During that week, I had acted normal, albeit emotionally distant, a bit less talkative and responsive. While I firmly believe there is no set time frame for expressing hurt and talking things through, this exchange has lingered in my mind, even all these years later.

"You're always playing chess. You wait to see how I respond before you respond. Or you come in and read the energy before you open your mouth. It makes me feel like you aren't being honest."

This is something my partner, John, said to me after a fight. He has expressed similar feelings multiple times throughout our relationship.

Hearing this from John wasn't easy. It shattered a part of my self-image. I had always seen myself as someone deeply invested in honest communication and relational harmony, so to hear that my attempts to "read the room" were perceived as dishonest shook me. The truth was my desire to avoid conflict wasn't rooted in harmony, but in fear—fear of rejection, fear of loss, and fear of vulnerability. The initial shock of this realization wasn't comfortable; in fact, it was painful. But what I've learned is that this discomfort is the doorway to deeper understanding and transformation.

Many of us are masters at this game of chess; we just don't realize we're playing. We grew up learning to assess how our parents or caregivers were feeling before deciding how we could feel or act. If Dad came home from work in a foul mood, I would know to be extra quiet and respectful to avoid setting him off. If I came home from school and Mom was happily chatting about her day and asking about mine, I could be loud, silly, and a bit more myself. Only after hearing similar feedback from both my friend and John—two very important people in my life—did I begin to understand that my skill of scanning for danger, keeping my cards close to my chest, and expressing myself only after weighing the risks and ensuring everyone was in the right energetic state made others feel unsafe around me.

This habit is incredibly hard to untangle. It is so deeply engrained that it happens mostly without conscious awareness, and it is a significant indicator of codependency. If I can feel a sense of control over a situation or dynamic—predict how this conversation might go, anticipate someone's response to me—I can prepare and protect myself from potential hurt, shame, or rejection. Sounds like a reasonable survival strategy, right? Possibly, but beneath this seemingly protective approach lies an addiction to an anxiety release valve that is unintentionally manipulative. I was avoiding the real challenge of building the resilience to experience anxiety without immediately needing to soothe it.

Developing emotional resilience means gradually building the capacity to experience anxiety without automatically reaching for that release valve. This could look like pausing before responding in a heated moment, practicing mindfulness techniques like deep breathing or body scanning when feeling activated or triggered, or even scheduling difficult conversation rehearsals with a therapist or trusted friend to build confidence. It also involves understanding that it's okay to feel overwhelmed, and that emotions are temporary. They don't have to dictate our actions or our sense of Self.

Looking back, that realization about my behavior was deeply unsettling. I remember feeling a wave of shame, confusion, and defensiveness as I grappled with the truth that my approach—something I believed to be protective and safe—was actually creating distance and mistrust. It was the first time I began to see that my way of relating wasn't as harmless or selfless as I had believed. This moment of discomfort was the starting point of a much longer journey, one where I had to confront the parts of myself I had long hidden or justified. It was not a linear path. The initial realizations felt more like losing footing than gaining insight, but I now see that those moments of destabilization were essential for growth. They were not signs of failure but invitations to step into a new way of being, to learn to relate from a place of safety within and authenticity rather than fear.

ALL ADDICTIONS SERVE THE SAME PURPOSE

Jung's work on addiction suggests that addicts are looking for spiritual experiences in the wrong places.[1] Codependency, much like addiction, stems from a deep need to regulate our emotional states through external sources. At their core, both are spiritual crises—attempts to find wholeness and connection in external validation, relationships, or control. Codependency manifests as basing our emotional well-being on someone else's state, seeking validation outside of ourselves, or using relationships (and sometimes our attempt to control a person or situation) to soothe our stress and anxiety. In essence, codependency and emotional control are coping mechanisms that mirror the addiction cycle—offering temporary relief while keeping us disconnected from our true needs, our sense of Self, and a deeper spiritual connection to something greater than us.

In recent years, I noticed the same maladaptive behaviors and relational struggles kept surfacing in my clients. They often described feeling like they had lost themselves in another person or their job, constantly playing the role of rescuer, savior, or fixer in their relationships, and feeling as if this was expected of them. Many struggled to speak up and communicate their feelings, lacked trust in themselves and others, and felt unseen, unheard, or undervalued. Most had low self-esteem and a sense of worthlessness, resulting in a cycle of unsatisfying relationships or unfulfilling jobs. And most notably, there was a common thread running through all of these stories: resentment. Lots and lots of resentment.

Through my years of facilitating weekly codependency recovery groups, I have come to believe that the most overlooked aspect of codependency is that it is not just a personal issue; it's a societal one. Culture profoundly shapes how we view ourselves within the constructs of relationships, community, needs, purpose, and values. In Western culture, we are conditioned to view relationships—not just romantic ones, but especially romantic ones—as the ultimate source of identity and fulfillment. This "soulmate model" encourages us to place the burden of our happiness on others, creating fertile ground for codependent dynamics. Love becomes something to lose ourselves in, hide behind, or use to fill our voids. We are taught that love should always feel good and fulfill our needs, turning it into a transactional exchange for the ego rather than a space for genuine connection.

In contrast, cultures that emphasize communal well-being and interdependence—like many Indigenous societies—teach us that emotional health is a collective responsibility, reducing the pressure on individual relationships to meet all our emotional needs.

At its core, codependency *is* an addiction, and healing the self-abandoning behaviors that maintain the unhappy status quo in our relationships requires recognizing this. While substance abuse is often stigmatized when it is the go-to for soothing anxiety, numbing deep-seated fear, or escaping uncomfortable feelings, the more socially acceptable addictions—shopping, scrolling social media, immersing ourselves in work or our children, or handing over our autonomy and relational power to romantic partners—are just as damaging. As Canadian physician and addiction expert Gabor Maté points out, an addiction is "manifested in *any* behavior that a person craves, finds temporary relief or pleasure in but suffers negative consequences as a result of, and yet has difficulty giving up."[2]

I will never forget my first Al-Anon meeting when the group facilitator opened with, "We're not here to talk about them and their disease; we're here to talk about you and your disease." It was the wake-up call I didn't realize I desperately needed, as I had been previously blaming all my relationship dissatisfaction on my romantic partner at the time.

Many clients come to me pointing the finger at the other person—partners, family members, bosses—believing that these people need to change in order for them to be happy. The truth is you don't need anyone to change or be anything other than what or who they are for you to be who you are. This understanding is crucial in codependency recovery. Most of us don't know who we are outside of our relationships, and that's where the real work begins—reconnecting with ourselves so we can stand in our power, regardless of how others show up.

ATTACHMENT VERSUS AUTHENTICITY

Gabor Maté frequently discusses two fundamental needs of every human being: attachment and authenticity. Human beings, born the least developed of all mammals, *need* attachment figures to care for them physically and emotionally in order to develop into healthy adults. However, the other half of the equation is a need to be authentic—to be seen, loved, and valued for who we truly are. Yet, because we need attachment to survive in infancy and early childhood, our system will sacrifice authenticity to secure attachment. Parent or caregiver thinks you are too dramatic? You will learn to stuff your expression down. Society tells you that your creativity is frivolous? You will learn to hide it and instead focus on being more productive. Little League coach tells you crying is weak? You will learn to cut off your emotions. Codependent behaviors develop in childhood as strategies to defend against the potential for rejection and abandonment. Ironically, by choosing not to show up as ourselves as a way to fit in or out of fear of rejection or abandonment, we end up rejecting and abandoning ourselves.

Fast-forward decades later and you're dissatisfied in your relationships, work, or life, but you can't pinpoint why. After another unhealthy relationship expires. In the throes of depression or an anxiety disorder. When you wake up and realize there has to be more to life than just getting through it—that you want to thrive, not just survive. This is often the point when clients find me. It's in that moment when the feeling that you *cannot* continue like this crystallizes the ability to take responsibility for changing your life.

Understanding codependency as an addiction to emotional control was both enlightening and deeply unsettling. It forced me to see how I was hooked on these patterns, much like any other addict. The first step toward recovery from any addiction is admitting there is a problem, and that admission can feel like everything is falling apart. But in that falling apart, there is space for something new to emerge. The discomfort of these realizations is not a sign that we are broken, but rather a signal that something in us is ready to break open, grow, and evolve.

THE BIRTHPLACE OF THE FALSE SELF

> "While the needs of the child's soul must be balanced with her need for safety and physical care and with carefully examined notions about 'civilized behavior,' I always worry for those who are too well behaved; they often have that 'faint soul' look in their eyes. Something is not right. A healthy soul shines through the persona on most days and blazes through on others. Where there is gross injury, the soul flees."
>
> —Clarissa Pinkola Estés, *Women Who Run with the Wolves*[3]

Somewhere along the way, most of us learned it wasn't okay to be ourselves. We learned not to communicate our hurts, desires, and needs. We learned that managing others' emotional responses was our responsibility. We learned that we could only show up in certain ways to be loved and accepted. We learned to label some emotions as good, while others were bad or shameful. We learned to stay small.

Most of our parents and caregivers were not bad people. Yes, some of them were undoubtedly harmful, even abusive. But for most of us, it is crucial to hold the tension of two conflicting truths: many of our parents and caregivers did the best they could with what they had, and yet many of their behaviors and choices still hurt us. Acknowledging this paradox is vital in our healing work. Many clients come to me clinging to an ideal of loyalty to their family of origin, believing loyalty is synonymous with not being honest about how their upbringing negatively affected them. That being honest somehow equates with being a "bad kid" or ungrateful. This is not the truth. What is true is that healing our childhood wounding and gaining a deeper understanding of why we think, respond, and act the way we do cannot happen until we can look at our upbringing objectively.

When I first began my therapy journey around age twenty-five, I was deeply committed to preserving the idea of my mother as perfect. At that time, our relationship was highly enmeshed; we were speaking about three to five times a day, and there was almost nothing about me or my relationships she did not know or have comments on. I struggled to make decisions without her input or approval. I found it difficult to be honest and open with my therapist about things she had said or done that had a profound, lasting negative impact on me. The power of the universal paradox—that two opposing truths can exist at once—became clear when I heard American Buddhist psychologist and teacher Tara Brach say something like this in her podcast: "Yes, your mother or father loved you, but did they *enjoy* you?"[4]

Reflecting on that question, I was reminded of my earlier reflections on my upbringing and my young single mother's struggles, which I shared in chapter 4. Much of my childhood was centered around making sure my mom was emotionally okay, and keeping her happy became my life's goal—a classic example of what we would call a "parentified child." But this is only one of the many roles we might assume in childhood that puts us on a path toward codependency. Whether you were the peacekeeper, the jokester, the golden child, the scapegoat, or some combination of these roles, the underlying theme remains the same: we learn that we must perform for our belonging. This belief that we cannot be fully ourselves and still be fully loved is often the root of our relational struggles as adults.

This is not to say that you must justify or "forgive" hurtful or abusive behaviors in order to heal, especially if forgiveness does not feel true for you in this moment. I am not one of those therapists who believes everything must start with forgiveness. It's okay to be angry. In fact, much healing comes from exploring and accepting our anger. Anger can be a powerful gateway into deeper self-understanding and can be a springboard into action. Now, if you've spent thirty years consumed by anger with no progression into action, that is a different conversation. As Glennon Doyle says in *Untamed*, "If we cannot forgive and move on, perhaps we need to move on first and forgiveness will follow."[5]

THE UNSPOKEN RULES

I often open my codependency workshops with a quote from Melody Beattie, an addiction counselor and pioneer in the world of addiction and codependency. In her book *Codependent No More: How to Stop Controlling Others and Start Caring for Yourself*, she writes:

> It's common to have unwritten, silent rules that usually develop in the immediate family and set the pace for relationships. Those rules prohibit discussion about problems; open expression of feelings; direct, honest communication; realistic expectations, such as being human, vulnerable, or imperfect; selfishness; trust in other people and one's self; playing and having fun; and rocking the boat through growth or change.[6]

These unspoken rules are critical in understanding why and how we develop behaviors that trap us in codependent ways of relating to each other. Keeping in mind Gabor Maté's point about humans having conflicting needs for both attachment and authenticity, these unspoken rules teach us to only express the parts of ourselves that our caregivers or society find acceptable. The rest—those feelings and parts deemed unacceptable—are pushed into the shadow.

These unspoken rules tangibly impact our ability to:

- Know what we are truly feeling.

- Identify what our needs and wants even are.

- Listen to our intuition.

They also lead to maladaptive emotional strategies, such as:

- Staying in our heads and rationalizing experiences instead of feeling emotions.

- Feeling shame around normal emotions and labeling some as unacceptable.

- Experiencing shame for simply being who we are or having needs at all.

- Fearing vulnerability.

- Struggling with emotional resilience.

As a result, many of us develop a false Self, one that is carefully crafted from years of field research. Test, get feedback, learn, pivot, test again, get feedback, learn, pivot, and so on. While it is necessary for children to learn what is socially acceptable to survive in a social culture, there is a risk in becoming too identified with this "persona." While developing a persona—our social face or external mask—is an imperative part of adapting and relating to that culture, the longer we live behind this mask and the more we become obsessed with others' perceptions, the further we stray from our true selves. Jung warned about this, noting that when we become overly concerned with external validation, the patterns of self-abandonment become nearly imperceptible. We lose the ability to see ourselves objectively and become incapable of differentiating between the Self and the societal expectations imposed upon us.

In Western societies, children are often taught to be self-reliant and independent, but this often comes with a hidden contradiction. They are also socialized to derive much of their self-worth from external validation—achievements, appearance, or romantic relationships. This dichotomy can lead to emotional confusion, where dependency on others for validation is mistaken for love. In contrast, cultures like those of Japan, South Africa, and many other African societies have concepts like "amae" (a sense of dependency and trust in the care and benevolence of others) or "Ubuntu" (an emphasis on common humanity and community connection). These approaches and cultural concepts offer a healthier, more balanced approach, allowing for a form of dependency that's rooted in mutual respect, care, and communal harmony rather than control and manipulation.

The challenging part of reconnecting with our true Self—unearthing her and developing and strengthening a relationship with her—is that it isn't as simple as recognizing self-abandoning behaviors. The knowing is one thing; the doing is another thing entirely. Fifteen years into my codependency recovery journey, I still struggle not to sweep things under the rug to avoid rocking the boat. I still say yes when I want to say no. I still put others' needs ahead of my own to the point of overwhelm and resentment.

Through years of therapy, reading, and practice, I've learned that speaking up about a hurt or grievance in my intimate relationships can ultimately lead to a deeper, more fulfilling connection—or reveal that a relationship isn't conducive to honesty and authenticity and should fall away. However, my ego often registers the potential loss of that attachment as a threat to my survival. It forgets that I have been with myself through some hard and uncomfortable conversations that led to more satisfying relationships. It also seems to forget that I have been with myself through painful dissolutions of relationships that created more space, freedom, and self-love on the other side. Every day, we come upon multiple crossroads. Go right, and do the hard thing that leads to expansion and fulfillment (short-term pain for long-term gain). Go left, and do what feels easier (short-term gain for long-term pain). The behavior you know so well. No one can make this choice for us. No one can grow for us. And no amount of relational knowledge can replace the need for lived, felt, and integrated experience.

Emotional resilience is not just about the ability to "bounce back" from difficult emotions; it's about building the capacity to stay with discomfort without immediately seeking to soothe it through familiar, often unhealthy patterns. For example, when feeling anxious about a partner's reaction, emotional resilience means resisting the urge to placate or manipulate to keep the peace. Instead, it could mean sitting with that anxiety, breathing through it, and speaking your truth even if the outcome is uncertain. It's recognizing that the discomfort of an honest conversation is temporary, while the effects of suppressing your voice can be long-lasting. Over time, this practice of tolerating discomfort helps build a stronger, more grounded sense of Self.

RESENTMENT IS OURS TO OWN
Andrea, a thirty-four-year-old Polish American mother of three, entered our session with a heavy sigh.

"I'm just so fed up with Aaron," she began, her frustration clear. "He's never around when I need him. I'm managing the kids, the house, and work, and when he does step in, it's only after I practically beg him. It's exhausting."

As Andrea continued to describe her frustration with Aaron, a familiar thread started to appear. She felt unsupported, unappreciated, and as though she had to carry the emotional load of their relationship on her own.

"You know, it's not just Aaron. Leah's been doing this to me too." She went on to explain that Leah, her best friend since college, had become distant. "I've always been there for her," Andrea said, "but when I needed her the most this past year, she wasn't there for me. I kept thinking, 'If she really cared, she would make time for me.' It's like I'm the one always holding everything together in all my relationships."

As Andrea spoke, she began to see a pattern—not just with Aaron and Leah, but in many of her relationships. "Why do I keep ending up here? Why do I always feel like I'm giving everything and not getting anything back?" she asked, the realization hitting her hard.

In that moment, I gently suggested, "Andrea, do you think you're wishing and waiting on Aaron and Leah to prove that you're lovable by giving love back to you in the same way you give it to them? Wanting them to acknowledge and validate all that you do as a way to tell you that you are worth something? That you are seen and appreciated as a person?"

Tears filled her eyes as the words settled. "I guess I've been thinking that if they loved me, they would make time for me. But it's not just them, is it? It's like I'm always waiting for someone to prove that I matter. For someone to give me permission to just . . . be. And for that to be enough."

This was a turning point for Andrea. As we unpacked her feelings, I explained, "Here's the uncomfortable truth: your resentment is entirely yours to own. That doesn't mean letting people off the hook for bad behavior. It means recognizing that this dynamic is part of a larger pattern that you play a part in maintaining. You're expecting Aaron and Leah to show up as your 'ideal parent.' The one we all wish we had, who saw us and validated us and made us feel worthy and chosen. But they are not your parent, and you are asking them to show up in ways they may not be capable of. And when they don't, it's confirming this belief that you're not worthy of love and care."

Andrea sat in silence for a moment, letting this sink in. "So I'm not seeing them for who they really are," she said slowly. "I'm seeing them for who I want them to be."

"Exactly," I replied. "It's not about their *desire* to support you; it's about their *capacity* to do so. When you depersonalize it, when you see their behavior—and honestly everyone's behavior—as a reflection of their own limitations instead of a statement about your worth, you can make a choice. You can decide whether this relationship is fulfilling for you or if it's not in alignment with what you need. This is the scary part that keeps most of us stuck in these dynamics. When you ask for what you need in a relationship, the other person has the chance to either agree and step up or disagree and disappoint you. By not asking, you think you're avoiding the disappointment and pain, but you're instead choosing to stay in resentment and, honestly, a bit of a victim state."

Andrea seemed to take that insight to heart and made a concrete plan. She reached out to Leah: "I miss our time together, and I'd love to set up a regular catch-up." Leah responded enthusiastically, and they agreed to a biweekly coffee date where she learned that Leah was feeling overwhelmed and somewhat depressed in her life and had been struggling to reach out and ask for connection and support because she felt like a burden.

With Aaron, she watched how she seemed to be waiting for him to notice her struggle or be attuned to her needs, and instead of staying in that place, she asked him to take charge with the kids on Saturday mornings so she could have time for herself. It wasn't perfect; she still felt like their co-parenting relationship was lopsided, but she came to another session and expressed, "It's funny. Now that I'm not expecting him to read my mind, things have improved. I used to think he wouldn't follow through, but asking for what I needed has actually brought us closer. There's more work to do here, but this feels like a start."

By owning her 100 percent, Andrea's relationships transformed along with her mindset. Not all of them rose to meet her where she was. In particular, a close work relationship actually fell away when she began to speak up more. But when she stopped expecting others to prove her worth and instead trusted herself to ask for what she needed, she began to build more tolerance for disappointment by allowing space for others' humanity, creating a foundation of honesty and authenticity. This work felt harder to her in some ways, but ultimately much more fulfilling.

WHAT'S YOUR 100 PERCENT?

The concept of "owning your 100 percent" comes from twelve-step programs, emphasizing personal responsibility in one's growth and recovery. In every dynamic and situation, there is *something* we can own. Always. Healing our self-abandoning and codependent tendencies is deeply personal work, but it actually happens on the stage of our relationships. It is in relationships that we have the opportunity to investigate our fears and activations, practice new skills and emotional language, and ride the waves of discomfort rather than relying on others to soothe us or regulate our emotional state.

We often fall into the trap of believing that relationships should primarily offer warmth, safety, and comfort. While healthy relationships should indeed provide a foundation of kindness, respect, and support, depth psychology suggests that their true purpose goes beyond comfort; it is growth. As Jung proposed, relationships act as mirrors, reflecting back our unconscious selves and challenging us to face and integrate our shadow aspects. They foster self-transformation by revealing areas of personal growth. When a relationship only serves as a security blanket, it may feel safe, but it misses the opportunity to catalyze our evolution.

Our egos crave comfort and the certainty of being right, not the discomfort of activation or the challenge of taking ownership and evolving. It is much easier (short-term gain) to believe that someone else is responsible for my feeling unloved or unappreciated than it is to sit with the reality that worth and value can be sourced from within—and that I have played a role in surrounding myself with people who reinforce those false beliefs. If building a strong sense of Self is like building a house, personal accountability is the foundation. We cannot control anyone or anything in this world except ourselves. So we must be willing to ask ourselves: What is my role in this struggle, pain, discomfort, relational dissatisfaction, or upset? In every single dynamic and situation, there is always something we can own or take responsibility for. Unfortunately, our egos are more concerned with being right than with growth. Growth requires seeing ourselves objectively and recognizing how we have contributed to our own suffering. It requires stepping out of a victim mentality and reclaiming our power, even if that means admitting our weaknesses, faults, and the ways we keep ourselves stuck.

Many spiritual and psychology teachers share that while the wound is not our fault, the healing of the wound is our responsibility. This is the hardest pill to swallow for every client I have ever worked with. Over the years, I've been accused of victim blaming and have earned the nickname the "cold water in the face" therapist from my clients and colleagues. No, we are not responsible for the traumas inflicted on us by others; we have no control over other people. But we are responsible for what we do next. We are responsible for going inward, examining our wounds, understanding how these wounds have shaped the way we show up in the world, and, most importantly, unearthing and working to course-correct the addictive tendencies and behaviors we developed as survival strategies that now block us from receiving the love we are all worthy of.

When I find myself in a space of righteousness, believing others should change for me to find peace or happiness, I frequently repeat Oprah Winfrey's famous quote: "Nothing is happening to me; it's happening for me."[7] This shift in perspective reminds me that my growth lies not in controlling others but in learning from every experience and taking full ownership of my responses.

MYTHS AS MAPS
Kali's Dance of Destruction and Rediscovering Spirit

The Hindu goddess Kali is a complex symbol, both feared and revered, embodying the dual forces of destruction and death as well as creation and salvation. She is characterized by her association with time, change, power, destruction, death, sexuality, violence, and motherly love. Kali also represents *shakti*—the divine feminine energy, creativity, and fertility.

Kali's name derives from Sanskrit, meaning "she who is black" or "she who is death," and there are several versions of her creation story found in sacred Hindu texts such as the *Devi Mahatmya* and the *Skanda Purana*. In one popular account, Durga—the warrior incarnation of Parvati, wife of the great Hindu god Shiva—becomes so enraged during a battle with the buffalo demon Mahishasura that her anger bursts from her forehead in the form of Kali. Once born, Kali's rage is uncontainable; she devours not only all demons she encounters, but also any wrongdoers, whose severed heads form the chain she wears around her neck.

No one—neither god nor human—can quell her bloodlust or halt her rampage. Fearing that Kali might destroy the entire universe,

Shiva himself lies down in her path. When Kali realizes she is standing on Shiva's chest, she finally calms down. This act illustrates the balance of destruction and creation, the wild and the divine.

Kali serves as a reminder that death, destruction, and chaos are part of the natural order, and she symbolizes the complex, multifaceted nature of the feminine within all of us. Before the rise of patriarchal societies, spiritual connections were often represented by powerful feminine figures. Jungian analyst Marie-Louise von Franz describes these archetypes as embodying "absolutely complete, yet unreflecting femininity," encompassing both nurturing and destructive aspects—from the light and sublime to the dark and fearful.[8]

Our disconnection from these fierce feminine archetypes—along with the multitudes they represent within us—mirrors our broader disconnection from the world of spirit. This separation has, in part, contributed to our modern struggles with addiction. In times of uncertainty and fear, we often seek external comforts—whether through substances, relationships, or distractions—to soothe anxieties that might once have been eased by a deeper reverence for the mysteries of the divine and an understanding of life's cyclical nature.

Rather than suggesting that ancient women did not seek distractions from life's difficulties, it is more useful to consider how modern women might reconnect with these complex, multifaceted aspects of the feminine today. Embracing the full spectrum of the feminine—including both nurturing and destructive forces—can be a path toward reclaiming power and self-awareness. By honoring these ancient archetypes like Kali, women today can begin to embrace their own complexities, recognizing that both creation and destruction are necessary for growth and transformation.

SEEING OURSELVES IN THE MYTH

Throughout this book, I have discussed the lack of initiations and rituals in modern culture and the lasting impact on emotional maturity. In the chapter on the Mother Wound, we explored how our fear of natural rhythms and cycles of death and rebirth is the root existential cause of the anxiety that drives us to try and control others. Simply put, an initiated woman understands the life-death-life cycle. She does not fear Kali or her destruction because she knows that only through destruction can new growth emerge. An initiated woman sees Kali in all of her destructive glory and understands that a complete feminine Soul has both light and dark aspects and welcomes all parts of the Self as purposeful and necessary. She accepts all the natural and human cycles of the universe.

As Clarissa Pinkola Estés writes, "One's desire for nearness, and for separations, waxes and wanes. The life/death/life nature not only teaches us to dance these, but teaches that the solution for malaise is always the opposite; so new action is the cure for boredom, closeness is the cure for loneliness, solitude is the cure for feeling cramped."[9]

For growth, newness, creativity, passion, meaning, or aliveness to flourish in our lives, we must constantly examine how our fear of withering, stagnation, lack of inspiration, lethargy, triviality, and lifelessness keeps us desperately clinging to, and attempting to control and manipulate, everything and everyone, including ourselves. Addictions arise from our inability to be with overwhelming feelings and from our ego's fear of dissolution (in other words, death). Kali reminds us of death's inevitability—not as a call to worship death, but as a challenge to transcend the ego's self-centered view of reality. Where did we learn that we should not experience fear, pain, or suffering?

When facing these fears, it can be helpful to ask ourselves some probing questions: What parts of my life or identity need to be released to make space for growth? What am I clinging to, even though I know it no longer serves me? What beliefs or behaviors must I let go of to fully embrace love and authenticity? What aspects of myself or my life do I fear confronting because they feel messy or imperfect? How can I find strength in those imperfections? What needs to end so something new can begin? What dreams or possibilities am I afraid to bring to life? And if not now, when will I finally take the leap?

GOING DEEPER

Cultivate

Moving from codependency to interdependence requires cultivating emotional resilience. This involves building the capacity to stay present with discomfort, manage anxiety, and respond consciously rather than react impulsively. Here are some strategies to start building this capacity:

1. Mindful Self-Check-ins: Set aside time daily to check in with your emotional state without judgment. Ask yourself: "What am I feeling right now?" and "Where is this feeling coming from?" This practice can help you recognize and name emotions rather than be driven by them.

2. Tolerate Uncertainty: Engage in small everyday practices that build tolerance for uncertainty. This could be something as simple as not checking your phone the moment a text arrives or delaying a decision that you feel pressured to make immediately.

3. Reframe Negative Self-Talk: When a difficult emotion arises, notice how quickly you jump to negative self-talk and gently reframe it. For instance, instead of thinking, "I can't handle this," try, "I am learning to handle discomfort and grow from it."

4. Embrace "Productive Discomfort": Seek out situations where you can practice staying present with discomfort, such as taking a cold shower or holding a challenging yoga pose. These exercises can translate into greater emotional resilience over time.

Examine the Rules
Reflect on the unspoken (or spoken) rules that have shaped your behaviors and beliefs. Consider the following:

- What were some of the unspoken rules in your family? What about the rules you learned from society?

- How did you know these were rules?

- In what ways do these rules still impact you today?

- Is it possible to begin establishing your own rules? Start noticing the behaviors and actions influenced by rules that were imposed on you but were never truly yours.

Own Your Part
Notice the ways you put yourself in the victim space, where you give away your power. When you feel slighted, annoyed, angry, upset, or resentful, take a breath and notice how the thoughts immediately turn to the other person—what they did wrong, how they upset you, what they should do differently. Now, ask yourself, "What is my part in this? What is my 100 percent?" Even if you believe you did nothing wrong, challenge yourself to sit with that question. Owning even a tiny part of the dynamic is a significant step toward strengthening the muscle of personal responsibility and ownership. If you walk into every tough dynamic with the understanding that there is *always* something you can own (this means owning your part, not owning more than is yours), it quiets the ego a bit and allows you to show up as a more mature and integrated Self.

10

belonging to ourselves

> "The building of the true and beautiful means
> the destruction of the good enough."
>
> —Glennon Doyle, *Untamed*[1]

As I sat down in the chair and laid my arm across the table, every fiber of my being screamed, "Nope! Don't do this. I don't like this. I want to leave!" I turned my face away as the tattoo gun started up, and the familiar deep scraping sensation began on the small spot next to my inner elbow. The actual process of receiving the tattoo was quick and only mildly irritating. After he wrapped my arm in plastic wrap, I got up, gave him my credit card, and left, never uttering a single complaint or expressing any dissatisfaction.

Earlier that week, my sister had come to visit me in Los Angeles during the early days of the pandemic. My daughter had been born only four months earlier, just as the city went into lockdown, and neither my brother nor my sister had met their niece yet. We spent our time walking outside, sitting in parks, and visiting places that were still open as long as everyone was masked. It was early enough in the pandemic that we were unaware of the severity of what would unfold over the next few years. One morning, my sister suggested getting small matching tattoos. I loved the idea, and we found small, delicate images of hands, one holding a sun and the other a moon, which we felt beautifully represented our personalities and connection. I searched online for tattoo studios, finding most of them closed, except for one in Highland Park. Usually I would research tattoo artists to death, but I thought, "Meh, Highland Park is a cool neighborhood. I'm sure they're fine for a small single-needle tattoo." We hopped in the car during my daughter's nap and drove over.

The moment we stepped into the studio, my body tightened. The tattoo artist, the only one working, listened to what we wanted and glanced at the pictures we showed him.

"Oh, that's easy! I can totally do that. And yeah, I work with single needle!" His energy felt erratic, and he made a few comments to my little sister that had a sexual undertone, with a laugh. He was pushy and seemed irritated as I emphasized that we wanted something delicate, fine-lined, and small. "Yes, I will make it single needle and just like the picture. It's easy," he insisted.

In reality, the tattoo turned out thick, black, and most certainly NOT single needle. It is the darkest and thickest tattoo I have, so much so that when I consulted with a laser removal center, they told me it would be very difficult to remove, and some of it would likely remain.

Since that experience, which lasted all of thirty minutes in 2020, I refer to my "ugly tattoo" regularly in my client sessions and codependency groups when discussing people-pleasing and the ways we override our body's signals to keep the peace, be liked, avoid upsetting people, or protect someone else's ego—all in the name of keeping ourselves safe. This may not have been a hugely traumatic or dangerous situation, but that's not the point. We begin self-abandoning in small ways from a young age, becoming so disconnected from our intuition that we barely register its signals, let alone act on them. We are so desperate to be chosen that we actively reject ourselves at every turn.

THE "CHOOSE ME" WOUND

> "I wanted to be a good girl, so I tried to control myself. I chose a personality, a body, a faith, and a sexuality so tiny I had to hold my breath to fit myself inside."
>
> —Glennon Doyle, *Untamed*[2]

One of the deepest wounds I see among my female clients is what I call the "choose me" wound. For many of us, the fear of abandonment and rejection drives our codependent ways of relating to one another. In a patriarchal society, women are taught that they are nothing if not partnered, while this same emphasis on partnership is not applied to men. We see it in the language we use: Men are playboys, but women are sluts. Men are celebrated for their sexual conquests, but women are shamed for having too many partners. Men joke about wives being a "ball and chain," while women are told their wedding day is the most important and special day of their lives. We might not use the term "spinster" anymore, but the message remains: find and be chosen by a man, or there is something wrong with you. Regardless of sexual orientation, our culture of mononormativity tells us that coupled is better than single and that one committed, lifelong partnership is better than multiple. Monogamously partnered is not only considered the base line, but is also portrayed as the ultimate source of satisfaction, love, and worthiness.

This belief—that women are nothing if not partnered—combined with the belief that we need to be chosen to have value shapes the way we groom our little girls to be good, quiet, agreeable, sweet, and perfect. Being taught to be a "good girl" fosters people-pleasing and perfectionist tendencies rooted in the belief that our value lies in how others perceive us. Although talked about in different ways, perfectionism, people-pleasing, and the "choose me" wound are all wrapped up together in one pretty little package. Performing, pretending, and not showing up authentically in order to be more likeable or agreeable are tactics to shield and protect against the pain of blame, judgment, shame, failure, and imperfection. We learn that we must sing for our supper, perform for our love and belonging. Raising our girls through the lens of perfectionism and performance creates women who are driven by the fear of failure, fear of vulnerability, and a lack of resilience.

If patriarchy would have us believe that a woman's value is in being chosen by a man, then women will spend much of their energy on finding a man, locking down a relationship, and maintaining it at all costs. This is a perfect way to keep women preoccupied with external validation instead of focusing on self-development, nurturing community, or seeking deeper Soul fulfillment. It also leads us to see people as objects whose sole purpose is to make us feel seen and valued. I have seen many women desperately struggle to find a partner, only to find one and then wish the partner was different. Many talk about "falling in love with potential" as if it were a virtuous trait, but in many ways, it is quite self-serving. Due to our conditioning, many of us believe it is better to be in a "good enough" relationship, hoping to mold the other person into who we want them to be, than to be alone and self-partnered.

TRANSACTION AND OWNERSHIP

Relating to each other from a place of fear is not love. Fear and love cannot coexist, just as judgment and curiosity cannot thrive together. When we engage with others driven by a frantic fear of being alone, a compulsion to be chosen to find value, or anxiety over abandonment or rejection, we end up clinging, controlling, and struggling to see and love the other person for who they truly are. This leads to inauthenticity, a lack of intimacy, and behaviors rooted in self-abandonment. It leads to *codependency*. When we source our worth and sense of belonging from another person, and they do the same, it creates a transactional relationship dynamic. It creates a dynamic of objectification in which we stop seeing the other person as an individual Soul with their own dreams and desires but as an object to serve our needs.

Transactional relationships rooted in fear say:

- "I will do for you if you do for me."

- "I will wait for you to act before I act."

- "I will love you if you behave in the way I feel you should."

- "You will stay the same and not evolve or grow so you don't reflect back to me the ways in which I need to evolve or grow."

- "You should always make me feel seen, heard, and loved, regardless of what is happening for you."

- "You are mine (i.e., I own you)."

Relational connections rooted in love say:

- "I will act out of love without needing something in return."

- "I will be brave and honest with both you and myself, always."

- "You are free to be yourself, and I am free to be myself."

- "I will support your growth, evolution, and happiness, even when it challenges me to grow and evolve in return."

- "I will strive to see, hear, and love you, even when I am struggling."

- "I recognize that you are your own person, and you don't owe me constant validation or attention. We are both responsible for our own emotional well-being."

- "You are a sovereign being. I do not own you."

HARD IS BETTER THAN NUMB

Sam, a thirty-five-year-old Venezuelan American with three small children, came to me struggling to process her partner's infidelity. The revelation of his affair had completely destabilized her. Anxiety attacks, sleepless nights, and tears filled each day. He wanted to work things out, she wasn't sure. While she felt terrified of the idea of their marriage ending, she confessed that discovering the affair had awakened something in her.

"I don't even think I'm mad at him, if I'm being honest. I kind of understand why he did it. I'm actually kind of jealous. I wish it had been me that had the affair."

"What about it makes you jealous?" I asked.

"For the few months it was going on, he looked and acted in a way that I haven't seen in probably ten years, or maybe ever. He laughed more, went back to the gym, demanded a long overdue promotion at work and got it. He was more present with the kids. Even though I now know he was sleeping with someone else the whole time, I loved the person he seemed to be becoming. And I wish I could become a version of that myself. All of my friends and my mom want me to hate him. They want me to divorce him and throw him out. But I don't think that's what I want. And I don't hate him."

"It sounds like he shattered the veneer. Like he couldn't stand the cage you both had put yourselves in, and he was the one who broke the lock first. Maybe you're jealous that he seemed to be braver than you in that way."

"*Yes*. I feel like I've been in a cage for the past six years, at least. I don't remember who I am; I don't do anything for myself anymore. I'm so consumed with the kids and the house that I haven't read a book cover to cover in years. I find myself not wanting my kids to touch me, let alone him, and then swimming in shame about it for hours. I ask myself regularly, 'Is this it?' Is this what the rest of my life will feel like? And then I argue with myself. I should be grateful. He's a good guy. A good provider. A good dad." Sam started to cry.

"Do you feel inspired by him?"

"No."

"Are you curious about him, what's going on in his deeper world?"

"Not up until recently I wasn't, no."

"Do you want what's best for him, even if that's the seemingly harder thing?"

"Yes, I do actually. I really care about him as a person."

"Are you inspired by yourself?"

"God, no."

"What about curious about yourself?"

"Yes, right now for the first time, yes."

"Do you want what is best for yourself, even if that's the seemingly harder thing?"

"Yes. And I'm okay with it being hard. For the first time in my life, I think I'm realizing hard is better than numb."

"Good. We can work with that."

BREADCRUMBS ARE NOT A MEAL

Sam's realization that "hard is better than numb" reflects a deeper truth about relationships: settling for comfort, for the sake of security or fear of loss, often leads to emotional stagnation and deep dissatisfaction. Her journey mirrors a much larger pattern we all face: the choice between the difficult work of self-discovery and the numbing safety of external validation.

If we are convinced that being partnered is better than being alone—that being chosen is where we find our value—we settle for breadcrumbs and "good enough" relationships. This is true for all relationships, not just romantic ones. And this is true for all of us, not only women. The pipeline of the choose me wound to codependent and transactional relationships maintains the patriarchal and misogynistic social order. It keeps us tethered to external validation, afraid to explore the depths of our own love and our Soul's potential. Men, too, are trapped in this system, conditioned to derive worth from achievement, status, or control, reinforcing structures that value possession over authenticity.

Our fear prevents us from showing ourselves fully because "What if they leave?" Well, what if they do? Until you can sit with the fear and pain of that thought and not allow it to govern your actions, you will never live or love authentically. A relationship sustained only by the fear of loss is not a relationship; it is an attachment. You must begin the process of choosing yourself in micro moments until your sense of Self becomes so strong that relating out of fear feels more painful than the potential end of a relationship.

MYTHS AS MAPS
Eros and Psyche, the Eternal Story of Love and the Soul

The myth of Psyche and Eros, which appears in Greek art as early as the fourth century BC, has been retold through poetry, drama, and opera across the centuries. Psyche, whose name means "soul" or "breath of life," is the youngest and most beautiful daughter of a King and Queen. So captivating is her beauty that mortals begin praying to her instead of Aphrodite, the goddess of love. Enraged, Aphrodite asks her son, Eros—known also by his Roman name, Cupid, representing desire and life force energy—to exact revenge by making Psyche fall in love with a hideous creature. However, Eros accidentally pricks himself with his own arrow and falls deeply in love with Psyche instead.

Despite being worshiped by many, Psyche remains unmarried. She represents the uninitiated and immature Maiden—desired only for her physical beauty and the projections that men place upon her, without any understanding or desire to know her true Self. Her father, distraught over her unmarried state, prays to the gods for a husband for his daughter. The oracle, responding to his plea, instructs him to prepare Psyche for a marriage that symbolically demands her death, a rite of passage indicating her initiation into womanhood. This metaphorical union of marriage and death speaks to the profound transformation she must undergo.

Rather than being thrown into the sea as foretold, the west wind carries Psyche to a meadow, where she is lulled into a deep sleep. Upon awakening, she discovers a magnificent palace that fulfills all her earthly desires. There, she is united with Eros in a secret marriage, though she is never allowed to see her husband in the light. Each night, Eros, cloaked in darkness, comes to her bed, where they consummate their union. Psyche, never allowed to see her lover, falls in love with her own projection of who he might be, becoming pregnant in the process.

Over time, Psyche becomes restless and, missing her previous earthly life, begs her still unknown love to allow her sisters to visit her. Jealous of her luxurious surroundings, her sisters, who can be seen as embodiments of Psyche's shadow, or the unacknowledged aspects of herself, convince her that she needs to see her lover's face, lest he be a monster destined to devour her and her unborn child. Psyche's curiosity and doubt lead her to light an oil lamp one night, revealing the beautiful Eros. In her shock, she accidentally pricks her finger on one of his arrows, spilling hot oil that wakes him. Feeling betrayed, Eros flees to his mother Aphrodite, leaving Psyche grief-stricken.

Furious at her son for marrying a mortal, Aphrodite devises four seemingly impossible tasks for Psyche, with her handmaidens Worry and Sadness sent to torment her along the way. Psyche's journey through these trials symbolizes the path of individuation—the process of integrating the unconscious with the conscious Self and transforming from the naïve Maiden into a mature, self-aware woman. Each task represents a challenge that mirrors the psychological journey of death and rebirth. With the aid of compassionate gods and beings, Psyche successfully completes the first three tasks and, on the fourth, ventures into the Underworld to retrieve a dose of beauty for Aphrodite.

Moved by Psyche's perseverance, Eros intervenes and seeks the help of Zeus, who convinces Aphrodite to relent. Zeus grants Psyche immortality, making her and Eros equals and legitimizing their marriage. In time, Psyche gives birth to a daughter named Pleasure, or

Bliss in some translations, symbolizing the fulfillment that arises from a fully realized Self and the union of love and Soul.

SEEING OURSELVES IN THE MYTH

> "The developmental tasks for a woman are to recognize the disclaimed and dissociated authority, competence, goodness, and/or power that she has seen as belonging to others, and to dissolve the persona of adolescent femininity."
>
> —Polly Young-Eisendrath, *The Cambridge Companion to Jung*[3]

Jung often spoke about the widespread spiritual crisis in modern times, a crisis born from our disconnection from the feminine and the divine coupled with an over-identification with the hypermasculine world of materialism and logic. This crisis leads to a profound emptiness, giving rise to anxiety, despair, a sense of meaninglessness, and addiction. This emptiness is what propels us into a longing for Eros—a longing for desire, love, and life force energy.

Through the myth of Eros and Psyche, we learn that Eros, while initially taking the form of passionate love, ultimately represents our desire for wholeness, transformation, and deep interconnection with both other humans and the divine. This yearning, if answered, propels us on a journey, a quest for wholeness marked by many trials, just as Psyche faced her four tasks. Each of these trials mirrors the cycle of death and rebirth, something we have seen in almost all our myths: entering into the darkness (the liminal space), confronting our shadow, and emerging as a more mature and integrated version of ourselves. Psyche's journey shows us that through real love—love for Self, for the divine, and for others—the Soul achieves union with the divine.

This love is not purely romantic. It is a love that transforms us at our core. The path from Maiden, the immature feminine, to mature Mother or Queen requires the grief and reckoning that come with realizing that we belong only to ourselves. It demands the understanding that where there is power over another, there cannot be love. No amount of being chosen by another will heal the wounds of attachment; these wounds are ours to soothe and, ultimately, to heal.

GOING DEEPER

Micro Moments

In my work with clients, I often emphasize the significance of micro moments—those small, everyday decisions where we choose ourselves. Each time we say no when our initial response is to say yes; each time we set and hold a boundary, even when we fear it might upset someone; each time we honestly tell someone, "That hurt my feelings" or "Please don't speak to me that way"; each time we say, "Actually, I've changed my mind. Thanks anyway," and leave the tattoo parlor, we lay a single brick on the foundation of a strong sense of Self. This foundation is built on personal accountability, trust, and authenticity.

Many people think inner work, self-development, or the path of individuation is forged in big aha moments or life-altering changes, but I strongly disagree. While those moments can be transformative, it is in the day-to-day micro moments where lasting change truly takes root. Every time we stand at those crossroads and tell our inner Self that we are listening, that we trust ourselves, that we respect and value ourselves enough to choose what feels true, we strengthen that foundation. No matter the consequence. Over time, these micro moments accumulate and shift our lives toward alignment with our authentic selves, making us braver, more grounded, and more self-assured.

Reflect

Write out and sit with some of the following questions and journal your responses: How much of my life do I feel is by my own design, and how much feels like I am just going along for the ride? What beliefs do I have about myself, relationships, and the world around me that are mine, and which ones have been passed down to me by family, culture, or society? How have these inherited beliefs shaped my choices today, and how might I consciously choose to reshape them? When was the last time I truly chose myself? In what relationships and interactions do I feel a sense of expansion, and in which do I feel contracted? Where and how do I perform in order to be liked? And finally, ask yourself: If I were perfect, would I matter more?

Feel All of It
Remember, as I mentioned in the introduction, "feelings are the portal"—the gateway to deeper understanding and transformation. I invite you to practice turning toward your uncomfortable feelings rather than distracting yourself or shying away from them. Head on. Arms wide open. If the reflection prompts brought up fear, anxiety, or a lump in your throat, this is good. Close your eyes and meditate on where you feel these emotions in your body—on the sensation of that lump, on the tightness in your chest. Be with it. Hold it gently, without judgment. Do not try to change it or make it go away. When we allow ourselves to fully experience and move through these sensations, we dissolve the power they hold over us. Remember, accepting Baba Yaga's hunger and Kali's destruction is part of reclaiming the Wild Woman within. The path to becoming an individuated woman—an authentic Self—includes embracing all aspects of ourselves, even those that feel uncomfortable or dark.

Commit
As you move forward, I encourage you to commit to practicing these steps daily. Choose one micro moment, one reflection question, or one emotional practice to engage with each day for the next week. Journal what you notice, what you feel, and what shifts begin to happen within you. This is how we build the muscles of self-belonging—one small choice at a time.

11

is it love or fear?

"No one will listen to us until we listen to ourselves."
—Marianne Williamson, *A Woman's Worth*[1]

Annoyance, irritation, anger, and even rage. This is what floods my body every time John expresses a 'need.' Every time he asks for praise, gentleness, acknowledgment of my harsh or mothering tone, or more physical affection, I feel repulsed. It's not just anger; it's a visceral recoil. Sitting across from him, hearing him ask for more acknowledgment, more touch, I want to scream. If we have one more conversation about our different love languages, I might scream."

"Vanessa, when was the last time you asked John for something?" My therapist's eyes were kind and concerned, which somehow only made me angrier.

"I know that's a trick question because of course the answer is probably almost never. I feel like I don't even know I have a need until it's not met or until I'm resentful. It's like I don't even know I have a boundary until it's been crossed and I'm suddenly pissed. All I know is I'm over here doing my best to care for a two-year-old, grow a new career, keep the house going, have friends, work out when I can, and he wants me to be more physically affectionate. I could punch him. He gets so upset about all of this, and I struggle to even feel empathy. I feel annoyed. I just want to tell him to stop being so damn needy, and then maybe I would want to lean in more. I'm a horrible person."

My therapist leaned in, unflinching. "You're not a horrible person; you're a person who grew up having to take care of everyone else's emotional needs, so when someone expresses their needs now or makes you feel like you aren't doing enough even though you feel like you're drowning, you get enraged. Your inner little girl gets enraged. Or maybe your adult Self gets enraged on behalf of your little girl, who probably wasn't allowed to be angry. This feeling isn't going to go away until you learn to feel that anger in a healthy way and express it. Until you learn how to feel into a boundary and firmly uphold it. Until you learn how to unapologetically ask for *your* needs to be met. Regardless of the feared outcome."

THE UNSPOKEN AGREEMENT

Through a lot of therapy and personal accountability practice in my relationships, I realized how deeply ingrained my tendency to overfunction was. Like so many women, I had been conditioned to believe that rescuing and meeting others' needs was not only my responsibility, but a measure of my worth as a human.

While overfunctioning and underfunctioning are not inherently gendered roles, societal norms often create an imbalance. In patriarchal societies, women are frequently groomed to overfunction, taught that their value lies in caregiving and rescuing. Misogynistic pseudoscience tells us women are the "natural-born caretakers," while socially constructed gender norms reinforce the idea that it's a woman's responsibility to meet everyone's needs. This conditioning leads many women to overfunction, striving for perfection and feeling overwhelmed by the expectation to be all things to all people, often at the expense of their own needs. Simultaneously, this same trap keeps men infantilized, disconnected from their emotions, and deeply unhappy, as they may underfunction in areas of emotional connection or domestic life.

Both overfunctioning and underfunctioning are behavioral responses to anxiety, fear of vulnerability and getting hurt, and difficulty communicating needs. They are both learned through family dynamics and societal conditioning and become deeply ingrained over time. If I am uncomfortable with others' struggles or big emotions, or I fear losing control, I will most likely overfunction as a way to soothe these anxieties. Conversely, if I am disconnected from my emotions or feel inadequate, believing I lack the ability or resilience to take care of myself, I will most likely underfunction, avoiding responsibility or relying on others for support.

These patterns are not fixed. People can fluctuate between overfunctioning and underfunctioning in different areas of their lives. Someone might overfunction at work but underfunction at home, or overfunction in day-to-day home management and underfunction in emotional communication and intimacy in the relationship. However, relationships often create a polarity; partners, friends, or colleagues tend to gravitate toward opposite roles, providing necessary friction for growth. One person may pull away emotionally, while the other leans in. If one bases their value on fixing and doing, the other may unconsciously agree that they need to be fixed. Two overfunctioners or two underfunctioners rarely form a dynamic together, just as two anxiously attached or two avoidantly attached individuals rarely pair up. It happens, but not often.

Contrary to the fairy tales where princes rescue princesses, it's often women in heteronormative dynamics who end up doing the saving. We are bombarded with images of damsels in distress, yet we simultaneously build our identities around the roles of savior, martyr, and caretaker. From a young age, many women learn to equate being needed with being loved, being delicate and demure with being female, and being chosen with being enough. This conditioning begins early, which is why I carefully monitor what my young daughter watches.

(Non-tablet moms, don't come for me. We're all out here doing the best we can!) I block any content with keywords like "wedding," "mother," "babies," "princess," or "rescued" that reinforces these outdated notions of womanhood, motherhood, and masculinity. Even today, the shows our little ones watch force-feed them patriarchal ideas of what it means to be a woman, mom, or a man.

CAREGIVING VERSUS CARETAKING

When I talk about stepping back and examining the ways we unconsciously try to fix and save in my therapy groups, I often get pushback from people who think I am saying we should not care for the people in our lives. Please hear me when I say there is nothing wrong with being a caring person. The problem begins when the caring is driven by low self-worth, a need to be needed, and a compulsion to create dependency—making oneself indispensable to provide a sense of safety, security, identity, and purpose. There is a big difference between caregiving and caretaking. One comes from a place of selflessness and love; the other comes from a place of fear and self-preservation.

To explore whether you are caregiving or caretaking, here are some questions to ask yourself:

- **Why am I doing this?** Is it because I genuinely want to support and empower the other person, or is it because I fear they might not need me if I don't? Caregiving feels like a choice; caretaking feels like an obligation or a compulsion.

- **How do I feel when the other person is struggling or uncomfortable?** Am I able to hold space for them without needing to jump in and fix it, trusting they have the capacity to handle their own emotions and challenges? Or do I feel anxious and compelled to step in, fearing what might happen if I don't?

- **Am I respecting their autonomy?** Caregiving allows the other person to make their own choices, even if they are different from what I think is best. Caretaking often involves overstepping boundaries, offering unsolicited advice, or trying to control the situation to make oneself feel safer.

- **How do I feel after helping?** If I feel drained, resentful, or frustrated after offering help, it might indicate caretaking rather than caregiving. Caregiving is energizing and rooted in mutual respect; caretaking can leave you feeling exhausted and unappreciated.

Reflecting on these distinctions can help you recognize whether your actions are grounded in love and connection or driven by a deeper need to control, be needed, or prove your worth. When you notice patterns of caretaking, it's an invitation to pause, reflect, and ask yourself what you truly need at that moment. Often, it's a signal to turn inward and focus on self-care and self-reflection.

In relationships built on dependency, there is danger for both the underfunctioner and the overfunctioner. In Harriet Lerner's book *The Dance of Anger*, she says of overfunctioners, "We may become reactive to every move that a person makes or fails to make, our emotions ranging from annoyance to intense anger or despair."[2] She continues, "The problem arises when we are excessively reactive to other people's problems, when we assume responsibility for things that we are not responsible for, and when we attempt to control things that are not in our control."[3] Not only are we stewing in our frustration and anger, but we are perpetuating the belief that we are victims of our circumstances, believing we have less control than we actually do. Stepping out of the overfunctioning role and changing our behavior, no matter the consequence, takes enormous strength and self-respect.

EMPATHY WITHOUT BOUNDARIES IS SELF-DESTRUCTION

Another common pushback I hear from clients is the justification of their codependent ways of relating by saying it's because they are an empath or a highly sensitive person. Many of us are hypervigilant to others' behaviors and moods because we had to be growing up. We obsess over what others are doing, saying, feeling, or needing as a way to avoid focusing on ourselves. This hypervigilance, often framed as "being an empath," begins as a survival mechanism to protect ourselves, but evolves into a way to escape our own discomfort with others' emotions. While all humans have mirror neurons that help us attune to others, empathy without boundaries is self-destruction. Being an empath is real, but it's not a spiritual gift bestowed upon us; it's a learned skill, often born from trauma.

There is nothing inherently wrong with any of these ways of being in relationships. It all comes down to the level of consciousness with which we examine and embody them. If either person in a dynamic becomes aware of their motivations and begins to challenge the existing patterns, it can upset the balance. Often, this disruption is exactly what is needed for both personal and relational evolution.

STEALING THEIR GROWTH AND STUNTING OUR OWN

> "If we're caretaking in the kitchen, we're probably caretaking in the bedroom."
>
> —Melody Beattie, *Codependent No More*[4]

No one likes to think of themselves as controlling or manipulative, yet this is often the essence of codependency. Many overfunctioning codependents *create* dependency in their relationships (including in their children) to avoid the fear of abandonment. Though usually unconscious and not overtly malicious, this dynamic involves significant manipulation and control. Overfunctioners often perform emotional gymnastics to avoid recognizing how self-serving their behavior is, instead casting themselves as the victim. To break this cycle, they must confront the reality that they are perpetuating the belief that others cannot care for themselves.

By constantly stepping in to provide what we believe others need, we end up overworking ourselves and underworking them. In our efforts to keep everyone else content, we deprive others of the opportunity to experience the stress, pain, or discomfort necessary for growth. When we swoop in and fix things or offer unsolicited feedback and advice, we send the message that we don't believe they have the ability to manage their challenges or grow. Over time, people start to believe you. They internalize this belief and stop trying because, consciously or unconsciously, they think, "Why bother? They do it better than I ever could." In this way, enabling becomes love turned to fear and help turned to control.

Control isn't always overt. Sometimes we proclaim our dependence, declaring ourselves the victim, weak or helpless to our circumstances. This can be a subtle form of manipulation, using guilt or pity to exert control. Ultimately, codependency is a self-defeating cycle. We have zero control over no one but ourselves. Attempts to rescue or control might work temporarily, but eventually, others push back because no one likes to be controlled. This pushback activates our fear of not being enough, not being needed, not having value, and ultimately being abandoned, perpetuating the cycle as we double down on our efforts to control.

When clients express feeling unseen, overworked, underappreciated, like a doormat, or like people only value them for what they do for them, I ask them to examine how they might be obstructing their own needs by stunting others' growth. This is part of owning "your 100 percent." While this accountability isn't always conscious, it's essential if we are to evolve.

To break free from these self-defeating cycles, we need to shift our approach from rescuing to supporting, creating space for both parties to grow. Instead of rushing to provide solutions or soothe discomfort, try asking open-ended questions that encourage others to articulate their needs and brainstorm their own solutions. For example, asking, "What do you think would help in this situation?" or saying, "I trust your judgment on this" promotes independence and reinforces their capacity to handle challenges. Practice sitting with your discomfort while allowing others to experience theirs; this fosters resilience. I tell my clients, the next time someone comes to you seeking your input, start by asking, "Would you like advice, or do you just need to vent?" This shows respect for their autonomy and nurtures problem-solving skills. By shifting from control to support, we empower others to grow, fostering healthier, more balanced relationships where both sides can thrive.

HIDING BEHIND OUR CODEPENDENT ROLES

If, during childhood, we learned to only express feelings that were acceptable to our caregivers, we also learned that showing needs or being "needy" would lead to judgment or shame. To avoid disapproval and disappointment, we kept our needs hidden, a strategy that often extends into adulthood, manifesting as low self-esteem, self-worth, or self-awareness. We bury our needs and develop coping strategies, such as overfunctioning or underfunctioning, to sidestep these uncomfortable feelings.

When we engage in the dance of overfunctioning and underfunctioning, neither party truly learns to know themselves. One hides from self-reflection by staying preoccupied with predicting the needs of the other person, while the other avoids introspection because someone else is managing it for them. Both remain disconnected from their true selves, failing to develop the skills needed to identify, communicate, and fulfill their needs, either independently or through healthy interdependence.

In *Facing Codependence*, Pia Mellody describes four common categories of how people relate to their wants and needs, particularly in the context of codependency:

1. **Too Dependent**: Knows what their wants and needs are, but expects others to fulfill them, leading to dependency and a lack of personal responsibility for one's emotional well-being.

2. **Antidependent**: Recognizes their needs and wants, but insists on meeting them alone, avoiding vulnerability or the discomfort of asking for help. This often results in isolation and burnout.

3. **Needless and Wantless**: Has wants and needs, but is unaware of them, often due to conditioning that suppresses or ignores them, leading to disconnection from oneself.

4. **Confused Needs and Wants**: Knows what they want, but not what they truly need. For example, they might seek comfort in material possessions ("stuff") when what they actually need is emotional or physical nurturing.

These categories illustrate how codependency distorts our relationship with our own needs and wants. A healthy approach to wants and needs involves recognizing, articulating, and taking responsibility for them in a balanced way. This would be a fifth category, where a person:

- **Identifies and Communicates Needs and Wants Effectively**: Being aware of and differentiating between needs and wants, and expressing them clearly. They understand the importance of meeting their own needs while also being open to receiving help or support in a reciprocal, non-demanding way. This requires **self-awareness, self-responsibility, and interdependence**.

This takes *a lot* of work for many, if not most, of us to achieve. Recognizing where we fall within these categories can be a helpful step toward removing the shame of disconnection from ourselves. Knowing I am not alone in these struggles has allowed me to offer myself grace while committing to the work needed to reconnect with my true needs. For example, I have come to understand that expecting others to read our minds, instead of doing the hard work to know the Self, is closely connected to the Mother Wound. It reflects our longing for that ideal parent who would see us, attune to us, and know us so deeply that they could anticipate our needs. But we cannot assign this task to others; they are not our parents and cannot heal that wound for us.

WE ARE NOT NEEDS-MEETING MACHINES

Over the past few years, there has been a lot of conversation in the wellness and therapy world about needs. What are your needs? Are you communicating your needs? Is your partner, friend, or family member meeting your needs? If not, why? Do you have different love languages? Can you adjust yourself or ask that they adjust themselves so you are better equipped to meet each other's needs? While I am glad we are having these conversations, I believe they often continue the ingrained, codependent ways of relating by focusing on three problematic areas: 1) not knowing the difference between needs and wants, 2) expecting those in our relationships to meet our needs, and 3) overemphasizing reparenting and co-regulation in our adult relationships, especially our romantic ones, as the primary means of meeting our needs.

We all have needs and wants. Needs are essential for survival—food, water, clothing, shelter. Wants, on the other hand, are things that enhance our lives but are not necessary for survival, like spontaneity, good communication, and shared interests. While some might argue that things like emotional safety or intimacy are needs (and according to Maslow's hierarchy, they can be), for the purpose of this discussion, I classify them as wants because, as adults, we are primarily responsible for ensuring they are met ourselves. We cannot *expect* another person to fulfill them for us.

For example, consider my clients Andrew, a second-generation Mexican American man, and Scott, a white man, both forty-four. Through the deeply ingrained patterns of over- and underfunctioning that were eroding their relationship, we unpacked a scenario where Andrew was engrossed in a project in his office, and Scott came home eager to share some exciting news. Scott was frustrated that Andrew didn't stop immediately to listen. This is a perfect example of a want—not a need.

Scott expressed, "I have a need in my relationships to feel prioritized and listened to." Fair enough. But my question to Scott was, "Is there room in your desire to feel prioritized to also respect your partner's needs in that moment?" Andrew's need to focus on his work at that time is just as valid. Emotional maturity means recognizing that sometimes we have to wait to share something, even if it feels disappointing. It's about balancing our wants with an awareness of our partner's needs.

When we expect another person to constantly fulfill our needs or, as I call it, function as our "needs-meeting machine," we place them in a parental role, making them responsible for our emotional equanimity and fulfillment, which are ultimately our own responsibilities as adults. As children, our parents ideally met our needs, often at the expense of their own, and could intuit what we needed before we were able to express it. In adult relationships, it is wonderful to feel seen, heard, or supported by a partner or friend, but these are not things we can *demand*.

Returning to Scott and Andrew's situation, if there is a recurring pattern where one partner consistently prioritizes work over everything else, dismisses the other, or shows little interest despite efforts to communicate, this reflects a difference in values and priorities, not a failure to meet needs. Even then, being listened to and prioritized are still wants. The important distinction here is that once you understand how your partner behaves, you can decide how to proceed.

Continuing to expect change from someone who has shown they are unwilling to meet certain wants is a form of self-abandonment. This is where boundaries, non-negotiables, and personal empowerment come into play. You can make decisions about whether the relationship aligns with your values rather than staying in a victim narrative, waiting for the other person to change. It may feel difficult, but this is where true empowerment lies.

This is a tough pill to swallow for many people. You might feel upset, angry, or even inclined to put the book down and dismiss everything I've said so far. I understand that reaction; I've encountered it many times when discussing this topic. A codependent society teaches us we are entitled to certain behaviors from others, and we have a right to demand them. It also conditions us to feel like victims of our circumstances rather than empowered agents of change. But remember, transactional relationships are about what I can get from you, while interdependence is about reciprocity. If reciprocity is not present, then there is no true relationship.

MYTHS AS MAPS
Demeter and Persephone, the Balance of Nurture and Surrender

In Greek mythology, Demeter is the Earth Mother, the goddess of fertility, harvest, and agriculture. She is often depicted with symbols of flowers, fruit, and grain, embodying the nurturing aspects of the earth. Demeter and her daughter, Persephone, were frequently worshipped together, emphasizing their inseparable bond.

The myth tells us that Demeter loves her daughter Persephone deeply. She keeps all men away from her only daughter, driven by a fierce desire to protect her. Hades, god of the Underworld, falls in love with Persephone but knows that Demeter would never approve of their union. He goes to Zeus, Persephone's father, for permission to marry her, and Zeus consents. One day, when Demeter allows Persephone to pick flowers with her friends, Hades seizes the opportunity. As Persephone strays far from her mother, the ground opens up, and Hades emerges from the Underworld in his chariot. He kidnaps Persephone and takes her back with him to be his queen.

For nine days, Demeter searches for her daughter, until the crone Hecate tells her she heard Persephone's cries but did not see where she was taken. Together, they approach Helios, the sun god who sees all of Earth. Helios reveals that Hades, with Zeus's blessing, abducted Persephone. Enraged and heartbroken, Demeter abandons her earthly duties. In some versions, she forgets them in her grief; in others, she purposefully stops in retaliation. Regardless, the earth begins to wither: seasons halt, harvests fail, no child is born, and famine spreads. The cries of humanity eventually reach Zeus, and faced with the extinction of life on Earth, he sends Hermes to the Underworld to bring Persephone back.

However, Hades tricks Persephone into eating a few pomegranate seeds (in some versions, she eats them willingly), knowing that anyone who consumes food from the Underworld is bound to it. In protest, Demeter threatens to let the world die. As a compromise, Zeus decides that Persephone will spend half the year on Earth with her mother and the other half in the Underworld with Hades as his queen.

SEEING OURSELVES IN THE MYTH

Like all myths and archetypal figures, there are many versions of the story of Demeter and Persephone, and just as many interpretations. Here, I want to focus on the relationship between Demeter and Persephone and the archetype of initiation seen in Persephone's kidnapping (yes, another map for initiation. Are you starting to see the pattern?).

On the surface, we see a loving relationship between mother and daughter. However, in some versions of the myth, Demeter's protectiveness borders on smothering. She reluctantly lets Persephone out of her sight only after much pleading and arguing. Archetypally, Demeter knows her daughter must face challenges to grow, but she resists letting go out of her own fear. Yet, despite her efforts, the very thing she fears most happens: Persephone is kidnapped. This event symbolizes a challenge that Demeter cannot solve for her daughter, highlighting the unavoidable journey each person must undertake toward self-realization. The support of Zeus can metaphorically represent the support of life itself, suggesting that great pain and challenges are often necessary steps on the path to maturity.

Persephone's abduction serves as a metaphor for the inner struggles within the journey of maturation, the conflicts between the Self and the act of leaving or differentiating from the Mother. This is why Persephone became the goddess of the Eleusinian Mysteries, the annual Greek initiation rituals that honored both Demeter and Persephone. These rituals, open only to women, represented a door to unknown worlds and the evolution of the psyche through initiatory rites.

The Eleusinian Mysteries were considered the most famous yet most secret religious rites in ancient Greece. Though the details of these rites were fiercely protected, with some accounts suggesting that anyone discovered trying to infiltrate the three-day-long ritual would be torn apart and killed, we know the Mysteries symbolized the myth of Demeter and Persephone. They included three phases: the descent, the search, and the ascent. These phases guided women initiates through a transformative path that mirrored the age-old cycle of death and rebirth while also paying homage to the stages of Maiden to Mother to Crone.

This cycle is not only natural, but imperative for growth (and not necessarily gendered). For those of us who hold too tightly to our loved ones, attempting to shield them, and ourselves, from the anxiety, trials, struggles, and pain *necessary* for spiritual and emotional evolution, we ensure not only more struggle for ourselves, but an unhealthy dependency in those we aim to protect. Each person has their own path and journey, and no one gets to dictate what that journey should or should not look like or include. Growth lies in the struggle. When we smother, overfunction, or enable, we think we are helping, but in reality, we are hindering. Hurting even.

GOING DEEPER

Resentment as Medicine

You've likely heard the saying, "Resentment is like drinking poison and waiting for the other person to die." There's deep truth in that statement, and yet . . . we still fall into its trap. In my codependency groups, I often point out that as we begin our recovery work, we might realize just how disconnected we are from our emotions. This is why I encourage people to regularly use a feelings wheel as part of their journey. And yet, even while being disconnected from nuanced emotions, most of us intimately know the feeling of resentment. So let's work with what we have. For the next week, turn up your awareness dial on the feeling of resentment. Notice every time this emotion washes over you or gives you a pang in your stomach. It doesn't have to be overwhelming; it could be the slightest twinge. I like to think of resentment as a signal that your codependency is being activated. It often means there is something that isn't being said, something you're doing or taking responsibility for that you shouldn't be. Feel the resentment, then try to uncover what's driving it. Where can you own your 100 percent?

Expand

Some of this work isn't sexy. It requires tangible effort, like list-making and hard conversations. This is one of those times. I want you to create a running list over one to two weeks. Start a note in your phone or journal—some place you can easily jot down notes in the moment. List all the things you are responsible for, not only around the home and with children, but also in your relationships. This isn't just a list of "I do the dishes every night and make all the kids' dentist appointments," but also "When the kids are upset, I soothe them and educate them on their emotions," or "When my partner is stressed out and snappy, I take the kids out of the house," or "When my mother is upset with someone in the family, I mediate between them to resolve it." It's not just the physical tasks we perform, but also the emotional labor we take on.

As you create this list, don't analyze whether you should or shouldn't be doing these things, or if you like or dislike them. Just write them down, plainly and factually. If your partner is willing to do this, have them create their own list in the same way and for the same length of time. If they aren't open to it, don't let that stop you; there's still plenty of value in doing this work on your own.

At the end of the week, review your list. What feelings come up around each item? Do any of them make you feel resentful? Are there things you actually enjoy being responsible for? Do some tasks bring you joy or fulfillment, while others drain or overwhelm you?

Explore

If your partner has created a similar list, you can sit together and discuss the higher-level themes that emerged from this exercise or any new awareness it brought you both. Set a time limit for each person to share their list and reflections; ten to fifteen minutes each is a good starting point. The goal here is to be succinct and focused. Pick a few key points or insights you had and share them. Remember, the spirit of this conversation should be about understanding and empathy, not accusation. Agree not to argue over whether something on the other person's list is actually their responsibility; if they feel it is, allow them that perspective. The purpose is not to go tit-for-tat on who does more, but to express where in the relationship you feel good, connected, valued, and fulfilled—and where you do not.

If you are not partnered, this can still be a productive exercise with insights gained. If you are partnered and the other person hasn't or won't make a list, you can still talk to them about your insights. You might say something like, "I've been reflecting on the responsibilities I take on and how they make me feel. I'd like to share some of my thoughts with you to help us understand each other better."

Keep in mind that this process can take time. You don't have to solve everything in one sitting. It's often beneficial to have these discussions in two or three parts, especially if you're not used to having such open, vulnerable conversations. The aim is to shift toward a style of communication that fosters empathy, understanding, and connection. Of course, we want some action and resolution to come from these talks, but that tends to come more easily when both partners feel seen, heard, and connected.

Experiment
Look at the items on your list that you *feel resentful about* and ask yourself if you do any of them because you don't trust the other person to do them "right," to do them the way you would, or to do them at all. Be honest with yourself. Why do you feel you can't trust them? Are there specific reasons, or is it more of a general feeling of not being able to rely on the ones you love? Is there a fear of being let down? Consider where this feeling originates—what is your historical experience with trust?

Now, and this might be challenging, I want you to choose one or two of those tasks and make a commitment to allow someone else to own or help with them. This could be part of one of your list conversations if you are partnered, where you openly discuss redistributing responsibilities. I would even challenge you to admit, "I've been holding onto this because I didn't trust you to do it 'right.'" This is probably going to feel uncomfortable. This level of honesty requires vulnerability—not only to admit this but to sit with the discomfort of allowing your partner to potentially feel hurt by this knowledge. They may step up and handle it—or they may not. Either way, it is valuable information for you both.

If you work with a therapist or coach, consider discussing this experiment with them. Many of us carry stories from our past about not being able to rely on others, leading us to rely solely on ourselves to avoid disappointment. By doing this, we unconsciously recreate and reinforce the very beliefs that keep us isolated. It's up to us to challenge these beliefs and the behaviors they produce.

Yes, it's true that by doing this experiment, your partner, friend, or family member might let you down. In fact, it's almost guaranteed that they will because they will never do things exactly as you would! This is all valuable information. Reflect on these possibilities:

- **Did they, in fact, do the thing, but just do it differently than you?** Now you have the opportunity to sit with your judgment and annoyance and ask yourself why you feel your way is the only right way (ick, I know).

- **Did they try but struggle, ask for your help, or not finish it?** Now you get to explore with them why they may feel judged, incompetent, or like they can't do anything right in your eyes.

- **Did they brush off the thing altogether and seemingly ignore it outright?** Now you get to tell them how this makes you feel dismissed and like your needs aren't important to them.

- **Did they get aggressive or defensive about having to do the thing at all, or about the list conversation from the jump?** Now you get to dig deeper into the relational dynamics, how you got here, and how you can change it moving forward.

In questioning and challenging the ways we overfunction to keep ourselves emotionally protected, we are also challenging the societal conditioning that keeps us isolated and unable to trust others—or ourselves. As counterintuitive as it may sound, it is better to trust in someone and have them let you down than to not even attempt to trust them and take everything on yourself. Trusting others provides valuable insights about our own capacity for vulnerability and communication and about their ability to engage meaningfully in our lives.

If we always rely only on ourselves, our relationships remain at a surface level. Depth in relationships requires intimacy, and intimacy requires risk.

12

the trouble with couples therapy

"Well, I've been afraid of changin'
'Cause I've built my life around you."

—Fleetwood Mac, "Landslide"[1]

During our first meeting with our new couples therapist, she mentioned being trained by a renowned relational therapist. While I didn't know much about his work, I liked her approach. She was somatically oriented, focused on grounding us in our bodies and helping us understand how our nervous systems influenced our relational behaviors. Being a therapist to other therapists is no easy feat, and she held her own. After our second session, she recommended we read one of her mentor's well-known books. Being the good student I am, I downloaded the audiobook that day and started working through it. The first part was quite helpful, covering much of what our therapist had already shared about the nervous system, attachment styles, and more.

However, as I continued listening, I became increasingly uncomfortable. The author began discussing the ways in which we are responsible for keeping our partner feeling safe and secure, suggesting that we must drop everything to "tend to them" whenever they are in distress. As he spoke of "governance" in relationships, involving a set of shared values and relationship rules, I started feeling a sensation of ick in my stomach. When he stated, "Your partner should have access to you 24/7," I recoiled, the sentence barely having a chance to land before I took out my AirPods and threw them across the kitchen, leaping out of my chair just as John was finding his way into the room, looking confused.

"I can't with this," I said. "There's a lot of good stuff here, but a lot of this is *crap*, in my opinion. It's all about how we are responsible for soothing each other, how we have to do things for our partner, even if we absolutely do not want to do them or even if they go against what we feel is best for ourselves. This is SO activating. It's like he's advocating for me to be your mother . . . and for you to be my father!" To his credit, John didn't argue; he just tried to talk me off the ledge.

WEIRD THERAPISTS

Listening to that audiobook that day, a fire was lit in me to reexamine the way we, as therapists, approach working with couples. What messages are we passing to our clients about what constitutes a "healthy," long-lasting relationship? Where do these messages originate, and are they genuinely helpful for *both* individuals in a couple?

What I discovered was a WEIRD (Western, Educated, Industrialized, Rich, Democratic) history behind relational psychology, a field researched, developed, and constructed by primarily white, middle- and upper-class men (and some women) from the United States and Europe. Because the foundational research in marital therapy focuses on such a narrow demographic—excluding women and families from diverse ethnic, socioeconomic, and Indigenous backgrounds, as well as various relational and living styles—its applicability is inherently limited. The research often reinforces existing structures and the status quo, something I am not interested in perpetuating in my work as a therapist.

Another trend I noticed is the disparity in focus between relationship books written by men and those by women. Men's books often center on rekindling and maintaining sex and intimacy after children, while the same category of books written by women tend to emphasize connection, support, and navigating the new identity as a mother and partner after children. Consider this: Why do these patterns persist, and what does it say about how we understand and value different aspects of relationships?

I'm not suggesting that all couples counseling is ineffective; in fact, it's been beneficial for my partner and me, and we plan to keep exploring different therapeutic approaches. However, I think it's worth questioning what we define as "effective" in a landscape where 40 to 50 percent of first marriages in the US end in divorce.[2] To be clear, I'm not saying therapy causes divorce or that it inherently fails. Instead, I wonder if high divorce rates might point to a larger need for improved social and cultural support systems for marriages, women, and families. Or perhaps we need to rethink our definitions of and expectations around marriage itself. Many might consider reducing conflict, improving communication, and fostering cooperation as "effective" outcomes, but I believe there's room to aim even higher.

The field's narrow focus often includes an overemphasis on attachment theory. It suggests our primary role is to "reparent" our partners to help heal their attachment wounds, without equally recognizing the value of acknowledging incompatibility and allowing relationships to evolve or expire. Additionally, couples therapy often upholds the idea that being partnered is the baseline for everyone, particularly women, and that relationships should always be maintained. This is a problematic assumption. Research shows that for about half of couples, the positive effects of therapy begin to dissipate after several years, even with follow-up care.[3] This raises the question: What are we calling "effective"? Should we reconsider what we define as a successful outcome in therapy? Perhaps we should even recognize that, in some cases, divorce or separation might actually be a healthier resolution.

THE WEIGHT OF PSYCHOLOGICAL HISTORY

As I have throughout this book, I want to offer historical context to ground these questions in an informed perspective. For over four thousand years, since Hippocrates coined the term "hysteria," women's mental health struggles have been pathologized and attributed to their lack of sex with men or their "effectiveness" at childbearing. This perspective has shaped much of what we consider "right" or "wrong" in our relationships, as mothers and as women. To clarify, these ideas did not come from women themselves or their communities, but from medical professionals and societal norms largely imposed by men. Even the origins of psychiatry are tied to this concept of "hysteria."

Fast-forward to 1889, when Freud claimed that hysteria was caused by the Oedipus complex: the idea that a child has an unconscious desire for their opposite-sex parent. Freud also perpetuated the myth that women who cannot orgasm solely from penetration are suffering from "psychosexual immaturity" or are "frigid," damaging ideas that still haunt women today.

These examples illustrate how deeply patriarchal, colonial, and misogynistic theories have influenced our understanding of mental health, relationships, and family dynamics. We must ask ourselves: How much of our inner wisdom have we outsourced to those who do not fully understand the experience of being a woman or mother, or those who have a vested interested in maintaining the outdated systems many of us are actively working to dismantle? Consider the connections between psychological research, books, and therapy itself; these are not separate entities but parts of a broader, intertwined system that shapes our beliefs and practices.

I WANT TO BELONG TO MYSELF AGAIN

Krista, a white woman in her forties, came to me after six months of couples therapy left her frustrated with the lack of progress in her relationship. Her decision to come to me was prompted by their therapist's recommendation to read a best-selling book by a Christian couples counselor. The book activated deep rage in Krista, as it seemed to push for more physical touch and loss of autonomy than she was comfortable with while overlooking a much deeper issue:

since becoming a mother, her sense of Self had fundamentally shifted. She had become acutely aware of the lack of autonomy she had always felt, now amplified by her husband's seemingly constant needs for touch, affection, validation, and sex. She saw the book's advice as superficial, failing to address her need for personal space, autonomy, and an authentic relationship that honored her individuality.

Their couples therapist was adamant that Krista's "avoidant attachment style" was a key problem in their marriage, advising her to start individual therapy that aligned with their couples work to help her desire more closeness with her husband. Krista felt cornered, as though the problem was solely hers to fix.

In our sessions, Krista and I focused on exploring her deep desire for more freedom and autonomy. She often used the word "untethered" to describe her longing. As a mom of a nine-month-old daughter and a three-year-old son who showed a clear preference for her over her husband, Krista expressed feeling like she was "constantly dripping with people clinging to her body." Much of our work centered on validating that her experience was completely normal and not a sign of something pathological. We discussed many of the themes that I explore in this book, including the impact of societal expectations on women and mothers.

We also dissected the book her couples therapist had recommended, which had sparked her feelings of rage. Krista felt a strong conviction that simply touching her husband more or offering more words of affirmation, strategies that the book suggested, were not going to save their marriage. She recognized that she did not owe her husband physical touch or sex, regardless of whether that was his "love language." Through coaching and support, she found the courage to express this to her partner.

Eventually, Krista articulated what she believed would give their marriage the best chance of success: both she and her husband needed to recognize that motherhood had fundamentally changed her as a person. She needed her husband to be more curious and respectful of her individual Soul's path and desires, and for him to explore his own social conditioning and Mother Wound that led him to seek sex as a form of validation. She found her voice and used it to advocate for herself in her couples work, pushing back on the counselor's notion that there is a one-size-fits-all approach to intimate relational health and satisfaction.

REPARENTING AND THE COLONIZATION OF THERAPY

As discussed in chapter 5, expecting our partner to co-regulate with us and play the part of the "Positive Mother" can have a detrimental impact on eros and passion. I won't belabor that point here, but I will emphasize that in our modern, Western, attachment-theory-obsessed psychology world, many relational therapists (and coaches) advocate reparenting our partners as an intervention or method of treatment for couples. As a depth psychotherapist, I see this approach as potentially harmful to the Soul's need for individuation, support, and autonomy. Convincing people that their partner is responsible for reparenting them perpetuates the "colonization of therapy," a concept that refers to how dominant cultural narratives and structures infiltrate therapeutic practices, often to the detriment of marginalized groups. (To unpack this further, refer to the work of Jennifer Mullan, founder of Decolonizing Therapy, who discusses how therapeutic practices can unconsciously uphold systems of oppression by centering dominant cultural norms and values.)

The underlying message of much of modern marital therapy goes something like this: The world is scary, we are helpless to change it, and we can't do it alone. Therefore, we need to find and keep a monogamous partnership at *all* costs, even to the detriment of the individual, children, extended family, and community. The nuclear family is presented as the best and only way to raise children, and through this structure, we are supposed to find our purpose and sense of Self.

This message is inherently colonial, most obviously because the nuclear family is a relatively new creation of the WEIRD world. For many relational therapists, their participation in a colonized paradigm of healing is unconscious. All clinicians, including those working with couples, must prioritize understanding how cultural dynamics and structures such as patriarchy, patriarchal capitalism, misogyny, white supremacy, and systemic oppression have historically affected and continue to affect the mental health of marginalized groups, including BIPOC individuals and women.

When the underlying approach to couples therapy places the romantic relationship as the center of everything—including our own personal healing—it diminishes the importance of developing a strong sense of Self and reliance on community. It also assumes that the mononormative structure is the best structure for everyone. This approach often centers the clinician's expertise, placing the couple (and even individuals) in a subordinate position, which can exacerbate feelings of disempowerment, especially for those with a history of marginalization or trauma. If therapists are to participate in the collective liberation of all people, we must each investigate our unconscious biases and beliefs that uphold current dominator systems.

WHAT ARE WE FIGHTING FOR?

"Enough! Time out!" My raised voice cut through the tension in the room, startling Julie and Scott into silence. "That's enough. Seriously. We've been meeting every week for months, and all either of you wants is to change the other person and remain the victim. Julie, Scott is not going to get down on his knees and declare his eternal gratitude to you for uprooting your life and moving across the country for him. No one forced you to make that choice. You made it. As an adult. Either stop holding it over his head or move back home. And Scott, Julie isn't going to change essentially *everything* about herself to fit into the exact mold of what keeps you comfortable and happy. This is who she is. Accept her or leave. You don't seem to even like who the other person is at their core. Why are you fighting to stay together? Staying together is a *choice*."

My heart was pounding. While I can be a direct and straightforward therapist (I mostly chalk it up to being from New York), I had never lost my cool like this in a session before.

"I want to have a baby," Julie said. Her eyes still wide.

"And?" I responded, not breaking eye contact with her. "Is this the dynamic you want to bring a child into? You are *miserable*."

"No, of course not. But I have no other option," she said, looking down. Scott looked hurt.

"You do have options. Both of you do. But it's terrifying to think outside of the box of 'shoulds,' to consider that you might have to grieve the idea of what you thought your life would look like. I don't have the right answer for either of you, but I made it clear when we first started working together that, as a couples therapist, my goal is not to keep the relationship together at all costs. My goal is to support what is life-giving. To champion the most fulfilling and respectful type of relationship for each individual Soul. If that means changing the form of the relationship container, then that's what I will advocate for. If your ultimate goals, after all this work, are to cling to the belief that each of you is the wronged party, that the other person is to blame for your unhappiness, and that you have to make them pay for that forever while maintaining the current structure of your relationship, then I think it's time I give you a few referrals to other therapists."

REDEFINING SUCCESS IN RELATIONSHIPS

You might be shocked by how I handled this moment with Julie and Scott, both white and in their late thirties. I know many clinicians would have approached it differently, and some might see my response as an obvious display of countertransference—a term used in therapy to describe when a therapist's personal feelings or unresolved issues affect their professional work. When that session ended, I walked out to where my partner was sitting and reading emails. I climbed into his lap, curled up, and began to sob. I was emotionally drained, overwhelmed by the venom, disrespect, and outright disgust these two people, who supposedly "loved" each other, constantly expressed. I felt a heaviness around why so many of us choose to stay in unhappy relationships because we are terrified to step outside the cultural narratives of what we "should" do.

As of writing this book, both Krista and her husband and Julie and Scott have separated. That might seem like a sad ending, but perhaps it isn't. Krista feels confident in her decision and has expressed a newfound sense of freedom and self-confidence she hadn't experienced before. She and her soon-to-be ex-husband have maintained a wonderful friendship, establishing mutual respect as the foundation of their relationship, knowing they will co-parent for life. Their decision came after about two years of individual and couples therapy, during which they realized they were simply no longer compatible as romantic partners. Instead of spending their lives trying to change each other into someone they'd feel good being married to, they chose a different path. They prioritized their friendship, their love of their children, and their own personal growth and fulfillment over maintaining the marriage in its original form. Of course, there was anger and grief, but eventually, there came peace and acceptance.

Julie and Scott are not friends, per se, but they are not enemies either. Julie decided she would rather rely on the support of her mother and sisters and get pregnant on her own. And so that's what she did.

I am emphatic about the need to stop celebrating longevity as the sole measure of success in relationships. When a friend tells me they are heading to their grandparents' fiftieth wedding anniversary party and I know those grandparents haven't spoken kindly to each other in twenty years, I don't see that as cause for celebration. However, when another friend, or even a client, tells me they've chosen to lovingly divorce, or "consciously uncouple" if you will, I stand up and applaud. Our grandmothers did not have the option to prioritize their personal fulfillment, to choose long-term happiness for themselves, their partners, or even their children. Their options were severely limited. Even today, many still believe being unhappily married is better than being happily single. Why? Because society teaches us so. It is all *learned* programming. It's time to unlearn it.

We need to challenge the narratives we've been taught about relationships and ourselves. It's time to push back against the systems that benefit a select few by keeping the rest of us overworked, overwhelmed, unhappy, unfulfilled, trapped in conflict, chasing, and pointing the finger at each other. It's all a distraction. Patriarchy, colonialism, white supremacy—none of these dominator systems can continue to thrive if we stop propping them up and sacrificing our lives to sustain them. And in a late-stage capitalist society, where the cost of living often demands two incomes to support a family, prioritizing well-being over mere survival can feel impossible. But perhaps that's exactly why it's even more important that we try.

MYTHS AS MAPS
The Little Mermaid, Sacrifice, and Selfhood

The 1989 Disney film *The Little Mermaid* is far from the first version of the tale of a girl who is half-fish, half-human and marries a human. As discussed earlier, it is essential to trace back our modern fairy tales to understand their original symbols and themes because it is in these original stories that we find the true "soul maps." The simplified versions we often see today have been transformed so extensively that all the mythic and numinous elements have been stripped away, leaving us with mere entertainment rather than a map to navigate life's complexities.

The animated version many of us know is based on Hans Christian Andersen's 1837 Danish fairy tale of the same name. Following the mythic thread, Andersen was inspired by a fairy tale novella named *Undine*, written by Friedrich de la Motte Fouqué. The term "undine" itself was coined by the occultist Paracelsus in his *Book on Nymphs*, published in 1566, which was based on the character from twelfth-century European folklore known as Melusine—a female water spirit depicted as a woman who is a serpent or fish from the waist down.

A common theme among these versions is that Melusine, undines, or mermaids do not possess eternal souls. In some versions, they live for three hundred years, but when they die, their souls dissolve into ocean foam and cease to exist. However, if a mermaid marries a human, she gains an immortal soul. For the Little Mermaid, a combination of her love for the prince, her desire for adventure and a life beyond the sea, and her longing for an immortal soul drives her to become human. The prince is a means to an end—a way to transcend her current existence.

Both Andersen's and Disney's versions have been presented to generations of young girls as a story about what to expect and desire in womanhood. Ursula, the sea witch (originally spelled Ursilla), traces back to the myths of the Selkies, the Inuit version of the mermaid. In both Andersen and Disney's versions, Ursula is a man-eater, with two water snakes as pets. In Andersen's version, she lives in a house built of the white bones of shipwrecked men; in Disney's, she lives in a dark cave lined with the trapped souls of the merfolk she has tricked.

In both versions, the mermaid must give up her voice to gain legs. In Andersen's version, her tongue is cut out, and she endures excruciating pain as her fins transform into legs; every step feels like walking on shards of glass, and her feet are always bleeding. The prince takes her in and loves her, as one would love a faithful pet, having her sleep on a cushion on the floor outside his bedroom door at night. He never discovers it was she who saved him from a shipwreck.

When he decides to marry another girl, the mermaid is heartbroken. (Unlike the happily-ever-after ending in the Disney version, Andersen's story takes a much darker turn.) Her sisters and grandmother tell her that if she kills the prince, she can become a mermaid again and return to her family. Instead, she sacrifices herself, and through this act, her Soul becomes eternal, allowing her to transcend to heaven.

SEEING OURSELVES IN THE MYTH

How does Hans Christian Andersen's version of *The Little Mermaid* (or at least this very truncated version) sit with you? Throughout this book, I have presented myths, fairy tales, and archetypal feminine figures that are meant to teach us how to navigate life as a woman, how to move through the world, and how to avoid pitfalls that may divert us from our Soul's path of individuation. In this final myth of the book, I offer a story, both modern and not, that appears to show women a path to redemption, but is, in fact, a patriarchal trap disguised as a tale of love and bravery. I present this story not as a map to follow, but as an example of why we should critically examine not just our modern fairy tales but also our cultural assumptions and the messages embedded within them.

The message in both Disney's and Andersen's versions of this fairy tale appears to be one of love and self-sacrifice, but the deeper message is a cautionary tale about the dangers of accepting treatment that minimizes our very being in the name of love. Mute and tormented, the mermaid dutifully attends to a prince who fails to see her true value.

On the surface, we are presented with a young, rebellious girl seeking adventure, willing to defy her father and leave everything she knows behind in order to "find herself." However, this facade of rebellion hides a more insidious message: the idea that a girl's ultimate focus should be on finding and marrying the ideal partner to achieve her "happily ever after." Both Andersen's and Disney's versions portray the mermaid as fifteen or sixteen years old, like many coming-of-age fairy tales where a young girl grapples with her newfound sexuality and the responses of men to her beauty.

The Little Mermaid gives up everything for the prince: her family, her voice, her autonomy—without love or even appreciation in return. This presents a suffocating combination of selflessness, silence, and penance as standards for female behavior. In Andersen's tale, when the Little Mermaid is not chosen, she is left with seemingly no alternative but to take her own life, reinforcing the idea that a woman's value is tied solely to her relationship with a man.

If we are not careful, these messages will continue to seep into the unconscious minds of our youth, just as they have with ours. Without open and hard conversations with our partners and children about what we see, what we are challenging, and what structures we refuse to live within, these narratives will continue to shape our lives, holding our happiness and fulfillment hostage.

My daughter has seen the Disney version of *The Little Mermaid*. She knows the songs and wears a Princess Ariel dress when she plays pretend. She loves mermaids. I try to balance allowing her the entertainment and beauty of the vibrant colors and songs with teaching her about the deeper meanings of the original myths and engaging in conversations about what these stories truly represent. I cannot shield her entirely from society's "princessification," but I can equip her with the knowledge of the underlying messages and show her, through my actions and choices, that being "chosen" by a prince and staying silent and loyal, regardless of treatment, should not be the goal.

As a therapist, I also see how these myths and fairy tales tie into the cultural ideals that many clients bring into their sessions. The narratives we absorb from childhood about love, sacrifice, and worthiness continue to inform our expectations and struggles in adult relationships. It is crucial for therapists to help clients unpack these deeply ingrained stories and challenge the societal scripts that no longer serve them—scripts that often perpetuate inequality and limit true self-actualization.

GOING DEEPER

Be Alone

In our culture, there is a pervasive belief that we become "complete" once we partner, and the fear of being seen as "incomplete" often keeps us in relationships, regardless of whether they truly serve us. I am not suggesting we should not seek partnerships, but I am advocating for the necessity of cultivating a relationship with the Self that exists independently from our partners and our children. We must be vigilant against cultural messages that tell us that aloneness is something to be feared. Cultivating a relationship with ourselves requires intentional alone time. For women, especially mothers, this time must be fought for, demanded, and fiercely protected at all costs.

Clarissa Pinkola Estés tells us that "long ago the word *alone* was treated as two words, *all one*. To be *all one* meant to be wholly one, to be in oneness, either essentially or temporarily. That is precisely the goal of solitude, to be all one."[4] In periods of being "all one," we create the space to connect and converse with the deepest parts of ourselves, to inquire into the state of our relationships, and to reflect on the condition of our inner lives. These periods of solitude do not need to be long, nor do they require significant resources, but they must be intentional. They involve a deliberate tuning out of the world's distractions—distractions specifically designed to keep us frazzled, scared, and disconnected from our inner selves. If the idea of carving out intentional alone time, and fighting for it, scares you or makes you uncomfortable . . . that's good. Fear and discomfort are often the medicines we need most.

Explore

Solitude can sometimes feel uncomfortable or even frightening, especially if you have been taught to fear being alone. Use this discomfort as a doorway to growth. During your alone time, explore a practice that stretches you beyond your comfort zone—whether it's sitting at a cafe in silence without distractions, trying a new form of movement, or engaging in a creative activity without self-criticism or an end goal. Reflect on what comes up for you and what it reveals about your relationship with yourself.

Carve Out

We need to be boundaried about the ways we carve out and protect our alone time. And for many of us, we have forgotten what we like to do or who we were before children and partners came into the picture. At the end of every week, I look at my calendar for the week upcoming. On at least two of the days, I schedule in one to two hours on my calendar that are mine, typically filling them with a workout or yoga class or sitting with coffee and reading a book. Decide what would feel nourishing to you, schedule it in, and then treat it like any other meeting that can't be canceled.

Conclusion

the journey continues

This book has been an exploration of myths, cultural conditioning, and the complexities of relationships—both with others and with ourselves. This is not the end of the work; it is only the beginning. The journey of self-discovery and individuation is ongoing, a lifelong process that invites us to constantly evolve. This is the kind of evolution that requires many initiations, deaths, periods of darkness, and rebirths. Once we begin to uncover the layers of social programming and internalized beliefs that no longer serve us, we cannot unknow what we've discovered. Once we see, we cannot unsee. This awareness compels us to change—not just for ourselves, but for future generations. We are paving the way, not only for our own liberation, but for our children too.

Make no mistake, this path is difficult because, as way-showers, we often walk a road with no clear map. There are not many others who have come before us to follow, no clear examples of how to break free from the patterns of codependency, internalized misogyny, and emotional disconnection that have been passed down through generations. But we are not without guidance. If we spend time with and relate to myths, archetypes, and even our dreams, they will show us the way. These ancient stories offer us timeless wisdom, reminding us that every step we take toward healing, even in the micro moments, brings us closer to coming home to our true selves.

Ultimately, we must learn to reconnect with the numinous—that vast, mysterious force that exists beyond our control yet always within our reach. It is this connection that helps us loosen our grip on the illusion of control and embrace the unknown with less fear. The journey ahead is not one of certainty, but of trust—in ourselves, in the wisdom of the myths, in the divine, and in the cycles of life that guide all of us. As we move forward, may we continue to let go, surrender, and allow ourselves to be led by the deeper forces that have been guiding humanity for centuries. Only by doing this can we truly transform the way we see and participate in relationships, freeing ourselves and those who come after us.

acknowledgments

To Logan: Thank you for choosing me to be your mama and for lighting the fire (or rather inferno) underneath me (and in my belly) to take radical responsibility for my life as a mother and a woman so you can see what is possible.

To John: Thank you for being one of my greatest knowings, teachers, mirrors, and the ultimate corrective love experience. Without your support and guidance, I would not be where I am today in life, in love, in career, or in passion. I am forever grateful that the universe brought you to me and for your permission to be vulnerable and share some of our hardest moments with the world in hopes others will learn from our struggles. Here's to many more years of exploration, evolution, and a refusal to rip out any of our chapters.

To my mother: Thank you for teaching me to be a take-no-shit, self-reliant, and strong-ass woman in this world. I am forever grateful for the resilience and voice you gave me. To you, grandma, and to the lineage of women who came before: Thank you for showing me what *wasn't* possible or available for you so I could demand it for myself and my daughter.

To my New York sister for life and the best literary agent around, JL Stermer: Thanks for always being my no-nonsense go-to for support through this process. Your honesty, humor, and compassion are unmatched.

To Diana Ventimiglia (and Sounds True) for believing in this book and to Sarah Stanton who adopted it as if it were her own and pushed it to become everything it could possibly be. Without the belief in and guidance of you two, this idea would never have been birthed into the world.

And to all of my chosen family who have supported me through this birthing process—not just of the book, but of the version of myself who needed to be birthed along with it. Who have listened to me rant and cry, and have watched me grow, stumble, want to give it all up, and then stand up again. I love all of you so much. Emily, Christina, Lena, Nami, Meridith, Taune, and especially my soul sister Dené. You're etched in my heart forever.

notes

EPIGRAPH
1 Rebecca Solnit, *The Mother of All Questions* (Haymarket Books, 2017), 2.

INTRODUCTION
1 Harriet Lerner, *The Dance of Anger: A Woman's Guide to Changing the Patterns of Intimate Relationships* (Harper & Row, 1985), 129.
2 Maureen Murdock, *The Heroine's Journey: Woman's Quest for Wholeness* (Shambhala Publications, 1990), XVII.
3 Pew Research Center, "More Childless US Adults Now Say They Don't Expect to Ever Have Children," November 19, 2021, pewresearch.org/short-reads/2021/11/19/more-childless-u-s-adults-now-say-they-dont-expect-to-ever-have-children/.
4 bell hooks, *The Will to Change: Men, Masculinity, and Love*, narrated by Janet St. John (Washington Square Press, 2004), at 11 min., 34 sec.
5 Maddy Savage, "How Covid-19 Is Changing Women's Lives," *BBC Worklife*, June 30, 2020, bbc.com/worklife/article/20200630-how-covid-19-is-changing-womens-lives; Maddy Savage, "Why the Pandemic Is Causing Spikes in Break-ups and Divorces," *BBC Worklife*, December 3, 2020, bbc.com/worklife/article/20201203-why-the-pandemic-is-causing-spikes-in-break-ups-and-divorces.

6 Aimee Picchi, "Even 'Breadwinner' Wives Do More Housework than Husbands," *CBS News*, April 13, 2023, cbsnews.com/news/women-breadwinners-tripled-since-1970s-still-doing-more-unpaid-work/.

7 Richard Fry, "Almost 1 in 5 Stay-at-Home Parents in the US Are Dads," Pew Research Center, August 3, 2023, pewresearch.org/short-reads/2023/08/03/almost-1-in-5-stay-at-home-parents-in-the-us-are-dads/.

8 Population Reference Bureau, "Why Is the US Birth Rate Declining?," May 6, 2021, prb.org/resources/why-is-the-u-s-birth-rate-declining/.

9 Clarissa Pinkola Estés, *Women Who Run with the Wolves: Myths and Stories of the Wild Woman Archetype* (Ballantine Books, 1992), 390.

10 Lisa Miller, *The Awakened Brain: The New Science of Spirituality and Our Quest for an Inspired Life*, narrated by Lisa Miller (Random House, 2021), at 5 mins., 40 sec.

11 Joseph Campbell, *The Hero with a Thousand Faces*, 3rd ed. (New World Library, 2008), 87.

PART 1: THE MYTHS OF MOTHERHOOD

1 Kavita Ramdas, "Radical Women, Embracing Tradition," TEDIndia, November 2009, ted.com/talks/kavita_ramdas_radical_women_embracing_tradition.

CHAPTER 1: FROM MAIDEN TO MOTHER

1 Marion Woodman, *The Pregnant Virgin: A Process of Psychological Transformation* (Inner City Books, 1985), 14.

2 World Health Organization, "Caesarean Section Rates Continue to Rise amid Growing Inequalities in Access," June 16, 2021, who.int/news/item/16-06-2021-caesarean-section-rates-continue-to-rise-amid-growing-inequalities-in-access.

3. Amanda S. Morris, et al., "The Role of the Family Context in the Development of Emotion Regulation," *Social Development* 16, no. 2 (2007): 361–88, doi.org/10.1111/j.1467-9507.2007.00389.x.
4. Ann Lazarus and Pieter Rossouw, "Understanding the Emotional Experience of Women Following Stillbirth and Neonatal Death," *BMC Pregnancy and Childbirth* 15 (2015): 125, doi.org/10.1186/s12884-015-0683-0.
5. Clarissa Pinkola Estés, *Women Who Run with the Wolves: Myths and Stories of the Wild Woman Archetype* (Ballantine Books, 1992), 191.
6. Woodman, *The Pregnant Virgin*, 285.
7. Pew Research Center, "Millennial Life: How Young Adulthood Today Compares with Prior Generations," May 27, 2020, pewresearch.org/social-trends/wp-content/uploads/sites/3/2020/05/PDST_05.27.20_millennial.families_fullreport.pdf.
8. Dana Raphael, *The Tender Gift: Breastfeeding* (Schocken Books, 1973).
9. Daniel N. Stern, *The Motherhood Constellation: A Unified View of Parent-Infant Psychotherapy* (Basic Books, 1995).
10. Valerie Coumont Graubart, "Changes and Transitions," in *Transpersonal Psychotherapy: Theory and Practice*, ed. Valerie Coumont Graubart (SAGE Publications, 2004), 124–42, doi.org/10.4135/9781446212264.
11. Graubart, "Changes and Transitions."

CHAPTER 2: THE LOSS OF THE VILLAGE... AND OURSELVES

1. Michaeleen Doucleff, *Hunt, Gather, Parent: What Ancient Cultures Can Teach Us about the Lost Art of Raising Happy, Helpful Little Humans* (Avid Reader Press/Simon & Schuster, 2021); World Health Organization, *Maternal Mental Health and Child Health and Development in Low and Middle-Income Countries* (World Health Organization, 2018).
2. Silvia Federici, *Witches, Witch-Hunting, and Women* (PM Press, 2018); Marija Gimbutas, *The Civilization of the Goddess:*

The World of Old Europe (HarperSanFrancisco, 1991); Jared Diamond, *Guns, Germs, and Steel: The Fates of Human Societies* (W. W. Norton & Company, 1997).
3 Federici, *Witches, Witch-Hunting, and Women*.
4 Federici.
5 Smithsonian Institution, *Homo sapiens*, Human Origins Program, updated January 3, 2024, humanorigins.si.edu/evidence/human-fossils/species/homo-sapiens.
6 Silvia Federici, *Caliban and the Witch: Women, the Body, and Primitive Accumulation* (Autonomedia, 2004); Barbara Ehrenreich and Deirdre English, *Witches, Midwives, and Nurses: A History of Women Healers*, 2nd ed. (Feminist Press, 2010); Anne L. Barstow, *Witchcraze: A New History of the European Witch Hunts* (Pandora, 1994); United Nations Human Rights Office of the High Commissioner, *Reports on Witch Hunts and Gender-Based Violence* (UNHRC, 2021).
7 Federici, *Caliban and the Witch*, 23.
8 Barbara Ehrenreich and Deirdre English, *Witches, Midwives, and Nurses*, 20.
9 Federici, *Witches, Witch-Hunting, and Women*, 46–49.
10 Ehrenreich and English, *Witches, Midwives, and Nurses*, 38.
11 Ehrenreich and English, 50.
12 Ehrenreich and English, 53.
13 Ehrenreich and English, 46.
14 Ehrenreich and English, 66.

CHAPTER 3: THE CULT OF BUSY

1 Thomas Merton, *Conjectures of a Guilty Bystander* (Doubleday, 1968), 86.
2 Clarissa Pinkola Estés, *Women Who Run with the Wolves: Myths and Stories of the Wild Woman Archetype* (Ballantine Books, 1992), 302.

3 R. F. Baumeister, et al., "Bad Is Stronger than Good," *Journal of Personality and Social Psychology* 81, no. 4 (2001): 323–39, doi .org/10.1037/0022-3514.81.4.323.
4 Betty Friedan, *The Feminine Mystique* (W. W. Norton & Company, 1963); Barbara Ehrenreich and Deirdre English, *For Her Own Good: Two Centuries of the Experts' Advice to Women* (Anchor Books, 2005).
5 Estés, *Women Who Run with the Wolves*, 236.
6 Glennon Doyle, *Untamed* (Dial Press, 2020), 113–34.

CHAPTER 4: MARTYRDOM IS NOT MOTHERING

1 Carl Jung, *The Development of Personality*, trans. R. F. C. Hull, vol. 17, in *The Collected Works of C. G. Jung* (Princeton University Press, 1954), originally published in 1934.
2 Meredith Small, *Our Babies, Ourselves: How Biology and Culture Shape the Way We Parent* (Anchor Books, 1998).
3 Sarah Blaffer Hrdy, *Mothers and Others: The Evolutionary Origins of Mutual Understanding* (Belknap Press, 2009).
4 S. Gaskins, "Children's Daily Lives in a Mayan Village: A Case Study of Culturally Constructed Roles and Activities," in *Children's Engagement in the World: Sociocultural Perspectives*, ed. A. Göncü (Cambridge University Press, 1999).
5 J. Henrich, et al., "The WEIRDest People in the World?," *Behavioral and Brain Sciences* 33, nos. 2–3 (2010): 61–83, doi .org/10.1017/S0140525X0999152X.
6 Philip Greven, *Spare the Child: The Religious Roots of Punishment and the Psychological Impact of Physical Abuse* (Vintage Books, 1991).
7 Barbara Ehrenreich and Deirdre English, *For Her Own Good: Two Centuries of the Experts' Advice to Women* (Anchor Books, 2005).
8 Sigmund Freud, *The Ego and the Id*, in *The Standard Edition of the Complete Psychological Works of Sigmund Freud*, ed. and trans. James Strachey, vol. 19 (Hogarth Press, 1923).

9 Freud, *The Ego and the Id.*
10 Alice Miller, *For Your Own Good: Hidden Cruelty in Child-Rearing and the Roots of Violence* (Farrar, Straus and Giroux, 1983).
11 Michaeleen Doucleff, *Hunt, Gather, Parent: What Ancient Cultures Can Teach Us about the Lost Art of Raising Happy, Helpful Little Humans* (Avid Reader Press/Simon & Schuster, 2021).
12 Glennon Doyle, *Untamed* (Dial Press, 2020), 128.
13 Kathleen Gallagher Elkins, *Mary, Mother of Martyrs: How Motherhood Became Self-Sacrifice in Early Christianity* (Columbia University Press, 2018), xxxi.
14 Adrienne Rich, *Of Woman Born: Motherhood as Experience and Institution* (W. W. Norton & Company, 1976).
15 Margie E. Lachman, et al., "Stress Control Beliefs and Psychological Distress: The Moderating Role of Age," *Psychology and Aging* 10, no. 3 (1995): 3–8, doi.org/10.1037/0882-7974.10.3.405.
16 Marina Warner, *Alone of All Her Sex: The Myth and the Cult of the Virgin Mary* (Weidenfeld and Nicolson, 1976); Joseph Campbell, *The Hero with a Thousand Faces* (Princeton University Press, 1949).
17 René Laurentin, *The Question of Mary: History and Theology* (Holt, Rinehart and Winston, 1963).
18 Alphonsus Liguori, *The Glories of Mary* (Redemptorist Fathers, 1868).
19 Elkins, *Mary, Mother of Martyrs*, 26.
20 Elkins, 28.
21 Clarissa Pinkola Estés, *Women Who Run with the Wolves: Myths and Stories of the Wild Woman Archetype* (Ballantine Books, 1992), 282.
22 Doucleff, *Hunt, Gather, Parent.*

PART 2: THE MYTHS OF SEX

1 Marion Woodman, *Addiction to Perfection: The Still Unravished Bride* (Inner City Books, 1982), 139.

CHAPTER 5: THE MOTHER WOUND

1. James Hollis, *Under Saturn's Shadow: The Wounding and Healing of Men* (Inner City Books, 1994), 38.
2. Adrienne Rich, *Of Woman Born: Motherhood as Experience and Institution* (W. W. Norton & Company, 1976); Paula J. Caplan, *Don't Blame Mother: Mending the Mother-Daughter Relationship* (Harper & Row, 1989).
3. Carl G. Jung, *The Collected Works of C. G. Jung*, vol. 9, part 1, *The Archetypes and the Collective Unconscious*, trans. R. F. C. Hull (Princeton University Press, 1968).
4. Erich Neumann, *The Great Mother: An Analysis of the Archetype*, trans. Ralph Manheim (Princeton University Press, 1955).
5. Carl G. Jung, *Two Essays on Analytical Psychology*, trans. R. F. C. Hull (Princeton University Press, 1966), originally published in 1953.
6. Marion Woodman, *Addiction to Perfection: The Still Unravished Bride* (Inner City Books, 1982).
7. Hollis, *Under Saturn's Shadow*, 42–43.
8. Jay Belsky and John Kelly, *The Transition to Parenthood: How a First Child Changes a Marriage; Why Some Couples Grow Closer and Others Apart* (Dell Publishing, 1994).
9. Carolyn Pape Cowan and Philip A. Cowan, *When Partners Become Parents: The Big Life Change for Couples* (Lawrence Erlbaum Associates, 2000).
10. James Hollis, *The Eden Project: In Search of the Magical Other* (Inner City Books, 1998), 36.
11. Paul H. Wright, "Men's Friendships, Women's Friendships, and the Alleged Inferiority of the Latter," *Sex Roles* 8, no. 1 (1982): 1–20.
12. Hollis, *Under Saturn's Shadow*, 54.

CHAPTER 6: THE FATHER WOUND

1. Carl G. Jung, *The Collected Works of C. G. Jung*, vol. 7: *Two Essays on Analytical Psychology*, ed. Herbert Read, Michael Fordham,

and Gerhard Adler, trans. R. F. C. Hull (Princeton University Press, 1966), para. 78.
2 James Hollis, *Under Saturn's Shadow: The Wounding and Healing of Men* (Inner City Books, 1994).
3 Terrence Real, *How Can I Get Through to You? Reconnecting Men and Women* (Scribner, 2002).
4 Hollis, *Under Saturn's Shadow*, 84.
5 Joseph H. Pleck, "The Gender Role Strain Paradigm: An Update," in *A New Psychology of Men*, ed. Ronald F. Levant and William S. Pollack (Basic Books, 1995), 11–32; Ronald F. Levant, "Desperately Seeking Language: Understanding, Assessing, and Treating Normative Male Alexithymia," in *The New Handbook of Psychotherapy and Counseling with Men: A Comprehensive Guide to Settings, Problems, and Treatment Approaches*, vol. 1, ed. Gary R. Brooks and Glenn E. Good (Jossey-Bass, 2001), 424–43.
6 Hollis, *Under Saturn's Shadow*, 22.
7 Clarissa Pinkola Estés, *Women Who Run with the Wolves: Myths and Stories of the Wild Woman Archetype* (Ballantine Books, 1992), 282.
8 Michael Gurian, *The Prince and the King: Healing the Archetypal Wounds of Men* (Shambhala Publications, 1992), 58.
9 Sophie Strand, *The Flowering Wand: Rewilding the Sacred Masculine*, narrated by author (Inner Traditions, 2022), at 7 min.
10 Marion Woodman, *Leaving My Father's House: A Journey to Conscious Femininity* (Shambhala Publications, 1992), 16.
11 bell hooks, *The Will to Change: Men, Masculinity, and Love* (Washington Square Press, 2004), 7.
12 Amy Gallo, "What Is Psychological Safety?," *Harvard Business Review*, February 15, 2023, hbr.org/2023/02/what-is-psychological-safety#:~:text=New%20research%20by%20Edmondson.

CHAPTER 7: SEX WAS NEVER ABOUT ME

1 Cory Muscara (@corymuscara), "Craving and addiction is not desire," Instagram, July 29, 2024, instagram.com/p/C -AjXY9p7j9/?igsh=MzRlODBiNWFlZA==.
2 Jaak Panksepp, *Affective Neuroscience: The Foundations of Human and Animal Emotions* (Oxford University Press, 1998).
3 Michelle Fine and Sara I. McClelland, "Sexuality Education and Desire: Still Missing After All These Years," *Harvard Educational Review* 76, no. 3 (2006): psycnet.apa.org/record/2006-20049-001.
4 Jennifer Barker, "The Orgasm Gap: Simple Truth of Sexual Solutions," *Psychology Today*, October 14, 2015, psychologytoday.com/gb/blog /stress-and-sex/201510/the-orgasm-gap-simple-truth-sexual-solutions.
5 bell hooks, *The Will to Change: Men, Masculinity, and Love* (Washington Square Press, 2004), 82.
6 hooks, *The Will to Change*, 82.
7 *Alphabet of Ben Sira* (also known as *Alphabet of Sirach*).

CHAPTER 8: THE WILD WOMAN'S ROLE IN OUR EVOLVING FEMINISM

1 bell hooks, *Feminism Is for Everybody: Passionate Politics* (South End Press, 2000), 7.
2 Marion Woodman, *Addiction to Perfection: The Still Unravished Bride* (Inner City Books, 1982,) 121.
3 hooks, *Feminism Is for Everybody*, 9.
4 Clarissa Pinkola Estés, *Women Who Run with the Wolves: Myths and Stories of the Wild Woman Archetype* (Ballantine Books, 1992), 43.
5 Estés, *Women Who Run with the Wolves*, 5.
6 Estés, 6.
7 Estés, 322.
8 Estés, 117.
9 Estés, 333.

PART 3: THE MYTHS OF RELATIONSHIPS
1. "Grace Hopper Discusses Data Processing and Innovation," *ComputerWorld*, October 1976.

CHAPTER 9: LIBERATION THROUGH RESPONSIBILITY
1. Carl Jung, "Letter to Bill Wilson, January 30, 1961," *in Alcoholics Anonymous: The Story of How Many Thousands of Men and Women Have Recovered from Alcoholism* (Alcoholics Anonymous World Services, 1984).
2. Gabor Maté, "Opioids and the Universal Experience of Addiction," *Dr. Gabor Maté Blog*, October 24, 2017, drgabormate.com/opioids-universal-experience-addiction/.
3. Clarissa Pinkola Estés, *Women Who Run with the Wolves: Myths and Stories of the Wild Woman Archetype* (Ballantine Books, 1992), 194.
4. Tara Brach, *Tara Brach Podcast*, accessed October 17, 2024, tarabrach.com/talks-audio-video.
5. Glennon Doyle, *Untamed* (Dial Press, 2020), 263.
6. Melody Beattie, *Codependent No More: How to Stop Controlling Others and Start Caring for Yourself* (Hazelden Publishing, 1986), 46.
7. Oprah Winfrey, *Super Soul Sunday* [TV series], OWN: Oprah Winfrey Network.
8. Marie-Louise von Franz, *The Interpretation of Fairy Tales* (Shambhala Publications, 1996), 25.
9. Estés, *Women Who Run with the Wolves*, 173.

CHAPTER 10: BELONGING TO OURSELVES
1. Glennon Doyle, *Untamed* (Dial Press, 2020), 74.
2. Doyle, *Untamed*, 5.
3. Polly Young-Eisendrath, "Gender and Contrasexuality: Jung's Contribution and Beyond," in *The Cambridge Companion to Jung*, ed. Polly Young-Eisendrath and Terence Dawson (Cambridge: Cambridge University Press, 1997), 223–39.

CHAPTER 11: IS IT LOVE OR FEAR?

1 Marianne Williamson, *A Woman's Worth* (Ballantine Books, 2013), 17.
2 Harriet Lerner, *The Dance of Anger: A Woman's Guide to Changing the Patterns of Intimate Relationships* (Harper & Row, 1985), 138.
3 Lerner, *The Dance of Anger*, 139.
4 Melody Beattie, *Codependent No More: How to Stop Controlling Others and Start Caring for Yourself* (Hazelden Publishing, 1986), 62.

CHAPTER 12: THE TROUBLE WITH COUPLES THERAPY

1 "Landslide," track 8, *Fleetwood Mac*, Warner Bros. Records, 1975.
2 Rose M. Kreider and Renee Ellis, *Number, Timing, and Duration of Marriages and Divorces: 2009* (US Census Bureau, 2011), census.gov/library/publications/2011/demo/p70-125.html.
3 Thomas N. Bradbury and Guy Bodenmann, *Interventions for Couples (Handbook of Couple and Family Therapy)* (Cambridge University Press, 2020).
4 Clarissa Pinkola Estés, *Women Who Run with the Wolves: Myths and Stories of the Wild Woman Archetype* (Ballantine Books, 1992), 316.

about the author

Vanessa Bennett, LMFT, is a licensed depth psychotherapist, facilitator, mental health content creator, and lifelong seeker who brings radical transparency and authenticity to her practice. Known for her down-to-earth approach, Vanessa uniquely translates complex psychological and spiritual ideas into relatable, practical insights. She's been called the "cold water in the face therapist," serving up compassionate but direct truths that foster transformation without shame.

Alongside her partner, John Kim, LMFT, Vanessa coauthored the relationship book *It's Not Me, It's You*. She leads soul-centered retreats, facilitates growth-oriented workshops for nonprofits and corporations, and cohosts the podcast *Cheaper Than Therapy*. A native New Yorker now based in Los Angeles, she's also a mother to a tenacious and far *too* wise daughter who continually inspires her work.

In both her life and practice, Vanessa is committed to walking her walk and removing the therapist from the pedestal of "expert." She's transparent about her own journey, empowering clients as the true experts of their own Soul's path. Holding a vision of each client's highest potential, she guides them toward living a life aligned with their truest selves.

about sounds true

Sounds True was founded in 1985 by Tami Simon with a clear mission: to disseminate spiritual wisdom. Since starting out as a project with one woman and her tape recorder, we have grown into a multimedia publishing company with a catalog of more than 3,000 titles by some of the leading teachers and visionaries of our time, and an ever-expanding family of beloved customers from across the world.

In more than four decades of evolution, Sounds True has maintained our focus on our overriding purpose and mission: to wake up the world. We offer books, audio programs, online learning experiences, and in-person events to support your personal growth and awakening, and to unlock our greatest human capacities to love and serve.

At SoundsTrue.com you'll find a wealth of resources to enrich your journey, including our weekly *Insights at the Edge* podcast, free downloads, and information about our nonprofit Sounds True Foundation, where we strive to remove financial barriers to the materials we publish through scholarships and donations worldwide.

To learn more, please visit SoundsTrue.com/freegifts or call us toll-free at 800.333.9185.

Together, we can wake up the world.